STEP BY STEP INDIAN COOKBOOK

MRIDULA BALJEKAR

Photographed by Peter Barry
Recipes prepared and styled by
Bridgeen Deery
and Wendy Devenish
Edited by Jillian Stewart
and Jane Adams
Designed by Philip Clucas
and Claire Leighton

Author's Acknowledgement

I wish to thank all my pupils for the inspiration they gave me by showing tremendous interest in and appreciation for my recipes.

I offer my sincere thanks to my close friends Gek Starkey and Louise Read for looking after my children when I was busy compiling the recipes for this book.

A multitude of loving thanks goes to my husband for his support and understanding during the entire period of writing this book.

Lastly, I must mention the book *Herbs, Spices and Flavourings,* which proved to be an invaluable guide in compiling the glossary. The author, Tim Stobart, deserves special thanks for an excellent piece of work.

2462

This edition published in 1993 by Coombe Books for
Parragon Book Service Ltd,
707 High Street, Finchley, London N12 0BT

Printed and bound in Singapore
ISBN 1-85813-410-2

STEP BY STEP

INDIAN COOKBOOK

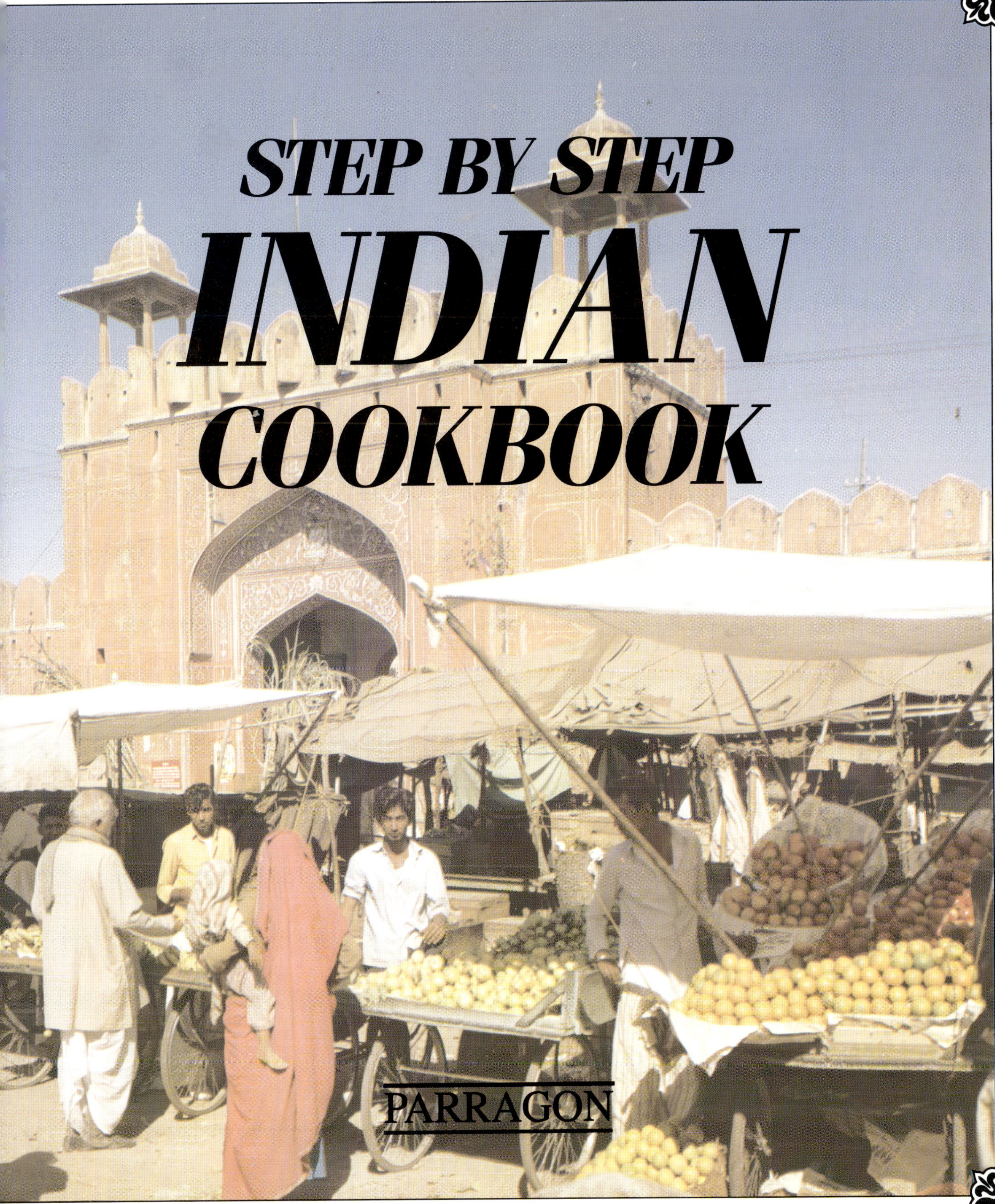

PARRAGON

contents

introduction

India is a country full of striking contrasts; this is evident not only in its cuisine, but also in its climate, geography, culture and customs. The vastness of the country, together with its great regional diversity, is the main factor that places Indian cuisine in its unique and interesting position in the culinary history of the world. Indian food reflects the colourful and varied life led by its people as well as the external and internal influences that have shaped its particular style of cooking.

The Mughals, a regal race of Muslims, invaded India from their traditional homeland in Afganistan and the Middle East, bringing with them exotic spices and dried fruits and nuts, which they combined with milk and cream to concoct rich 'Mughlai' dishes. These are amongst the finest in Indian regional cuisine.

During their journey to India via Persia (modern-day Iran), the Mughals adapted the much-admired Persian cooking to their own style and later introduced this into India. They then settled in northern India and made 'Mughlai' cuisine famous throughout the country. Dishes cooked in this particular style, with their delicately flavoured, rich, smooth sauces, include kormas, pasandas and wonderfully fragrant birianis and pilaus, all of which have become extremely popular both in India and the West.

The Kashmiris from the north, used saffron and other rare condiments, giving Indian recipes, especially sweets and puddings, a festive touch. It is also in Kashmir that the origins of the Saraswat community are found. They originally lived in the valley of the Saraswati river in Kashmir and journeyed southward, finally settling down in the districts of North and South Kanara. Their contribution to the cuisine of the country has been considerable. Kashmiris are mainly vegetarians, though most will eat the beautiful fresh fish found along the vast coastline. Most Saraswat recipes, as is evident from those contained in this book, are quick, easy, delicious and, above all, very healthy.

About thirteen centuries ago, a group of Persians came to India and made their home in the southern half of the country. They adapted to the rich and varied culture they found there, but made their own particular contribution to the Indian culinary world. Persian food has a very distinctive flavour which the Parsees, as they are known in India, cleverly integrated into the exotic and colourful cooking of the Indian subcontinent. A fine example of their contribution is the 'Dhansak' style – chicken or mutton cooked with lentils and spices and served with brown rice.

The influence of religion on the country's cooking has been, and continues to be, quite profound. There are many religions practised in India, of which the major ones are Hinduism with its three main divisions – Buddhism, Jainism and Sikhism – and Islam, which was first brought to India by foreign traders.

There are a number of taboos, or restrictions, that apply to the food eaten by followers of the different religions. Devout Hindus, for example, will not eat beef because Indian mythology depicts the cow as a sacred animal, while Muslims will not eat pork and their religion requires that animals are killed by the halal method.

In the early days, when travel and communication between different areas were virtually nonexistent, each region used the herbs and spices that were to be found growing naturally. As a result, housewives were compelled to experiment by using the same ingredients, but frying, grinding and mixing them in different sequences and proportions. The same ingredients, when cooked differently, gave dishes their diverse tastes, colours and textures, and resulted in the same recipes having quite a few variations. Today, though certain recipes have specific geographic strongholds, a large number of the dishes and cooking methods have spread the length and breadth of the country.

People are often confused by the different ways in which the names of ingredients and dishes are spelt in English. Should it be Tandoor or Tandur? Aloo Ghosh or Alu Ghosht? Because all the fourteen main Indian languages and their 144 dialects are phonetic, the translation of Indian phonetics into non-phonetic English spelling causes this confusion.

Since ancient times Indians have known about the medicinal properties of herbs, spices and other ingredients used in cooking. Garlic, for example, is known to control the level of cholesterol in the blood and, therefore, reduces the risk of high blood pressure and heart attacks. Cloves and cinnamon act against coughs and colds and help to keep the body warm in extreme weather. Ginger reduces acidity in the stomach and thus minimises the risk of ulcers. Green chillies, which normally thrive in dry, arid areas where not much else grows, are a good source of vitamins; cumin helps settle an upset stomach; turmeric purifies the blood; mustard, which grows in cooler climates, has a warming effect and prevents hypothermia – the list is endless!

These different properties created a varied, healthy cuisine that is now known by the all-embracing term 'Indian food' or, 'curry'. It is a common misconception, however, that everything that is spicy is a curry. The word curry means sauce and dry-spiced Indian dishes cannot therefore strictly be called curries. Dishes all have their own identifying terms. For example, a vegetable dish that has no gravy is known as a bhaji, while food cooked by the dum method, which creates little or no gravy, is simply referred to as, say, Dum Aloo (potatoes) or Dum Murghi (chicken).

Indian recipes are generally handed down from one generation to the next. A fair attempt has now been made to formalise and record all recipes. Weights and measures were never used and the quantities of all the ingredients were simply estimated. It therefore took a long period of apprenticeship for anyone to become a good cook. This practice is followed even to this day in India.

For the Western world, however, the recipes have to be written down, which involves the laborious measuring of estimated quantities; skill and experience have had to give way to the urgency and mass-production needs of today's busy lifestyle.

INDIAN SPICES AND CONDIMENTS

The range of Indian spices and condiments is vast and varied. The selection of spices that go into any given recipe has evolved through the generations and great care has to be taken to ensure that the chosen spices complement, rather than counteract, each other. Correct use of spices is the key to successful Indian cookery.

Spices usually add taste and texture to the dish. They integrate totally into the sauce or gravy and cannot be identified at the end of the cooking process; examples are asafoetida, ginger, garam masala and most ground ingredients.

Condiments generally add flavour and bouquet to the dish. They do not blend into the sauce and are put to one side after cooking, not eaten. Examples are whole chillies, cinnamon stick, whole cloves and cardamom.

Interestingly, whether an item is a spice or condiment is sometimes determined by its usage rather than by the ingredient itself: coriander seed is a condiment, but ground coriander is a spice.

Spices are usually freshly ground just before cooking to ensure that the best possible results are obtained. In many cases meat is marinated overnight in the spice mixture so that the spices have a chance to reach the innermost 'grain' of the meat. Careful and correct use of previously ground and stored spices, if a few tips and hints are followed, will produce perfectly good results. These tips have been included in most of the recipes.

Once the spices to be used are selected, the cook is faced with several options:

1 The quantity of each spice to use.
2 Which of these spices to roast and grind.
3 In what sequence to add these spices to the dish.

Thus, even if only three spices are chosen, it is still possible to concoct dozens of different flavours! Obviously only a few of these have found favour through the generations, but this point serves to illustrate the vast number of combinations that are possible. The process can be likened to musicians playing a piece of music; even with the same notes and the same players the end result can be totally different depending on the skill of the conductor in blending, mixing and emphasising the different contributions made by individual players.

Some five thousand years ago, the sages of India discovered the medicinal properties of various roots, barks, leaves, seeds and flowers. They were the first to formalise and systemise the effects and usage of these ingredients. Natural human reluctance to accept these dictats forced the sages to incorporate these instructions into the Holy Indian Scriptures, the *Vedas*. Once these instructions were given a religious bias they were more readily accepted into the Indian way of life.

THE TECHNIQUES OF PREPARING AND COOKING INDIAN FOOD

Maintaining the delicate balance of spice mixing is an art which can be acquired with a little care and imagination. The taste given to any dish by the spices depends on their combination and on the method of cooking used. The same basic spices used in different combinations and with different methods of cooking, will produce a dramatically different taste. The combinations are many and varied, but the best results can be achieved by following the simple guidelines below.

Preparing Spices

In India, spices are usually freshly ground before cooking each meal, as this ensures the best results. However, it is not always possible for today's busy cook to follow this method. Careful and correct use of ready-ground or home-ground, stored spices will produce perfectly delicious results.

Using whole spices Clean the spices, remove any debris, stalks and pieces of grit. Heat a cast-iron or other heavy-based pan without adding any fat, and dry-roast the spices gently until you can smell the aroma. Allow the spices to cool completely, then grind in a coffee mill and store in airtight jars. Use as required. These spices will remain fresh for three to four months.

Using ready-ground spices Ground spices have a limited shelf life as they tend to lose their essential flavour and aroma during storage. Better results can be achieved by revitalising dull spices. To do this, heat them through gently in a dry, heavy-based pan. Heat the spices just until you can smell the aroma being released, then cool thoroughly and store in airtight jars. Spices prepared in this way will produce a much more delicious dish than if used straight from the packet.

Frying Spices

It is essential to follow the timings given for frying spices at different stages of cooking. Frying and braising the spices at different temperatures for the same recipe is an art that ultimately helps to blend the flavours of the various spices that are used.

Frying dry spices Care should be taken in frying dry, ground or whole spices. The fat should not be allowed to overheat as this will burn the spices very quickly, imparting a bitter flavour to the dish.

Frying 'wet' spices This category consists mainly of puréed onions, ginger and garlic, to which other dry, ground spices are added during frying. It is crucial not to rush the process of frying. The raw smell, which will ultimately lead to a rancid curry, must be eliminated before adding the meat.

Frying onions When frying chopped or sliced onions to make a curry sauce, the onions should not be allowed to brown. They should be fried gently, over medium-low heat and stirred frequently to ensure that they are an even, pale golden colour. Sometimes onions have to be browned if they are to be used to garnish pilaus and birianis. For this purpose, the onions should be fried over medium heat, stirring frequently to ensure even browning.

The fat used for frying onions should be carefully measured because, in the beginning, when the moisture content of the onions 'cloud' the fat, it is tempting to add a little more. Once the moisture begins to evaporate, the fat will separate and become more visible, indicating that the onions are now ready to take on other spices. When dry spices are added at this stage the heat should be adjusted to low, and after two to three minutes, a little water (about one tablespoon) should be sprinkled over to ensure that the mixture does not stick to the bottom of the pan and that it fries evenly.

Using Water

The temperature of the water used in preparing a curry is an important consideration. Cold water should not be added to the carefully blended ingredients, as this will impair the flavour. Warm water helps to maintain the degree of flavour that has been achieved by blending the spices at a given temperature.

Using Salt

Most westerners seem to find the quantity of salt used in Indian recipes rather alarming. There are perfectly valid reasons for maintaining these levels of salt in the food, the most important being that salt subdues the flavour of the spices and chillies. Without the correct amount of salt, the spices taste rather overpowering. Unlike in Western cooking, salt in Indian cooking is used at the beginning of, or during the cooking process to ensure the proper blending of flavours created by the different spices used. Another reason is that when salt is added to some dishes, particularly vegetables, these release their own juices and the food is cooked entirely in these. This in turn dilutes the effect of the spices, creating a proper balance of flavours.

If the amount of salt is drastically reduced in a recipe, it is advisable to adjust the quantity of spices too. This, though, will carry the risk of losing the authentic taste of the dish.

Using a Pressure Cooker

The pressure cooker is an almost indispensable item in an Indian kitchen. A large proportion of the Indian population is vegetarian, and protein in their daily diet is therefore obtained from foods such as lentils, chickpeas, and all kinds of dried beans. In a pressure cooker, pulses as well as meat, will cook in less than half the time required by the conventional method. Peas and beans should be prepared according to the instructions in the recipe, but, instead of prolonged simmering, they can be cooked in a pressure cooker. Remember, however, to follow the manufacturer's instructions regarding cooking times.

Preparing Rice Before Cooking

Long grain rice is generally used in Indian cooking. There are different types of long grain rice and choosing a good quality rice is just as important as cooking it successfully.

Basmati is the superior long grain rice and is used in all pilaus and birianis. Basmati rice differs from other long grain rice in that it is matured for as long as four to five years after harvesting. The older the rice, the better it is, as it will cook easily without sticking. Basmati rice varies a great deal in quality and this largely depends on how mature the rice is. The best variety, grown in the foothills of the mighty Himalayas, is known as 'Tilda'. There are other varieties of good quality basmati rice, such as Dehra Dun Basmati, Patna Basmati and, of course, Pakistani Basmati.

Young long grain rice has a high proportion of starch and is more prone to sticking. However, as basmati rice tends to be expensive, other long grain rice, such as Patna rice, can be used successfully if it is washed and drained at least two to three times in cold water. After draining it, soak the rice in cold water for an hour or so, then stir it and drain thoroughly. This will reduce the starch content and prepare the grains to absorb the moisture during cooking without getting sticky. Basmati rice should also be washed at least twice, soaked for thirty minutes, and then drained.

One important point to remember for successful rice cookery is that the rice should never be stirred as soon as it is cooked. Freshly cooked rice tends to be fragile and it must be allowed to stand before being handled. The rice should be forked through gently before serving.

In India rice is also of significance in religious and social ceremonies. At weddings, for instance, small handfuls of rice are thrown, rather like confetti, at the bridegroom when he arrives at the bride's home for the wedding ceremony. Similarly, when the bride arrives at her new home, after the ceremony, a large bowl of rice is offered to her and she scatters some of it on the ground before entering the house. This signifies that the bride brings good fortune with her.

Preparing Dough for Indian Bread

The type of dough used for Indian bread tends to be easy to prepare, and can be prepared in advance. The point to watch out for is that the right amount of water is used to ensure that the dough has the correct elasticity without any stickiness. The level of absorbency varies a great deal between different types of flour. It is therefore advisable to add the water a little at a time until the correct consistency is achieved. Prepared dough should be wrapped in greaseproof paper and placed in a plastic bag if it is to be stored in the refrigerator. The dough will always benefit from a little standing time. If left at room temperature, wrap the dough first in greaseproof paper and then in a cloth to prevent it from drying out. It should not be left at room temperature for more than a few hours. Dough stored in the refrigerator should be brought to room temperature before rolling out.

Preparing Chicken

Chicken is never cooked with the skin left on and it is always cut into small pieces. This is because the skin does not allow the spices to permeate the meat, and the smaller the pieces are cut, the better the chances of the spices reaching the innermost grain of the meat. As well as removing the skin, all excess fat should be trimmed off. The chicken should then be washed and dried thoroughly with absorbent paper or a cloth. If not dried properly, the excess water content will not allow the chicken to fry with the spices and it will start braising instead. Frying the chicken with the other ingredients before adding the required amount of water is extremely important.

Chicken is also normally cooked on the bone, except when making kababs, because the flavour of the meat is always best nearest the bone. The bones also add flavour to the gravy. In India, a special bone stock, called *Yakhni*, is prepared for cooking certain types of curries and pilaus which use boned meat.

Preparing Meat

Meat is generally cooked on the bone for the reasons stated above. The same procedure for skinning, trimming off the fat, and washing and drying as for chicken, should be followed when preparing meat. Again, drying the meat is very important.

Cooking with Oil and Ghee

Traditionally, most of the cooking was done in ghee (clarified butter), but recently people have been made aware of the dangers of too much saturated fat in their diet and hence oil is now more commonly used. No particular recommendation is necessary as to which cooking oil to use. It is purely a matter of personal choice, though a light variety, such as sunflower oil is easier on the digestive system. Ghee, however, is necessary for certain dishes, such as pilaus, birianis and some Mughlai curries.

TECHNIQUES

Although full instructions accompany each recipe, a description of the techniques themselves is necessary to help understand them better. Once these techniques are fully understood, you will be completely at ease cooking Indian food and will be able to use your own creative skills to adapt the recipes.

Braising (Korma)

This is one of the most important techniques. Korma is essentially braised meat or vegetables, cooked using only a minute quantity of liquid. Traditionally, a korma is made by very slow cooking and hot charcoal is placed on the lid to ensure that even distribution of heat is maintained from both directions. To simplify this, a heavy-based pan with a tight-fitting lid should be used, because slow cooking is the key to success with this method. There are several different types of korma dishes, all of which use only prime cuts of meat. For most kormas, the meat or chicken is first marinated in a yogurt-based mixture and cooked in the marinade itself, with little or no water. The more elaborate kormas need an aromatic stock, or *Yakhni*, which is prepared by prolonged simmering of bones with whole spices. This is then strained and used to cook the meat.

The delicious creamy taste and the smooth velvety texture come from ingredients such as thick set natural yogurt, cream, ground almonds and coconut milk. These, of course, are not all used in the same dish.

Pot Roasting (The Dum Method)

Though this method is like western pot roasting, there is a very special technique involved. The dish is cooked over charcoal and hot charcoal is also placed on the lid of the pot. The pot is sealed using a sticky dough made of flour, to prevent any loss of steam. Accurate judgement of cooking times is necessary because the lid is removed only once the food is fully cooked. The food is not stirred during cooking, but the pot is gently shaken from side to side to ensure that the food does not stick to the pan.

To adapt this method for use in a modern kitchen, use a heavy-based saucepan which has a non-stick surface and a tight-fitting lid. The non-stick surface is essential because the food is generally cooked without any water. Sometimes a little water is added to cook certain dishes such as Kashmiri Dum Aloo, and this method is known as 'Dum Bhoona'. The meat and vegetables cooked by this method are normally cut into large pieces, and as little or no water is used in the dum method, a generous amount of ghee or oil is used to cook the food. For the health-conscious, present-day food habits make it difficult to follow this traditional method and the recipes contained in this book therefore tend towards the use of cooking liquid to replace some of the fat. To seal the saucepan, use a piece of aluminium foil or greaseproof paper, then put the lid on.

Frying (Bhoona)

This important technique produces beautifully aromatic, dry dishes. The most important stage in cooking a successful bhoona dish is frying the spices until they are a rich brown colour. Sometimes puréed onions, garlic and ginger root are fried first at varying temperatures to achieve the required colour, and the other spices are added halfway through. Chopped or sliced onions with crushed garlic and ginger, fried in the same way, produce a different flavour in a bhoona dish. The meat is cut into small pieces and very little water or stock is used to cook it. At the end of the cooking time, the meat is occasionally fried again, over a high heat to give it that final 'bhoona' flavour. Meat or fish is sometimes browned over a fairly high heat to form a crust, then the spices are fried separately and combined with the meat or fish to cook with a small amout of liquid, which forms a dryish dish such as Fish Bhoona. Meat or chicken can be cooked in a spicy liquid first until almost tender. The pieces are then lifted out of the liquid and fried in hot fat, and a little cooking liquid is added from time to time until the liquid has reduced to a paste-like consistency; Murghi Jhal Frezi is a perfect example.

Seasoning (Tarka)

Tarka simply means seasoning, and this method involves frying spices in hot oil and these are then incorporated into the dish after it has been cooked. Sometimes, only whole spices such as mustard and cumin seeds, dried red chillies and curry leaves are fried, and sometimes finely chopped or sliced onions and garlic are added to the whole spices, as in Tarka Dhal.

Tandoori Cooking

The word *tandoor* means clay oven; therefore, all food cooked in a tandoor is referred to as Tandoori food. A tandoor is cylinder-like in shape and charcoal is used to cook the food. The heat generated in the tandoor is rather fierce and the clay is able to retain this heat well and to distribute it evenly. This is the reason why Tandoori Chicken and kabab dishes such as Chicken Tikka and Boti Kabab, have a crust on the surface while the inside is beautifully moist and succulent. Small whole chickens and whole fish can also be cooked to perfection in a tandoor.

The preparation of Tandoori dishes involves marinating first to tenderise the meat, a process which also enables the flavour of the spices to penetrate deep inside. The pieces of meat, chicken or whole fish, are all threaded onto specially designed skewers and lowered into the oven. Food generally takes only a few minutes to cook because the tandoor is able to cook both the outside and the inside of the food simultaneously.

Besides cooking meat, fish and chicken, the tandoor is also used to bake breads such as Naan and Tandoori Roti. The dough is not rolled, but stretched to the desired shape and slapped onto the inner walls of the tandoor. The colour used in Tandoori food has no flavour, and is used simply to distinguish Tandoori dishes from others. The traditional colouring is a natural dye, though artificial Tandoori colour is widely used now. The colour does not add any flavour and can therefore be omitted from the recipe, if desired. On the other hand, if you like the colour, but are unable to buy it, tomato purée mixed with a few drops of red food colouring makes a good substitute. The food colouring on its own will turn the food pink rather than red. One tablespoon of tomato purée is generally enough for the recipes contained in this book.

There is no substitue for a tandoor, but they are fairly expensive to install and not economical to run for small amounts of food. A traditional tandoor is meant for commercial use where mass production is necessary, although smaller versions are now being manufactured. Perfectly delicious Tandoori food can be prepared in a very hot gas or electric oven, although the characteristic charcoal flavour will be missing. Food cooked in this way should be turned over and basted during cooking and the excess liquid should be shaken off before the food is removed from the cooking dish.

REFRIGERATING, FREEZING AND REHEATING

Indian food is ideal for entertaining because the preparation can be done in advance and the food refrigerated or frozen.

When refrigerating Indian food it is advisable to cover the dish with a piece of cling film or aluminium foil before placing the lid on it. This not only ensures freshness, but also prevents the leakage of strong smells inside the refrigerator.

Although freezing, defrosting and reheating need no special techniques, a few important points should be remembered for the most successful results.

Freezing and Defrosting Dishes with Gravy

The dish should be cooled thoroughly and chilled for several hours before freezing. Defrosting should be done slowly, preferably overnight in the refrigerator, and the dish should be thoroughly defrosted before reheating. The dish should also be reheated fairly slowly. This is most important in reheating Mughlai, or creamy, dishes.

When a dish is defrosted it can look rather alarming to the novice because the liquid separates and collects at the bottom of the container. At this stage, there is no need to stir and mix the food. Simply transfer the food to a saucepan and cover with a lid. Place the saucepan over a low heat and bring the contents to a gentle simmer. Then stir the food gently, replace the lid and allow the dish to simmer until it is heated through. This way, the meat will reabsorb all the liquid and the texture of the dish will return to its original state.

Freezing and Defrosting Dry Dishes

Foods such as kababs, Tandoori dishes, all types of pakoras, bhajiyas and samosas should be cooled and wrapped in a double thickness of aluminium foil to prevent them from drying out. Place the packed food in a freezer bag, then label and freeze it. The food should be defrosted slowly and thoroughly before reheating.

Reheat kababs and Tandoori dishes in the oven, in their foil package. The oven temperature should be moderately hot with the food placed in the centre. Most of these dishes will reheat adequately in ten to fifteen minutes, with the exception of Tandoori Chicken which will need approximately twenty to twenty-five minutes. These can also be successfully reheated in the microwave; the food must be covered to prevent dehydration during reheating. The pieces of meat and chicken should be turned over halfway through the reheating cycle.

Reheat pakoras and bhajiyas in the centre of a moderately hot oven in an open dish. The foil should be removed and the food arranged in a single layer. They can also be reheated under a preheated medium grill and turned over halfway through. Both methods will restore the crispness. The microwave is not suitable for this purpose. To reheat samosas, unwrap and arrange them on an open tray in a single layer. The tray should be placed in the centre of a moderate oven for fifteen to twenty minutes, turning the samosas over once. They can also be reheated under a preheated low grill for ten to fifteen minutes, turning frequently.

It is not strictly necessary to defrost bread before reheating. The foil package can be placed in the centre of a hot oven for about twenty minutes, and the package turned over halfway through. Allow ten to twelve minutes if the bread has been defrosted.

Breads such as Naan and Tandoori Roti can be reheated successfully in the microwave. Thinner varieties, such as Chapatties, become rather hard and dry if reheated in the microwave. Puris and Loochis are not recommended for freezing.

To reheat Cauliflower Cutlets and Masala Machchi, unwrap and reheat under a preheated low grill for eight to ten minutes, turning them over carefully halfway through.

All other dry dishes that are suitable for freezing can be reheated on top of the cooker over a low heat. The food should be stirred gently from time to time.

All rice dishes, whether refrigerated or frozen and defrosted, can be reheated as follows. Put the rice into an ovenproof dish and cover it first with a piece of greased greaseproof paper before putting the lid on. This will prevent the top layer of the rice from drying out during reheating. Preheat the oven to 180°C/350°F/Gas Mark 4. Reheat the rice in the centre of the oven; the time required will depend on the quantity. Usually, 275g/10oz of rice will heat through in thirty to thirty-five minutes.

The easiest way to reheat rice is in the microwave. It should be placed in a covered dish and the rice forked through once or twice during reheating to ensure that it heats evenly.

The best way to serve rice without having to reheat is to prepare it fully up to the stage of adding water. Do not add the water, but remove the pan from the heat, cover it and set aside until you are ready to serve the meal. Then place the pan of prepared rice over a medium-low heat and once it starts sizzling, stir gently, then add the water and follow the remaining instructions in the recipe. Cooked rice will keep hot for twenty-five to thirty minutes.

COOKING UTENSILS AND EQUIPMENT

No extra-special cooking utensils are required to produce the authentic flavour of Indian food. Traditionally, cast iron and earthenware pots and pans are used in India. A round-bottomed cast-iron pan (*Kadhai*), similar to a wok but smaller in size, is used for deep-frying. Its shape means that it does not require as much cooking fat or oil as a deep-fat fryer and the cast iron enables the food to cook at an even and steady temperature. A cast-iron griddle (*Tava*) is used to make most Indian breads. Heavy pots and pans with tight-fitting lids and a frying pan with a non-stick surface are ideal for Indian cooking because they enable the food to cook evenly without sticking.

For preparing the ingredients, an electric blender and a coffee grinder are absolutely necessary. In a modern kitchen, these replace the traditional grinding stone.

A blender is essential for pulverising onions, root ginger and fresh garlic while a coffee grinder is required for grinding special spice mixtures. It is advisable, however, not to use the same grinder for coffee unless you like coffee with a spicy flavour!

A pestle and mortar or a wooden pestle are useful for crushing garlic and root ginger.

If your budget will allow, a food processor is an excellent investment. Indian recipes call for finely chopped or sliced onions and these are the key to a successful, smooth sauce. To achieve the necessary degree of fineness manually can be rather difficult and time consuming. A food processor will do this in a few seconds, as well as chopping vegetables and making a beautiful purée of onions, root ginger and fresh garlic. This purée can be frozen in the required quantities. In fact, just about any ingredients that need blending can be prepared in the food processor in a few seconds.

The greatest advantage of a food processor is that it will mix and knead the dough for all Indian breads to perfection, saving you all the hard work.

PLANNING AND SERVING AN INDIAN MEAL

Unlike in the West, Indian dishes are not strictly categorised into starters and main courses. An Indian meal consists of several dishes, and the traditional style of serving these would be to bring all the dishes to the dining table and for everyone to help themselves, rather like a sit-down buffet. Generally, people have second helpings of most of the dishes. In the classic style, however, the food is actually served in a large plate known as a *thali*. The staple, such as rice or bread along with the dry dishes, is served on the thali and small bowls are used to serve dishes containing gravy. Traditional methods are being adapted to suit the changing pattern of life and there is no reason why a starter cannot be served before the main meal, indeed this practice is now becoming increasingly popular.

A carefully chosen starter is the way to fill guests with curiosity as well as enthusiasm for the meal to follow. With this in mind, enticing and delicious recipes have been chosen for the section entitled 'Snacks and Starters'.

Alcoholic drinks are not traditional accompaniments to an Indian meal; this is because the majority of the population in India prefer water which, they feel, better enables them to enjoy and appreciate the flavour of the spices. If you wish to serve alchohol, lager is by far the best drink to accompany an Indian meal. Well-chilled, dry white wine or dry cider are suitable alternatives. A chilled, light red wine can be served if desired, though red wine does not complement an Indian meal very well.

Nonalcoholic drinks, such as Nimbu Pani, Jeera Pani and Mango Sherbet, can all be enjoyed with Indian food.

MICROWAVE INDIAN COOKING

Cooking Indian food in the microwave oven might sound like an impossible idea. However, a careful analysis of the way in which spices are used in the conventional method, will show that adapting this to the microwave is actually fairly simple and straightforward.

In the conventional method of cooking, spices are fried first, both to eliminate their raw taste and to enhance their flavour before the meat, fish or vegetables are added. This is the very essence of successful Indian cookery. Two easy steps will ensure that these requirements are met when cooking in the microwave. Firstly, preroast the spices using the conventional cooker (full instructions for this are given in 'The Techniques of Preparing and Cooking Indian Food'). Then freshen up the spices just before using them. Instructions on how to do this are given with each recipe. This normally involves roasting or heating the spices at specified power levels for specified times and then allowing a certain amount of standing time.

When preparing Indian dishes in the microwave, you should bear in mind several factors:

1 Spices tend to taste much stronger than in conventionally cooked dishes. For this reason, they must be used only in the quantities specified. Fewer spices in smaller quantities is the key to success here. Pay particular attention to turmeric and saffron; if not used carefully in the specified quantities, these two spices will impart a bitter taste to the dishes.

2 Cooking the dishes in advance and reheating them will enhance their flavour by a significant amount. Whilst this is true of conventionally cooked recipes, it is particularly evident in microwave-prepared dishes.

3 Remember that it is important to stir the food as you would do in the conventional method.

4 It is very important to use the right size of cooking dish; the correct sizes are specified in most recipes.

5 Cut all meat, vegetables and fish into even-sized pieces so that the microwave energy is able to penetrate the food uniformly, thereby cooking all the pieces evenly and to the required degree.

6 Allowing standing time after cooking is another important point to remember, as the microwave energy will carry on cooking the food even when the oven is switched off.

Follow the above steps carefully and you will find that the food is just as delicious as that cooked in the conventional way. Microwave cooking is also the perfect way to prepare Indian meals without strong cooking smells.

The most important benefit, of course, is that the microwave cuts cooking time by at least a third and, in some cases, by as much as half. Last, but not least, food cooked in the microwave is healthier as it retains all its goodness as well as the fresh colours of the vegetables, making the dish look more attractive and appetising.

Microwave Indian cooking is sure to be an exciting new experience which will not only bring you a great deal of pleasure but also heaps of compliments from family and friends!

All microwave recipes featured in this book were prepared using a 700 watt oven. For ovens of a lower rating, timings should be increased accordingly:
500 watt: add 40 seconds to every minute stated in the recipe
600 watt: add 20 seconds to every minute stated in the recipe
650 watt: only a slight increase in the overall time is necessary

snacks and starters

Mutton Patties

MAKES 14 Patties

1kg/2.2lbs potatoes
½-1 tsp chilli powder
1½ tsps salt or to taste
3 tbsps cooking oil
½ tsp fennel seeds
1 large onion, finely chopped
½-inch cube of root ginger, peeled and finely grated
2-4 cloves garlic, peeled and chopped or crushed
325g/12oz fine lean mince, lamb or beef

Make a paste of the following 5 ingredients by adding 3 tbsps water
1 tsp ground cumin
1½ tsps ground coriander
1 tsp ground fennel
½ tsp ground turmeric
½ tsp garam masala

1 small tin of tomatoes
90ml/3fl oz water
1 fresh green chilli, finely chopped
2 tbsps chopped coriander leaves
1 egg, beaten
2 tbsps milk
2 tbsps flour
100g/4oz golden breadcrumbs
Oil for deep frying

1. Boil the potatoes in their jacket, peel and mash them. Add half the chilli powder and ½ tsp salt from the specified amount. Divide the mixture into 14 golf-ball sized portions, cover and keep aside.

2. Heat the oil over medium heat and fry the fennel seeds until they are brown.

3. Add the onions, ginger and garlic, and stir and fry until the onions are lightly browned (6-8 minutes).

4. Add the mince and fry until all moisture evaporates, stirring frequently (6-8 minutes).

5. Add the spice paste, stir and fry for 5-6 minutes reducing heat towards the last 2-3 minutes.

6. Add the tomatoes, stir and mix, breaking them up with the back of the spoon. Adjust heat to medium and cook for 3-4 minutes stirring frequently.

7. Add the water, the remaining chilli powder and salt, cover and simmer for 15 minutes. Adjust heat to medium, uncover and cook for 4-5 minutes or until the mixture is completely dry but moist. Stir frequently.

8. Stir in the chopped green chilli and the coriander leaves. Cook for 1-2 minutes stirring constantly, remove from heat and allow to cool completely.

9. Mix the beaten egg with the milk and keep aside.

10. Take a portion of the potato and roll it between the palms to make a neat smooth ball. Make a depression in the centre and form into a cup shape. Fill this cavity with the mince leaving approx. ¼-inch round the border. Cover the filling by gently pressing the entire circular border together. Roll between the palms and flatten to form a round cake, about ½-inch thick.

11. Dust the cake in the flour then dip in egg and milk mixture and roll in the breadcrumbs. Make the rest of the patties the same way.

12. Deep fry the patties until they are golden brown. Drain on absorbent paper.

TIME Preparation takes 45-50 minutes, cooking takes 35-40 minutes.

Chicken Tikka

Chicken Tikka is one of the most popular chicken dishes cooked in the Tandoor, the Indian clay oven. This recipe is adapted to cook the chicken in the conventional oven at a high temperature.

SERVES 4

450g/1lb boneless, skinned chicken breast
1 tsp salt
Juice of ½ a lemon
½ tsp tandoori colour or a few drops of red food colouring mixed with 1 tbsp tomato purée
2 cloves garlic, peeled and coarsely chopped
½-inch cube of root ginger, peeled and coarsely chopped
2 tsps ground coriander
½ tsp ground allspice or garam masala
¼ of a whole nutmeg, finely grated
½ tsp ground turmeric
125g/5oz thick set natural yogurt
4 tbsps corn or vegetable oil
½ tsp chilli powder

1. Cut the chicken into 1-inch cubes. Sprinkle with ½ tsp salt from the specified amount, and the lemon juice – mix thoroughly, cover and keep aside for 30 minutes.

2. Put the rest of the ingredients into an electric food processor or liquidiser and blend until smooth.

3. Put this marinade into a sieve and hold the sieve over the chicken pieces. Press the marinade through the sieve with the back of a metal spoon until only a very coarse mixture is left.

4. Coat the chicken thoroughly with the sieved marinade, cover the container and leave to marinate for 6-8 hours or overnight in the refrigerator.

5. Preheat the oven to 230°C/450°F/Gas Mark 8.

6. Line a roasting tin with aluminium foil (this will help to maintain the high level of temperature required to cook the chicken quickly without drying it out).

7. Thread the chicken onto skewers, leaving ¼-inch gap between each piece (this is necessary for the heat to reach all sides of the chicken).

8. Place the skewers in the prepared roasting tin and brush with some of the remaining marinade.

9. Cook in the centre of the oven for 6-8 minutes.

10. Take the tin out of the oven, turn the skewers over and brush the pieces of chicken with the remaining marinade.

11. Return the tin to the oven and cook for a further 6-8 minutes.

12. Shake off any excess liquid from the chicken. (Strain the excess liquid and keep aside for Chicken Tikka Masala)

13. Place the skewers on a serving dish. You may take the tikka off the skewers if you wish, but allow the meat to cool slightly before removing from the skewers.

TIME Preparation takes 30-35 minutes plus time needed to marinate, cooking takes 15-18 minutes.

Barrah Kabab (Marinated Lamb Chops)

A wonderful dish which can be served as a starter or a main course. The chops are marinated in a spice-laced yogurt mixture. The yogurt tenderises the chops and also prepares the meat to absorb the spices better.

SERVES 6-8

900g/2lbs lamb chump chops
½ tsp ground nutmeg
½ tsp ground black pepper
½ tsp ground cinnamon
½ tsp cayenne or chilli powder
½ tsp ground turmeric
2 cloves garlic, peeled
2 tbsps coarsely chopped onions
½-inch cube of root ginger, peeled and chopped
125g/5oz thick set natural yogurt
½ tsp salt or to taste
1 tbsp cooking oil
1 tsp ground cumin
1 tbsp sesame seeds

1. Trim off excess fat from the chops and flatten each chop with a meat mallet or a rolling pin. Wipe clean with a damp cloth.

2. Put all ingredients except chops, oil, cumin and sesame seeds, into an electric liquidiser or food processor and blend to a purée.

3. Put the chops into a large bowl and pour the blended ingredients over them.

4. Using your fingers, rub the marinade well into each chop.

5. Cover the container with cling film and leave to marinate for at least 8 hours in a cool place or overnight in the refrigerator.

6. Preheat oven to 219°C/425°F/Gas Mark 7.

7. Line a roasting tin with aluminium foil (this will help reflect heat and keep your roasting tin clean).

8. Arrange the chops on the roasting tin in a single layer (reserve any remaining marinade) and cook in the centre of the oven for 10 minutes – turning the chops over once. Reduce heat to 200°C/400°F/ Gas Mark 6.

9. Mix the remaining marinade with the oil and cumin. Brush the chops with this and sprinkle half the sesame seeds on top. Return the tray to the upper part of the oven for 10 minutes. Turn the chops over and brush this side with the remaining marinade mixture and sprinkle the rest of the sesame seeds as before. Cook for a further 10-15 minutes.

TIME Preparation takes 20-25 minutes plus 8 hours to marinate, cooking takes 30-35 minutes.

SERVING IDEAS Serve as a starter with plenty of raw onion rings, sprinkled with lemon juice, wedges of cucumber and crisp lettuce leaves; or as a main course with Plain Boiled Rice and Mixed Vegetable Curry.
Suitable for freezing.

Onion Bhajiyas

Onion Bhajiyas are popular all over India and have established themselves as a firm favourite in this country. They are made by coating finely shredded onions with a spicy batter.

SERVES 6-8

150g/6oz besan (gram or chick-pea flour)
1 tsp salt or to taste
Pinch of bicarbonate of soda
1 tbsp ground rice
2 tsps ground cumin
2 tsps ground coriander
½-1 tsp chilli powder
1-2 fresh green chillies, finely chopped and seeded if a milder flavour is preferred
2 large onions, sliced into half rings and separated
200ml/7fl oz water
Oil for deep frying

1. Sieve the besan and add the salt, bicarbonate of soda, ground rice, cumin, coriander, chilli powder and green chillies; mix well.

2. Now add the onions and mix thoroughly.

3. Gradually add the water and keep mixing until a soft but thick batter is formed and the onions are thoroughly coated with this batter.

4. Heat the oil over medium heat (*it is important to heat the oil to the correct temperature – 160-180°C*). To test this, take a tiny amount of the batter, about the size of a seed of a lemon and drop it in the oil. If it floats up to the surface immediately but without turning brown, the oil is at the correct temperature.

5. Using a tablespoon put in as many small amounts (about half a tablespoon) of the onion/batter mix as the pan will hold in a single layer. Take care not to make these amounts too large as this will result in the outside of the bhajiyas being overdone while the insides remain uncooked.

6. Reduce the heat to low as the bhajiyas need to be fried over a gentle heat to ensure that the batter at the centre of the bhajiyas is cooked, and stays soft, whilst the outside turns golden brown and crisp. This should take about 10-12 minutes for each batch.

7. Drain the bhajiyas on absorbent paper.

TIME Preparation takes 15-20 minutes, cooking takes 45-50 minutes.

SERVING IDEAS Serve on their own with drinks or with a selection of chutneys as a starter.
Suitable for freezing.

Chicken or Turkey Pakoras

These delicious pakoras can be made with cooked as well as raw meat and it is therefore an excellent and unusual way to use left over Christmas turkey or Sunday roast. Raw chicken breast has been used for the recipe below, as they remain more succulent than cooked meat.

SERVES 6-8

150ml/5fl oz water
1 medium-size onion, coarsely chopped
2-3 cloves garlic, peeled and coarsely chopped
1-2 fresh green chillies, coarsely chopped; remove the seeds if you prefer a mild flavour
2 tbsps chopped coriander leaves
125g/5oz besan or gram flour/chick pea flour, sieved
1 tsp ground coriander
1 tsp ground cumin
½ tsp garam masala
½ tsp chilli powder
1 tsp salt or to taste
Pinch of bicarbonate of soda
325g/12oz fresh, boneless and skinless chicken or turkey breast
Oil for deep frying

---

1. Put 90ml/3fl oz water from the specified amount into an electric liquidiser followed by the onion, garlic, green chillies and coriander leaves. Blend until smooth. Alternatively, process the ingredients in a food processor without the water.

2. In a large bowl, mix the besan, coriander, cumin, garam masala, chilli powder, salt and bicarbonate of soda.

3. Add the liquidised ingredients and mix thoroughly.

4. Add the remaining water and mix well to form a thick paste.

5. Cut the chicken into pieces and gently mix into the paste until the pieces are fully coated.

6. Heat the oil over medium heat; when hot, using a tablespoon, put in one piece of besan-coated chicken/turkey at a time until you have as many as the pan will hold in a single layer without overcrowding it. Make sure that each piece is fully coated with the paste.

7. Adjust heat to low and fry the pakoras for 10-15 minutes turning them over half way through. Remove the pakoras with a perforated spoon and drain on absorbent paper.

TIME Preparation takes 20 minutes, cooking takes 30 minutes.

SERVING IDEAS Serve with Tomato Chutney or Green Coriander Chutney. Suitable for freezing.

Boti Kabab

Tender boneless lamb is the traditional meat used for these kababs. They are marinated in a spice-laced yogurt dressing before cooking.

SERVES 6

700g/1½lbs boned leg of lamb
2 small cloves of garlic, peeled and chopped
2 tbsps chopped coriander leaves
2 tbsps lemon juice
75g/3oz thick set natural yogurt
Salt to taste
½ tsp ground turmeric
2 tbsps cooking oil

Grind the following 4 ingredients in a coffee grinder:
6 green cardamons (with the skin)
1 cinnamon stick, 1-inch long
2-3 dried red chillies
1 tbsp coriander seeds

To garnish
Thinly sliced onion rings, separated
Crisp lettuce leaves
Wedges of cucumber

1. Wash the meat and dry with a cloth.

2. Prick all over with a sharp knife and cut into 1½-inch cubes.

3. Put the garlic, coriander leaves, lemon juice and yogurt into a liquidiser or food processor and blend until smooth. Add the salt, turmeric and the ground ingredients.

4. Put the meat into a bowl and add the liquidised ingredients.

5. Mix thoroughly, cover and leave to marinate for 6-8 hours (or overnight in the refrigerator).

6. Preheat grill to high.

7. Line the grill pan with a piece of aluminium foil (this will reflect heat and also keep your grill pan clean).

8. Thread meat onto skewers leaving about ¼-inch gap between each piece.

9. Mix any remaining marinade with the oil and keep aside.

10. Place the skewers on the prepared grill pan and grill the kababs for 2-3 minutes.

11. Turn the skewers over and grill for a further 2-3 minutes.

12. Reduce heat to medium. Brush the kababs with the oil/marinade mixture and grill for 6-8 minutes.

13. Turn the skewers over and brush the kababs with the remaining oil/marinade mixture. Grill for a further 6-8 minutes.

TIME Preparation takes 20 minutes plus time needed for marinating, cooking takes 15-20 minutes.

SERVING IDEAS Serve as a starter, using ingredients given for garnishing. Serve on cocktail sticks with drinks or as a side dish for a dinner party.

VARIATION Use fillet of pork.

WATCHPOINT Do not overcook the Kababs: follow the cooking time precisely so that the Kababs remain succulent after cooking.

Seekh Kababs

Wooden skewers about 6-8-inches long are the best type of skewers for these kababs. You can use metal or steel skewers, but allow the skewers to cool before shaping the next batch of kababs onto them.

MAKES 18 Kababs

Juice of half a lemon
2 tbsps chopped fresh mint or 1 tsp dried or bottled mint
3-4 tbsps chopped coriander leaves
25g/1oz raw cashews
1 medium-sized onion, coarsely chopped
2 small cloves of garlic, peeled and coarsely chopped
1-2 fresh green chillies, finely chopped or minced; remove the seeds if you like it mild
700g/1½lb lean mince, beef or lamb
2 tsps ground coriander
2 tsps ground cumin
1 tsp ground ajwain (ajowan or carum) or ground caraway seeds
½ tsp garam masala
½ tsp Tandoori colour or a few drops of red food colouring mixed with 1 tbsp tomato purée
½ tsp freshly ground black pepper
1 egg yolk
¼ tsp chilli powder
1 tsp salt or to taste
4 tbsps cooking oil

Grind the following ingredients in a coffee grinder
2 tbsps white poppy seeds
2 tbsps sesame seeds

1. Put the lemon juice, mint, coriander leaves, cashews, onion, garlic and green chillies in an electric liquidiser and blend to a smooth paste. Transfer the mixture to a large bowl.

2. Using the liquidiser, grind the mince in 2-3 small batches until it is fairly smooth, rather like a paste. Add the meat to the rest of the liquidised ingredients in the bowl.

3. Add the rest of the ingredients, except the the oil and knead the mixture until all the ingredients are mixed thoroughly and it is smooth. Alternatively, put all the ingredients, except the oil, in an electric food processor and process until the mixture is smooth.

4. Chill the mixture for 30 minutes.

5. Preheat oven to 240°C/475°F, Gas Mark 9. Line a roasting tin with aluminium foil.

6. Divide the kabab mix into about 18 balls, each slightly larger than a golf ball.

7. Mould a ball onto a skewer and form into a sausage shape by gently rolling between your palms (about 4-5-inches long) and place on the prepared roasting tin. Make the rest of the kababs the same way.

8. Brush generously with the oil and place the roasting tin just below the top rung of the oven. Cook for 6-8 minutes. Remove the tin from the oven and brush the kababs liberally with the remaining oil and cook for a further 6-8 minutes.

9. Allow the kababs to cool slightly before removing them from the skewers.

TIME Preparation takes 15-20 minutes, cooking takes 35-40 minutes.

Potato Pakoras

The Indian love of snacks is apparent in the wide range of mouthwatering recipes created to suit different occasions. These spice-coated crunchy potato slices are easy to make and can be served in a number of different ways.

SERVES 4-6

50g/2oz besan (gram flour or chick pea flour)
1 tbsp ground rice
½ tsp salt or to taste
1½ tsps ground coriander
1 tsp ground cumin
½ tsp chilli powder
50ml/2fl oz water
450g/1lb medium-sized potatoes, peeled and cut into ¼-inch thick slices
Oil for deep frying

1. Mix all the dry ingredients in a large bowl.

2. Add the water and mix to thick paste.

3. Add the potatoes and mix until the potato slices are fully coated with the paste.

4. Heat the oil over medium heat in a deep pan (you can use a deep fat fryer or a chip pan without the basket) and put in as many of the coated potato slices as the pan will hold in a single layer.

5. Fry the pakoras until golden brown (6-8 minutes).

6. Drain on absorbent paper.

TIME Preparation takes 10-15 minutes, cooking takes 20 minutes.

SERVING IDEAS Serve on their own with drinks; as a side dish with any meat, fish or chicken curry; or as a starter with Avocado Chutney.

VARIATION Use sweet potatoes.

WATCHPOINT Do not overcrowd the pan. This is to prevent the pakoras from sticking together.

NARGISI KABABS

MAKES 14 Kababs

For the filling:
2 hard-boiled eggs, shelled and coarsely chopped
1 fresh green chilli, finely chopped and seeded for a milder flavour
2 tbsps finely chopped or minced onion
1 tbsp finely chopped or minced coriander leaves
¼ tsp salt
1 tbsp thick set natural yogurt

25g/1oz ghee or unsalted butter
1 large onion, coarsely chopped
3-4 cloves garlic, peeled and coarsely chopped
1-inch cube of root ginger, peeled and coarsely chopped
1 tsp ground cumin
1½ tsps ground coriander
1 tsp garam masala
½ tsp chilli powder
½ tsp freshly ground black pepper
50g/2oz thick set natural yogurt
1 tbsp fresh mint leaves or 1 tsp dried or bottled mint
2 tbsps chopped coriander leaves
¾ tsp salt or to taste
570g/1¼lbs fine lean mince, lamb or beef
1 egg
2 tbsps besan (chick pea flour or gram flour), sieved
1 tbsp water
90ml/3fl oz cooking oil

1. Combine all ingredients for the filling in a bowl, mix thoroughly and keep aside.

2. Melt the ghee or butter over medium heat and fry the onion, garlic and ginger for 3-4 minutes. Adjust heat to low and add the cumin, coriander, garam masala, chilli powder and pepper, stir and fry for 1-2 minutes, then remove from heat and allow to cool.

3. Put the yogurt into an electric food processor and add the fried ingredients, mint, coriander, salt and the mince. Blend until smooth.

4. If you are using a liquidiser, blend the ingredients first without the mince. Transfer the blended ingredients to a mixing bowl and grind the mince in 2-3 batches.

5. Knead the blended ingredients and the mince until smooth. Divide the mixture into about 14 golf ball-sized portions. Make a depression in the centre of each ball and form into a cup shape. Fill with 1 heaped tsp of the egg mixture and cover the filling by pressing the edges together. Now roll it gently between the palms to form a neat ball, press the ball gently and form a round flat cake about ¾-inch thick. Make the rest of the kababs the same way.

6. Beat the egg and gradually sprinkle the besan while still beating. Add the water and beat again.

7. Heat the oil over medium heat in a wide, shallow, preferably non-stick or cast iron pan. Dip each kabab in the batter and fry in a single layer without overcrowding the pan until they are brown on both sides (3-4 minutes each side). Drain on absorbent paper.

TIME Preparation takes 40-45 minutes, cooking takes 10-15 minutes.

Mushroom Bhaji

Although mushrooms are not widely used in India, the Indian restaurants in this country have popularised the use of mushrooms in Indian cookery. Mushroom Bhaji appears to be one of the most popular of them all.

SERVES 4

3-4 tbsps cooking oil
1 medium-sized onion, finely chopped
2-3 cloves garlic, peeled and crushed
½ tsp ground turmeric
½ tsp chilli powder
1 tsp ground coriander
1 tsp ground cumin
¾ tsp salt or to taste
1 tbsp tomato purée
225g/8oz mushrooms, chopped

1. Heat the oil over medium heat and fry the onions until they are lightly browned.

2. Lower heat and add the garlic, turmeric, chilli powder, coriander and cumin. Stir and fry the spices and add about 1 tbsp water to prevent the spices from sticking to the bottom of the pan. As soon as this water dries up, add a little more. Continue doing this until you have fried the spices for about 5 minutes.

3. Add the salt and tomato purée, mix well and add the mushrooms. Stir until the ingredients are thoroughly mixed.

4. Sprinkle about 2 tbsps water and cover the pan. Simmer for 10 minutes.

5. The finished dish should have a little amount of gravy, but it should not be runny. If it appears to be a little runny, take the lid off and let the liquid evaporate until the gravy is reasonably thick.

TIME Preparation takes 15 minutes, cooking takes 20 minutes.

SERVING IDEAS Serve with Plain Boiled Rice or any Indian bread accompanied by Chicken with Channa Dhal or Kofta Curry. Also excellent with Kofta Pilau.

Meat Samosas

The ever-popular Samosas make a wonderful treat on any occasion. In India, they are a familiar sight at wedding receptions and cocktail parties.

MAKES 18 Samosas

2 tbsps cooking oil
2 medium-sized onions, finely chopped
225g/8oz lean mince, lamb or beef
3-4 cloves garlic, peeled and crushed
½-inch cube of root ginger, finely grated
½ tsp ground turmeric
2 tsps ground coriander
1½ tsps ground cumin
½-1 tsp chilli powder
½ tsp salt or to taste
125ml/4fl oz warm water
150g/6oz frozen garden peas
2 tbsps desiccated coconut
1 tsp garam masala
1-2 fresh green chillies, finely chopped and seeded if a milder flavour is preferred
2 tbsps chopped coriander leaves
1 tbsp lemon juice

1. Heat the oil over medium heat and fry the onions until they are lightly browned.

2. Add the mince, garlic and ginger. Stir and fry until all the liquid evaporates and adjust heat to low.

3. Add the turmeric, coriander, cumin, chilli powder and salt. Stir and fry until mince is lightly browned.

4. Add the water and the peas, bring to the boil, cover and simmer for 25–30 minutes. If there is any liquid left, take the lid off and cook the mince over medium heat until it is completely dry, stirring frequently.

5. Stir in the coconut, garam masala, green chillies and coriander leaves.

6. Remove from heat and add the lemon juice. Cool thoroughly before filling the Samosas.

For the pastry

225g/8oz plain flour
50g/2oz ghee or butter
½ tsp salt
75 ml/2½ fl oz warm water
Oil for deep frying

1. Add the butter and salt to the flour. Rub in well.

2. Mix a soft dough by adding the water. Knead until the dough feels soft and velvety to the touch.

3. Divide the dough into 9 balls. Rotate each ball between your palms in a circular motion, then press it down to make a flat cake.

4. Roll out each flat cake into 4-inch discs and cut into two. Use each semicircle of pastry as one envelope.

5. Moisten the straight edge with a little warm water.

6. Fold the semicircle of pastry in half to form a triangular cone.

7. Join the straight edges by pressing them hard into each other. Make sure that there are no gaps.

8. Fill these cones with the filling, leaving about ¼-inch border on the top of the cone.

9. Now moisten the top edges and press them hard together.

10. Deep fry the samosas over gentle heat until they are golden brown and drain on absorbent paper.

CAULIFLOWER PAKORAS

These chunky cauliflower florets with a spicy coating make a versatile snack as they can be served in many different ways.

SERVES 4

75g/3oz besan (gram flour or chick pea flour), sieved
1 tbsp ground rice
¾ tsp salt or to taste
2 tbsps ground coriander
2 tsps ground cumin
½-1 tsp chilli powder
½ tsp ground turmeric
Pinch of bicarbonate of soda
1 medium-sized cauliflower, cut into about 1½-inch florets
150ml/5fl oz water
Oil for deep frying

1. Mix the dry ingredients in a large bowl.

2. Add the cauliflower and water. Mix until the cauliflower is fully coated with the spiced gram flour paste. If the florets are not completely covered with the batter, spread the batter over the uncovered areas with a spoon.

3. Heat the oil over medium heat and put in as many florets as the pan will hold in a single layer. You can use a deep fat fryer or a chip pan without the basket.

4. Fry until the pakoras are uniformly brown (6-8 minutes per batch).

5. Drain on absorbent paper.

TIME Preparation takes 15 minutes, cooking takes 20 minutes.

SERVING IDEAS Serve on their own with drinks, as a side dish with almost anything or as a starter with Carrot & Peanut Raita.

TO FREEZE Suitable for freezing. Defrost thoroughly before reheating under a preheated medium grill for 6-8 minutes, turning them once.

WATCHPOINT Use no more than a pinch of bicarbonate of soda, because any more than that will ruin the taste and appearance of the pakoras.

SPICED MIXED NUTS

These spiced nuts are delicious and irresistible. They are roasted with a little oil and coated with spices while they are hot.

SERVES 8-10

100g/4oz whole almonds
100g/4oz raw cashews
2 tsps cooking oil
½ tsp ground coriander
½ tsp ground cumin
¼ tsp chilli powder
½ tsp salt

1. In a heavy-based pan, cook the nuts over low heat until they are heated through (3-4 minutes).

2. Add 1 tsp oil, stir and mix thoroughly. Toast the nuts until they are evenly browned (10-12 minutes), stirring constantly.

3. Remove from the heat and sprinkle with the spices and salt immediately. Mix thoroughly and keep aside for 10 minutes.

4. Add the remaining oil, stir and mix until the nuts are fully coated by the spices.

5. Allow to cool completely before serving.

TIME Preparation takes 5 minutes, cooking takes 15 minutes.

SERVING IDEAS Serve with pre-dinner drinks.

VARIATION Use peanuts instead of almonds.

Spiced Potato Bites

In Indian cookery, potatoes are used very imaginatively. Here, boiled potatoes are cut into small pieces and sautéed until they are brown and then flavoured with a light sprinkling of spices.

SERVES 6-8

700g/1½lbs potatoes
4 tbsps cooking oil
½ tbsp salt or to taste
¼ tsp garam masala
½ tsp ground cumin
½ tsp ground coriander
¼ - ½ tsp chilli powder

1. Boil the potatoes in their jacket, cool thoroughly, peel and dice them into 1-inch cubes.

2. In a wide shallow pan, preferably non-stick or cast iron, heat the oil over medium heat. It is important to have the right pan otherwise the potatoes will stick.

3. Add the potatoes and spread them evenly around the pan. Brown the potatoes evenly, stirring them occasionally.

4. When the potatoes are brown, sprinkle over the salt, garam masala, cumin, coriander and the chilli powder. Stir gently and mix until the potatoes are fully coated with the spices. Remove from the heat.

TIME Preparation takes 30 minutes to boil the potatoes plus time to cool them, cooking takes 10-12 minutes.

SERVING IDEAS Serve on cocktail sticks with drinks.

WATCHPOINT The potatoes must be allowed to cool thoroughly. Hot or warm potatoes crumble easily and therefore cannot be cut into neat pieces.

Vegetable Samosas

As the majority of the Indian population is vegetarian, it is no wonder that the original recipe for samosas is a vegetarian one.

MAKES 18 Samosas

450g/1lb potatoes
2 tbsps cooking oil
½ tsp black mustard seeds
1 tsp cumin seeds
2 dried red chillies, coarsely chopped
1 medium-sized onion, finely chopped
1-2 fresh green chillies, coarsely chopped and seeded if a milder flavour is preferred
½ tsp ground turmeric
1 tsp ground coriander
1 tsp ground cumin
1 tsp salt or to taste
1 tbsp chopped coriander leaves

1. Boil the potatoes in their jacket, allow to cool thoroughly, then peel and dice them.

2. Heat the oil and add mustard seeds. As soon as they start crackling, add the cumin seeds and red chillies, and then the onions and green chillies. Fry till the onions are soft. Add the turmeric, coriander and cumin.

3. Stir quickly and add the potatoes and the salt.

4. Reduce heat to low, stir and cook until the potatoes are thoroughly mixed with the spices.

5. Remove from the heat and stir in the coriander leaves. Cool thoroughly before filling the samosas. Make the samosas as instructed in the pastry recipe given for Meat Samosas.

TIME Preparation takes about 60 minutes and cooking takes about 60 minutes.

VARIATION Use 225g/8oz cauliflower and 225g/8oz potatoes. Blanch the cauliflower in boiling salted water, drain and cut into small pieces (almost the same size as diced potatoes).

main meals

FISH BHOONA

SERVES 4

700g/1½lbs steak or fillets of any white fish
6 tbsps cooking oil

Mix the following 4 ingredients in a small bowl
1 tbsp plain flour
¼ tsp ground turmeric
¼ tsp chilli powder
¼ tsp salt

1 large onion, coarsely chopped
½-inch cube of root ginger, peeled and coarsely chopped
2-4 cloves garlic, peeled and coarsely chopped
½ tsp ground turmeric
¼ tsp chilli powder
1 tsp ground coriander
½ tsp garam masala
1 small tin of tomatoes
150ml/5fl oz warm water
100g/4oz frozen garden peas
1 tsp salt or to taste
1 tbsp chopped coriander leaves

1. Skin the fish, wash and dry thoroughly on absorbent paper and cut the fish into approximately 2.5 × 5cm/1 × 2-inch pieces.

2. Heat 2 tbsps oil from the specified amount, in a large frying pan, preferably non-stick or cast iron, over medium heat.

3. Lightly dust the fish, one piece at a time, in the seasoned flour and place in the hot oil. Put in as many pieces as the pan will hold in a single layer without overcrowding it and adjust heat to medium-high. Fry the fish until all the pieces are evenly browned. This has to be done quickly in fairly hot oil so that the fish is thoroughly sealed. Fry all the fish this way and drain on absorbent paper.

4. Put the onion, ginger and garlic into a liquidiser or food processor and blend until smooth.

5. Heat the remaining oil over medium heat in a wide, shallow pan. Add the onion mixture and stir. When the mixture is heated through turn heat down to low, stir and fry for 3-4 minutes.

6. Add the turmeric, chilli, coriander and garam masala and fry for 4-5 minutes, stirring continuously. During this time, from the tin of tomatoes, add 1 tbsp juice at a time to prevent the spices from sticking to the bottom of the pan.

7. Now add one tomato at a time, along with any remaining juice, breaking the tomato with the back of the spoon. Cook until the tomato is well incorporated into the rest of the ingredients. Use up the rest of the tomatoes in the same way.

8. Add the water, peas and salt. Bring to the boil and add the fish. Cover and simmer for 5 to 6 minutes.

9. Remove from heat and sprinkle the coriander leaves on top.

TIME Preparation takes 15-20 minutes, cooking takes 30-35 minutes.

TANDOORI FISH

A firm-fleshed white fish is ideal for this dish; it is not necessary to use an expensive fish. The fish should be handled carefully as most white fish tend to flake during cooking.

SERVES 4

450g/1lb fillet or steak of any white fish
2 cloves garlic, peeled and coarsely chopped
¼-inch cube of root ginger, peeled and coarsely chopped
½ tsp salt
1 tsp ground cumin
1 tsp ground coriander
½ tsp garam masala
¼-½ tsp chilli powder
¼ tsp Tandoori colour or a few drops of red food colouring mixed with 1 tbsp tomato purée
Juice of half a lemon
3 tbsps water
2 tbsps cooking oil

Mix the following ingredients in a small bowl
2 heaped tbsps flour
½ tsp chilli powder
¼ tsp salt

1. Wash the fish and dry on absorbent paper. Cut into 1-inch squares. If using frozen fish, defrost it thoroughly and dry on absorbent paper before cutting it.

2. Add the salt to the ginger and garlic and crush to a smooth pulp.

3. In a small bowl, mix together the ginger/garlic pulp, cumin, coriander, garam masala, chilli powder and Tandoori colour or tomato purée mix. Add the lemon juice and water and mix thoroughly. Keep aside.

4. Heat the oil over medium heat in a non-stick or cast iron frying pan. Dust each piece of fish in the seasoned flour and put in the hot oil in a single layer, leave plenty of room in the pan. Fry for 5 minutes, 2½ minutes each side, and drain on absorbent paper. Now return all the fish to the pan.

5. Hold a sieve over the pan and pour the liquid spice mixture into it. Press with the back of a metal spoon until the mixture in the sieve looks dry and very coarse; discard this mixture.

6. Stir gently and cook over medium heat until the fish is fully coated with the spices and the liquid dries up. Remove from heat.

TIME Preparation takes 15 minutes, cooking takes 15-20 minutes.

SERVING IDEAS Serve garnished with shredded lettuce leaves, sliced cucumber and raw onion rings.
Suitable for freezing.

Masala Machchi

Masala Machchi or spicy fish is made by marinating fish in lemon juice and spices. The lemon juice gives the fish a rather smooth and velvety texture.

SERVES 4

Juice of half a lemon
1 small onion, peeled and coarsely chopped
2-3 cloves garlic, peeled and coarsely chopped
1-inch cube of root ginger, peeled and coarsely chopped
1-2 fresh green chillies, chopped; seed the chillies if you like a milder flavour
3 tbsps chopped coriander leaves
1 tsp salt or to taste
450g/1lb fillet of any white fish
90ml/3fl oz oil for shallow frying

To coat the fish
3 tbsps plain flour
1 egg, beaten
¼ tsp salt
¼ tsp chilli powder

1. Put the lemon juice, onion, garlic, ginger, green chillies, coriander leaves and 1 tsp salt into an electric liquidiser and blend until smooth.

2. Wash the fish gently and pat dry with absorbent paper. If you are using frozen fish, defrost thoroughly and then dry as for fresh fish.

3. Cut the fish into 1½ × 1-inch pieces. Put a light coating of the spice paste on all sides of each piece of fish, cover the container and leave to marinate in a cool place for 2-3 hours, or overnight in the refrigerator.

4. Mix the flour with the salt and chilli powder. Dust each piece of fish lightly with this, then dip in the beaten egg. Shallow fry in a single layer over medium heat until brown on both sides (2-3 minutes on each side). Drain on absorbent paper. Alternatively, deep fry the fish until golden brown and drain on absorbent paper.

TIME Preparation takes 15-20 minutes, cooking takes 12-15 minutes.

SERVING IDEAS Serve with Bhindi (Okra) Raita or Aubergine Raita. Can be served as a side dish with rice and Tarka Dhal or Saagwalla Dahl. Suitable for freezing.

Spiced Sardines

Fresh sardines are easily available from early summer to late autumn. The preparation below is simple and tastes excellent.

SERVES 4

8 fresh sardines (about 700g/1½lb)
1 tsp salt or to taste
3-4 cloves garlic, peeled and coarsely chopped
The juice of half a lemon
½ tsp ground turmeric
½-1 tsp chilli powder
3 heaped tbsps plain flour
60ml/2½fl oz cooking oil

1. Scale and clean the fish. Wash gently in cold water and dry on absorbent paper.

2. Add the salt to the garlic and crush to a smooth pulp.

3. Mix all the ingredients together, except the fish, flour and oil, in a small bowl.

4. Put the fish in a wide shallow dish and pour the marinade over. Spread it gently on both sides of the fish, cover and refrigerate for 2-4 hours.

5. Heat the oil over medium heat. Dip each fish in the flour and coat it thoroughly. Fry until golden brown on both sides (2-3 minutes each side). Drain on absorbent paper.

TIME Preparation takes 20 minutes plus 2-4 hours to marinate, cooking takes 6-8 minutes

SERVING IDEAS Serve as a starter with Avocado Chutney and sliced cucumber.

Cod Roe Scramble

Fish roe makes a very nutritious dish and a few fairly standard ingredients transform the taste dramatically. Here the cod roe is browned gently with onions and other ingredients and the final flavour of the dish is subtle and delicious.

SERVES 4

225g/8oz fresh cod roe
2 tbsps cooking oil
1 medium-sized onion, finely chopped
1 fresh green chilli, finely chopped
2 tbsps ground coriander
½ tsp ground turmeric
½ tsp salt or to taste

1. Chop the cod roe coarsely.

2. Heat the oil over medium heat in a non-stick or cast iron pan and fry the onion and the green chilli until the onion is soft but not brown.

3. Add the coriander and turmeric, stir and fry for 1 minute.

4. Add the cod roe and salt, stir and fry for 3-4 minutes, breaking up the pieces with the spoon.

5. Adjust heat to low and let it cook until it begins to brown (6-8 minutes), stirring occasionally.

6. Remove from the heat and serve.

TIME Preparation takes 10-15 minutes, cooking takes 12-15 minutes.

SERVING IDEAS Serve with Plain Boiled Rice, Tarka Dhal and/or Boti Kabab.

FISH SHAHJAHANI

A rich, but easy to prepare fish dish which is named after the Mughal Emperor Shahjahan, who was noted for his love of good food.

SERVES 4

700g/1½lbs fillet of any white fish
75g/3oz roasted cashews
125ml/4fl oz single cream
50g/2oz unsalted butter
225g/8oz onions, finely sliced
2-inch piece of cinnamon stick, broken up
4 green cardamoms, split open the top of each pod
2 whole cloves
1-2 fresh green chillies, sliced lengthwise; seeded if a milder flavour is preferred
1 tsp ground turmeric
175ml/6fl oz warm water
1 tsp salt or to taste
1 tbsp lemon juice

1. Rinse the fish gently in cold water, dry on absorbent paper and cut into 2.5 × 5cm/1 × 2-inch pieces.

2. Put the cashews and the cream in an electric blender and blend to a reasonably fine mixture.

3. In a wide, shallow pan melt the butter over medium heat and fry onions, cinnamon, cardamom, cloves and green chillies until the onions are lightly browned (6-8 minutes). Stir in the turmeric.

4. Add the water and salt and arrange the fish in a single layer. Bring to the boil, cover the pan and simmer for 2-3 minutes.

5. Now add the cashew/cream mixture and stir gently until the pieces of fish are well coated. Cover the pan again and simmer for a further 2-3 minutes.

6. Remove from heat and gently stir in the lemon juice.

TIME Preparation takes 15 minutes, cooking takes 15-20 minutes.

SERVING IDEAS To appreciate the wonderful flavour of this dish fully, the rice served with it should not be too highly flavoured. Choose a mild flavoured rice such as Cardamom Rice or Fried Brown Rice. Serve Green Beans with Garlic Butter as a side dish.

VARIATION Use potatoes which have been boiled in their jackets, peeled and diced

WATCHPOINT It is important to use a wide shallow pan so that the fish can be arranged in a single layer to prevent them from breaking up during cooking.

Bengal Fish Curry

The abundance of fish in the Bay of Bengal has enabled the people of this north eastern part of India to develop many delicious dishes using fish. In the recipe below, the fish is cooked entirely in natural yogurt which, with the addition of a little gram flour, gives it an unusual touch.

SERVES 4

700g/1½lbs firm fleshed fish such as river trout, grey or red mullet
1 tsp ground turmeric
1¼ tsps salt or to taste
5 tbsps cooking oil
1 large onion, finely chopped
¼-in cube of root ginger – peeled and finely chopped or grated
1 tbsp ground coriander
½-1 tsp chilli powder
1 tsp paprika
275g/10oz thick set natural yogurt
4-6 whole fresh green chillies
1-2 cloves of garlic, peeled and crushed
1 tbsp besan (gram or chick pea flour)
2 tbsps chopped coriander leaves (optional)

1. Clean and wash the fish and pat dry.

2. Cut each fish in to 1½-inch pieces.

3. Gently rub into the fish ¼ tsp turmeric and ¼ tsp salt from the specified amount and put it aside for 15-20 minutes.

4. Meanwhile, heat the oil over medium heat; use a pan wide enough to hold the fish in a single layer and fry onion and ginger until the onions are lightly browned (6-7 minutes), stirring frequently.

5. Add coriander, remaining turmeric, chilli powder and the paprika – adjust heat to low and fry for 1-2 minutes, stirring continuously.

6. Beat the yogurt with a fork until smooth and add to the onion and spice mixture, adjust heat to medium, add the whole green chillies, the remaining salt and the garlic. Stir and mix well.

7. Arrange the pieces of fish in this liquid in a single layer and bring to the boil. Cover and cook over low heat for 5-6 minutes.

8. Blend the besan with a little water to make a pouring consistency. Strain this over the fish curry, stir gently, and mix. Cover and cook for 2-3 minutes.

9. Remove from heat and gently mix in half the coriander leaves.

10. Transfer the fish curry into a serving dish and garnish with the remaining coriander leaves (if used).

TIME Preparation takes 20-25 minutes, cooking takes 20 minutes.

SERVING IDEAS Serve with plain boiled rice and Cabbage with Gram Flour. For a dinner party or special occasion, serve with Fried Brown Rice and Spiced Green Beans. Carrot & Mooli Salad makes an interesting addition to the menu.
Suitable for freezing.

VARIATION Use chunky cod or haddock fillets, but take extra care as they can break easily during cooking.

PRAWN CHILLI MASALA

This is a delicate but richly flavoured dish. In India, only fresh and juicy king prawns will do, but standard peeled prawns can be used for this recipe.

SERVES 4

75g/3oz unsalted butter
6 green cardamoms, split open the top of each pod
1-inch cube of root ginger, peeled and finely grated
3-4 cloves garlic, peeled and crushed
1 tbsp ground coriander
½ tsp ground turmeric
450g/1lb fresh peeled prawns
125g/5oz thick set natural yogurt
90ml/3fl oz water
1 tsp sugar
1 tsp salt or to taste
25g/1oz ground almonds
4-6 whole fresh green chillies
100g/4oz finely chopped onions
2 fresh green chillies, seeded and minced
½ tsp garam masala
1 tbsp chopped coriander leaves

1. Melt 50g/2oz butter from the specified amount over gentle heat and add the whole cardamoms, fry for 30 seconds and add the ginger and garlic. Stir and cook for 1 minute, then add the ground coriander and turmeric. Stir and fry for 30 seconds.

2. Add the prawns, turn the heat up to medium and cook for 5-6 minutes, stirring frequently.

3. Beat the yogurt until smooth, gradually add the water and beat until well blended. Add this mixture to the prawns, stir in the sugar and the salt, cover the pan and simmer for 5-6 minutes.

4. Add the ground almonds and the whole green chillies and cook, uncovered, for 5 minutes.

5. Meanwhile, fry the onions in the remaining 25g/1oz butter until they are just soft, but not brown. Add the minced green chillies and the garam masala; stir and fry for a further 1-2 minutes. Stir this mixture into the prawns along with any butter left in the pan. Remove the pan from the heat.

6. Put the prawns in a serving dish and garnish with the coriander leaves.

TIME Preparation takes 15 minutes, cooking takes 20-25 minutes.

SERVING IDEAS Serve with Mushroom Pilau or Fried Brown Rice. Green Beans in Garlic Butter or Spiced Green Beans are ideal as a side dish.

TO FREEZE Suitable for freezing if fresh prawns are used.

Smoked Mackerel Salad

In Assam and Bengal, this salad is made with a fish which is very similar to mackerel. As smoked fish is not readily available there, the smoking is usually done at home.

SERVES 4

225g/8oz smoked mackerel
50g/2oz finely chopped onions
1 fresh green chilli, seeded and finely chopped
2 tbsps finely chopped coriander leaves
1½ tbsps lemon juice

1. Remove skin and bones from the fish and mash it with a fork.

2. Add all ingredients and mix thoroughly. Cover the container and refrigerate for 2-3 hours before serving.

TIME Preparation takes 10 minutes.

SERVING IDEAS Serve garnished with Tarka Dhal and Fried Brown Rice or on small savoury biscuits with drinks.
Suitable for freezing.

MIXED VEGETABLE CURRY

A variety of seasonal vegetables are cooked together in a gravy flavoured by a few ground spices, onions and tomatoes. Whole green chillies are added towards the end to enhance the flavour of the dish and also to retain their fresh green colour.

SERVES 4-6

4-5 tbsps cooking oil
1 large onion, finely chopped
½-inch cube of root ginger, peeled and finely sliced
1 tsp ground turmeric
1 tsp ground coriander
1 tsp ground cumin
1 tsp paprika
4 small ripe tomatoes, skinned and chopped or a small can of tomatoes with the juice
225g/8oz potatoes, peeled and diced
75g/3oz french beans or dwarf beans, sliced
100g/4oz carrots, scraped and sliced
75g/3oz garden peas, shelled weight
450ml/15fl oz warm water
2-4 whole fresh green chillies
1 tsp garam masala
1 tsp salt or to taste
1 tbsp chopped coriander leaves

1. Heat the oil over medium heat and fry the onions until they are lightly browned. (6-7 minutes).

2. Add the ginger and fry for 30 seconds.

3. Adjust heat to low and add the turmeric, coriander, cumin and paprika. Stir and mix well.

4. Add half the tomatoes and fry for 2 minutes, stirring continuously.

5. Add all the vegetables and the water. Stir and mix well. Bring to the boil, cover and simmer until vegetables are tender (15-20 minutes).

6. Add the remaining tomatoes and the green chillies. Cover and simmer for 5-6 minutes.

7. Add the.garam masala and salt, mix well. Stir in half the coriander leaves and remove from heat.

8. Put the vegetable curry into a serving dish and sprinkle the remaining coriander leaves on top.

TIME Preparation takes 25-30 minutes, cooking takes 30 minutes.

SERVING IDEAS Serve with Tandoori Roti or Naan and Kababs, Masala Machchi or Tandoori Fish. Can also be served with Meat Biriani.

TO FREEZE Suitable for freezing, but omit the potatoes. Add pre-boiled diced potatoes during reheating.

WATCHPOINT Frozen peas and beans may be used for convenience, but the cooking time should be adjusted accordingly. Cook the fresh vegetables first and follow cooking time for frozen vegetables as per instructions on packets.

EGG & POTATO DUM

Hard-boiled curried eggs are very popular in the northeastern part of India. Here, the eggs are cooked with potatoes and they are both fried first until they form a light crust. Slow cooking, without any loss of steam, is the secret of the success of this dish.

SERVES 4-6

6 hard-boiled eggs
5 tbsps cooking oil
450g/1lb medium-sized potatoes, peeled and quartered
⅛ tsp each of chilli powder and ground turmeric, mixed together
1 large onion, finely chopped
½-inch cube of root ginger, peeled and grated
1 cinnamon stick, 2-inch long; broken up into 2-3 pieces
2 black cardamoms, split open the top of each pod
4 whole cloves
1 fresh green chilli, chopped
1 small tin of tomatoes
½ tsp ground turmeric
2 tsps ground coriander
1 tsp ground fennel
¼-½ tsp chilli powder (optional)
1 tsp salt or to taste
225ml/8fl oz warm water
1 tbsp chopped coriander leaves

1. Shell the eggs and make 4 slits lengthwise on each egg leaving about ½-inch gap on either end.

2. Heat the oil over medium heat in a cast iron or non-stick pan (enamel or steel pans will cause the eggs and the potatoes to stick). Fry the potatoes until they are well browned on all sides (about 10 minutes). Remove them with a slotted spoon and keep aside.

3. Remove the pan from heat and stir in the turmeric and chilli mixture. Place the pan back on heat and fry the whole eggs until they are well browned. Remove them with a slotted spoon and keep aside.

4. In the same oil, fry the onions, ginger, cinnamon, cardamom, cloves and green chilli until the onions are lightly browned (6-7 minutes).

5. Add half the tomatoes, stir and fry until the tomatoes break up (2-3 minutes).

6. Add the turmeric, ground coriander, fennel and chilli powder (if used); stir and fry for 3-4 minutes.

7. Add the rest of the tomatoes and fry for 4-5 minutes, stirring frequently.

8. Add the potatoes, salt and water, bring to the boil, cover the pan tightly and simmer until the potatoes are tender, stirring occasionally.

9. Now add the eggs and simmer, uncovered for 5-6 minutes, stirring once or twice.

10. Stir in the coriander leaves and remove from heat.

TIME Preparation takes 15 minutes, cooking takes 35-40 minutes.

SERVING IDEAS Serve with Parathas, Puris or Loochis.

TANDOORI CHICKEN

The Tandoor, because of its fierce but even distribution of heat, enables meat to cook quickly, forming a light crust on the outside but leaving the inside moist and succulent.

It is possible to achieve perfectly satisfactory results by using a conventional gas or electric oven at the highest temperature setting, though the distinctive flavour of clay-cooked chicken will not be achieved.

SERVES 4-6

1.2kg/2½lbs chicken joints, legs or breast or a combination of the two

1 tsp salt or to taste

Juice of half a lemon

½-inch cube of root ginger, peeled and coarsely chopped

2-3 small cloves of garlic, peeled and coarsely chopped

1 fresh green chilli, coarsely chopped and seeded if a milder flavour is required

2 tbsps chopped coriander leaves

75g/3oz thick set natural yogurt

1 tsp ground coriander

½ tsp ground cumin

1 tsp garam masala

¼ tsp freshly ground black pepper

½ tsp Tandoori colour (available from Indian grocers in powder form), or a few drops of red food colouring mixed with 1 tbsp tomato purée

1. Remove skin from the chicken and cut each piece into two. With a sharp knife, make 2-3 slits in each piece. Rub salt and lemon juice into the chicken pieces and set aside for half an hour.

2. Meanwhile, put the ginger, garlic, green chillies, coriander leaves and the yogurt into a liquidiser and blend until smooth. Add the rest of the ingredients and blend again.

3. Pour and spread the marinade all over the chicken, especially into the slits. Cover the container with cling film and leave to marinate for 6-8 hours or overnight in the refrigerator.

4. Preheat oven to 240°C/475°F/Gas Mark 9. Line a roasting tin with aluminium foil (this will help to maintain the high level of heat required to cook the chicken) and arrange the chicken pieces in it. Place the roasting tin in the centre of the oven and bake for 25-30 minutes, turning the pieces over carefully as they brown and basting with juice in the roasting tin as well as any remaining marinade.

5. Remove from the oven, lift each piece with a pair of tongs and shake off any excess liquid.

TIME Preparation takes 20-25 minutes, cooking takes 25-30 minutes.

SERVING IDEAS Serve as a starter with lettuce, cucumber, tomatoes and sliced raw onions; or as a side dish with Plain Pillau, Mushroom Bhaji and Mint & Onion Raita.

Suitable for freezing.

MURGHI NAWABI

This is a classic example of the popular Mughal cuisine which is noted for its delicate flavourings and rich smooth sauces. The chicken is marinated in yogurt and turmeric and simmered in delicately flavoured coconut milk.

SERVES 4-6

1kg/2.2lbs chicken joints, skinned
125g/5oz thick set natural yogurt
½ tsp ground turmeric
3-4 cloves garlic, peeled and coarsely chopped
1-inch cube of root ginger, peeled and coarsely chopped
4-6 dried red chillies
50g/2oz ghee or unsalted butter
2 large onions, finely sliced
1 tsp caraway seeds
1 tsp garam masala
1¼ tsps salt or to taste
225ml/8fl oz warm water plus 90ml/3fl oz cold water
85g/3½oz creamed coconut, cut into small pieces
75g/3oz raw cashews
2 hard-boiled eggs, sliced
¼ tsp paprika

1. Cut each chicken joint into two pieces (separate leg from thigh and cut each breast into two pieces). Wash the chicken and dry on absorbent paper.

2. Beat the yogurt and turmeric powder together until smooth. Add to the chicken and mix thoroughly, cover the container and leave to marinate for 4-6 hours or overnight in the refrigerator.

3. Put the garlic, ginger and red chillies in an electric liquidiser and add just enough water to facilitate blade movement and mixing. Blend until the ingredients are smooth. Alternatively, crush the garlic, ginger and finely chop the chillies.

4. Melt the ghee or butter over medium heat and fry the onions until they are brown (8-10 minutes). Remove the pan from heat and, using a wooden spatula, press the onions to the side of the pan in order to squeeze out excess fat. Transfer the onions onto a plate and keep aside.

5. Place the pan back on heat and fry the caraway seeds and garam masala for 30 seconds. Add the blended ingredients. Stir briskly and add the chicken, fried onions and salt. Fry the chicken for 5-6 minutes, stirring frequently and lowering heat as the chicken is heated through. If there is any yogurt marinade left in the container add this to the chicken.

6. Add the water and the creamed coconut. Bring to the boil, cover the pan and simmer until the chicken is tender and the gravy is thick (30-35 minutes). Stir occasionally during this time.

7. Meanwhile, put the cashews into an electric blender and add the cold water and blend until smooth. Add the cashew paste to the chicken during the last 5 minutes of cooking time. Simmer uncovered for 4-5 minutes, stirring frequently.

8. Put the chicken into a serving dish and garnish with the sliced eggs. Sprinkle the paprika on top.

CHICKEN CHAAT

Recipes do not have to be elaborate to be tasty, and Chicken Chaat is a perfect example. Cubes of chicken meat, stir-fried with a light coating of spices look impressive with a colourful salad and taste superb.

SERVES 4

700g/1½lbs chicken breast, skinned and boned
1 tsp salt or to taste
2-3 cloves garlic, peeled and coarsely chopped
2 tbsps cooking oil
1½ tsps ground coriander
¼ tsp ground turmeric
¼-½ tsp chilli powder
1½ tbsps lemon juice
2 tbsps finely chopped coriander leaves

1. Wash the chicken and dry on absorbent paper. Cut into 1-inch cubes.

2. Add the salt to the garlic and crush to a smooth pulp.

3. Heat the oil in a frying pan, preferably non-stick or cast iron, over medium heat.

4. Add the garlic and fry until it is lightly browned.

5. Add the chicken and fry for 6-7 minutes, stirring constantly.

6. Add the ground coriander, turmeric and chilli powder. Fry for 3-4 minutes, stirring frequently. Remove from heat and stir in the lemon juice and coriander leaves.

TIME Preparation takes 15 minutes, cooking takes 12-15 minutes.

SERVING IDEAS Serve as a starter garnished with crispy lettuce leaves, sliced cucumber, raw sliced onion and wedges of lemon or with a selection of chutneys. Chicken Chaat can also be served with drinks on cocktail sticks, hot or cold.
Suitable for freezing.

SABJI MASALA MURGH

This chicken dish is wonderful when time may be short to cook a separate vegetable dish, because a selection of vegetables are added to the chicken at different stages. Frozen vegetables are used in this recipe; if fresh vegetables are used, the cooking time should be adjusted accordingly.

SERVES 4-6

1kg/2.2lbs chicken portions
200ml/7fl oz water
75g/3oz roasted cashews
50g/2oz ghee or unsalted butter
1-inch cube of root ginger, peeled and finely grated
4-6 cloves garlic, peeled and finely chopped

Grind the following 4 ingredients in a coffee grinder
¼ tsp ground nutmeg
6 green cardamoms with the skin
1 tsp caraway seeds
4-6 dried red chillies

1¼ tsps salt or to taste
50g/2oz whole baby carrots
50g/2oz frozen garden peas
50g/2oz frozen sweetcorn
4 spring onions, coarsely chopped
1 small green pepper, seeded and finely shredded

1. Skin the chicken and separate legs from thighs; wash and pat dry.

2. Put 125ml/4fl oz water from the specified amount, into an electric blender and add the cashews, blend to a smooth paste.

3. Melt the ghee or butter over medium heat and fry the ginger and garlic for 1 minute.

4. Adjust heat to low and add the ground ingredients, stir and fry for 1 minute.

5. Add the chicken, adjust heat to medium-high and fry the chicken until it changes colour (5-6 minutes).

6. Add the cashew paste, stir and mix thoroughly. Rinse out the blender container with the remaining water and add to the chicken.

7. Add the salt, mix well, cover the pan and cook over low heat for 15 minutes, stirring occasionally.

8. Add the carrots, stir and mix; cover and cook for a further 15 minutes.

9. Add the peas and the sweetcorn, mix well, cover the pan and cook over medium heat for 5 minutes.

10. Reserve half the spring onions and add the rest to the chicken along with the green pepper. Cook, uncovered, for 5-6 minutes, stirring frequently. Remove from the heat.

11. Put the chicken in a serving dish and garnish with the reserved spring onions.

TIME Preparation takes 20-25 minutes, cooking takes 45-50 minutes.

SERVING IDEAS Serve with Plain Fried Rice or Cardamom Rice.

Chicken Kohlapuri

This delicious chicken dish comes from Kohlapur in southern India. The original recipe has a large amount of chillies as people in this part of India prefer a very hot flavour. For this recipe, however, the quantity of chillies has been reduced.

SERVES 4-6

1.4kg/2½lbs chicken joints, skinned
1 large onion, coarsely chopped
3-4 cloves garlic, peeled and coarsely chopped
1-inch cube of root ginger, peeled and coarsely chopped
6 tbsps cooking oil
1 tsp ground turmeric
2 tsps ground coriander
1½ tsps ground cumin
1-1¼ tsps chilli powder
1 small tin of tomatoes
1¼ tsps salt or to taste
180ml/6fl oz water
4-6 whole green chillies
1 tsp garam masala
2 tbsps chopped coriander leaves

1. Cut each chicken joint in two (separate legs from thighs or cut breast into 2-3 pieces); wash and dry on absorbent paper.

2. Place the onion, garlic and ginger in an electric food processor or liquidiser and blend to a smooth purée. You may need to add a little water if you are using a liquidiser.

3. Heat the oil over medium heat and add the liquidised ingredients. Stir and fry for 5-6 minutes.

4. Add turmeric, ground coriander, cumin and chilli powder; adjust heat to low and fry for 4-5 minutes stirring frequently.

5. Add half the tomatoes, stir and cook for 2-3 minutes.

6. Now add the chicken, stir and cook until chicken changes colour (4-5 minutes) and add the rest of the tomatoes, along with all the juice.

7. Add salt and water, bring to the boil, cover and simmer until the chicken is tender. Stir occasionally to ensure that the thickened gravy does not stick to the bottom of the pan.

8. Add the whole green chillies and garam masala, cover and simmer for 5 minutes.

9. Remove the pan from heat and stir in the coriander leaves.

TIME Preparation takes 15-20 minutes, cooking takes 55 minutes.

SERVING IDEAS Serve with Plain Boiled Rice and Mixed Vegetable Bhaji. Suitable for freezing.

WATCHPOINT In stage 3, it is important to fry the ingredients for the specified time so that the raw smell of the onions, ginger and garlic can be eliminated before adding the rest of the ingredients.

Chicken with Channa Dhal

Channa dhal has a distinctive flavour which goes particularly well with chicken. As channa dhal is only available from Indian grocers, yellow split peas, which is similar to channa dhal, can be used.

SERVES 6-8

225g/8oz channa chal or yellow split peas
1kg/2.2lb chicken joints

Make a paste of the following 6 ingredients by adding 55ml/2fl oz water
1 tbsp ground coriander
1 tsp ground turmeric
½ tsp cayenne or chilli powder
½ tsp freshly ground black pepper
1 tsp ground cinnamon
½ tsp ground nutmeg

2 tbsps cooking oil
1-inch cube of root ginger, peeled and grated
3-4 cloves garlic, peeled and crushed
1 fresh green chilli, finely chopped
1¼ tsps salt or to taste
450ml/15fl oz warm water
40g/1½oz ghee or unsalted butter
1 large onion, finely sliced
2 tbsps chopped coriander leaves
1 medium-sized ripe tomato, sliced

1. Clean and wash the channa dhal or the split peas and soak them in plenty of cold water for about 2 hours. Drain well.

2. Cut each chicken joint into two, separating leg from thigh. Wash and pat dry.

3. In a heavy-based pan, heat the oil gently over low heat and fry the ginger, garlic and green chilli for 1 minute.

4. Add the spice paste, stir and fry for 2-3 minutes.

5. Add the chicken, adjust heat to medium-high, stir and fry the chicken until it changes colour (3-4 minutes).

6. Add the dhal or split peas, stir and fry for a further 3-4 minutes.

7. Stir in the salt and add the water. Bring to the boil, cover the pan and simmer until the chicken and the dhal are tender (35-40 minutes).

8. Meanwhile, in a separate pan, melt the ghee or butter over medium heat and fry the onions until they are golden brown (8-10 minutes), stirring frequently.

9. Add the onions to the chicken along with any remaining ghee in the pan. Add half the coriander leaves and stir until all the ingredients are mixed thoroughly. Cover the pan and simmer for 10 minutes.

10. Put the chicken in a serving dish and garnish with the tomatoes and the remaining coriander leaves.

TIME Preparation takes 25 minutes plus time needed to soak the dhal, cooking takes 55 minutes.

Chicken Korma

Korma is a classic north Indian dish and there are many variations, some of which are quite elaborate. The recipe below, though simple and prepared with readily available ingredients, has all the characteristic features of this classic dish.

SERVES 4-6

1.4kg/2½lbs chicken joints, skin removed
1-inch cube of root ginger, finely grated
125g/5oz thick set natural yogurt
1 small onion, coarsely chopped
3-4 dried red chillies
2-4 cloves garlic, peeled and coarsely chopped
5 tbsps cooking oil plus 2 tbsps extra oil
450g/1lb onions, finely sliced
1 tbsp ground coriander
½ tsp powdered black pepper
1 tsp garam masala
1 tsp ground turmeric
225ml/8fl oz warm water (reduce quantity if using boneless chicken)
75g/3oz creamed coconut, cut into small pieces
1¼ tsps salt or to taste
2 heaped tbsps ground almonds
Juice of ½ a lemon

1. Cut each chicken joint into half, separating leg from thigh and cutting each breast into two.

2. Mix with ginger and yogurt, cover and leave to marinate in a cool place for 2-4 hours or in the refrigerator overnight.

3. Place the chopped onion, red chillies and garlic in a liquidiser or food processor and liquidise to a smooth paste. You may need to add a little water if you are using a liquidiser.

4. Heat the 5 tbsps oil over medium heat and fry the sliced onions till they are golden brown. Remove the pan from the heat and using a slotted spoon, transfer the onions to another dish, Leave any remaining oil in the pan.

5. Place the pan in which the onions have been fried, over medium heat and add the other 2 tbsps cooking oil.

6. When hot, add the ground coriander, powdered pepper, garam masala and turmeric, stir rapidly (take the pan off the heat if the oil is too hot) and add the chicken along with the marinade. Adjust the heat to medium-high and fry the chicken for about 10 minutes, stirring frequently.

7. Add the liquidised spices and continue to fry for 6-8 minutes on low heat.

8. Add the water and the coconut and bring to the boil. Stir until coconut is dissolved. Add fried onion slices and salt.

9. Reduce heat to low, cover the pan and simmer until the chicken is tender (25-30 minutes). Sprinkle the ground almonds and mix well. Remove from heat and add the lemon juice.

TIME Preparation takes 15 minutes plus time needed to marinate, cooking takes 55 minutes.

SERVING IDEAS Serve with Pilau Rice or Mushroom Pilau and Carrot & Peanut Raita.
Suitable for freezing.

CHICKEN DO-PIAZA

A fairly easy dish to prepare in which more than the usual quantity of onions are used. The name itself suggests the quantity of onions required, Do means twice and Piaz means onion. The literal translation would, therefore, be 'chicken with twice the amount of onions'.

SERVES 4-6

1.4kg/2½lbs chicken joints, skin removed
1 large onion, coarsely chopped
1-inch cube of root ginger, peeled and coarsely chopped
3-4 cloves garlic, peeled and coarsely chopped
4 tbsps cooking oil
1 tsp ground turmeric
1 tsp ground coriander
1 tsp ground cumin
¼-½ tsp chilli powder
1 small tin of tomatoes
175ml/6fl oz warm water
2 cinnamon sticks, each 2-inches long; broken up
4 green cardamoms; split open the top of each pod
4 whole cloves
2 dried bay leaves, crumpled
1¼ tsp salt or to taste
2 level tbsps ghee or unsalted butter
1 large onion, finely sliced
1 tbsp chopped coriander leaves (optional)

---

1. Cut each chicken breast into 3 pieces. If you are using legs, separate leg from thigh. Wash and dry on absorbent paper or a cloth.

2. Place the chopped onion, ginger and garlic into a liquidiser or food processor and liquidise to a smooth paste, add a little water, if necessary, to facilitate blade movement.

3. Heat the oil over medium heat and add the liquidised ingredients. Stir and fry for 4-5 minutes.

4. Add turmeric, coriander, cumin and chilli powder. Fry for 4-5 minutes stirring frequently. During this time, from the tin of tomatoes, add 1 tbsp juice at a time to prevent the spices from sticking to the pan. When you have used up all the tomato juice, add the chicken and fry it over medium-high heat until the chicken has changed colour.

5. Add the water, cinnamon, cardomom, cloves, bay leaves, salt and the whole tomatoes. Bring to the boil, cover and simmer until the chicken is tender and the gravy is fairly thick (about 25 minutes). Cook uncovered, if necessary, to thicken the gravy.

6. Heat the ghee or butter and fry the sliced onion for 5 minutes. Add the onions along with the ghee to the chicken. Remove from heat and stir in the coriander leaves.

TIME Preparation takes 15 minutes, cooking takes 45 minutes.

SERVING IDEAS Serve with Naan or Tandoori Roti and Potato Raita or with Plain Boiled Rice and Potatoes with Garlic & Chillies.
Suitable for freezing.

VARIATION Use lamb, but adjust cooking time.

Chicken with Whole Spices

This recipe is the answer to a good, tasty curry in a hurry! With this curry on the menu, you can present a whole meal in approximately one hour.

SERVES 4-6

1kg/2.2lbs chicken joints, skinned
4 tbsps cooking oil
1 tsp cumin seeds
1 large onion, finely chopped
½-inch cube of root ginger, peeled and finely chopped
2-4 cloves garlic, peeled and crushed or finely chopped
2-3 dried red chillies, whole
2 cinnamon sticks, 2-inches long each, broken up
2 black cardamoms, split open the top of each pod
4 whole cloves
10 whole allspice seeds
½ tsp ground turmeric
1 tsp paprika
150ml/5fl oz warm water
1¼ tsp salt or to taste
2 ripe tomatoes, skinned and chopped
2 fresh green chillies, whole
1 tbsp ground almond
2 tbsps chopped coriander leaves (optional)

1. Cut each chicken joint in two; separate leg from thigh and cut each breast in two.

2. Heat the oil over medium heat and fry the cumin seeds until they pop, then add the onions, ginger, garlic and red chillies. Fry until the onions are soft but not brown, stirring frequently.

3. Add the cinnamon, cardamom, cloves and allspice, stir and fry for 30 seconds.

4. Stir in the turmeric and paprika and immediately follow with the chicken. Adjust heat to medium-high and fry the chicken until it changes colour (5-6 minutes), stirring frequently.

5. Add the water and salt, bring to the boil, cover the pan and simmer until the chicken is tender (about 30 minutes).

6. Add the tomatoes, green chillies and the ground almonds. Stir and mix well, cover the pan and simmer for a further 6-8 minutes.

7. Stir in half the coriander leaves and remove the pan from heat.

8. Transfer the chicken into a serving dish and garnish with the remaining coriander leaves, (if used).

TIME Preparation takes 15-20 minutes, cooking takes 50 minutes.

SERVING IDEAS Serve with Plain Boiled or Plain Fried Rice, Cucumber Raita and/or Cauliflower Masala.
Suitable for freezing.

VARIATION Add peeled and diced potatoes about 20 minutes before completion of cooking time.

Dahi Murghi

Dahi Murghi or chicken in yogurt needs little effort to cook and is simply gorgeous. The chicken is marinated in a yogurt-laced mixture and simmered until tender. Its simple method of cooking means that it can easily be fitted into a busy life style.

SERVES 4-6

1kg/2.2lbs chicken joints, skinned
125g/5oz carton of thick set natural yogurt
3-4 cloves garlic, peeled and coarsely chopped
1-inch cube of root ginger, peeled and coarsely chopped
2-3 dried red chillies
½ tsp ground turmeric
1 tbsp ground coriander
4 tbsps cooking oil
1 large onion, finely sliced
2-4 fresh green chillies, whole
1 tsp salt or to taste
½ tsp garam masala
2 tbsps chopped coriander leaves

---

1. Cut each chicken joint into two, separate leg from thigh and cut each breast into two pieces. Wash the chicken and dry on absorbent paper.

2. Put the yogurt, garlic, ginger, dried red chillies, turmeric and ground coriander in a liquidiser and blend until smooth.

3. Put the chicken in a large mixing bowl and pour the marinade over. Mix thoroughly, cover the container and leave to marinate for 6-8 hours, or overnight in the refrigerator.

4. Put the chicken into a heavy-based pan with a lid and place over medium heat, stirring occasionally until the chicken is heated through. Cover the pan and simmer gently until the chicken is tender (about 25-30 minutes). Remove the pan from heat.

5. Heat the oil over medium heat in a wide shallow pan and brown the onions.

6. Add the chicken and cook uncovered for 5-6 minutes stirring frequently.

7. Add the whole green chillies, salt and garam masala and cook for a further 3-4 minutes.

8. Remove the pan from the heat and stir in half the coriander leaves.

9. Put the chicken into a serving dish and sprinkle the remaining coriander leaves on top.

TIME Preparation takes 15 minutes plus time needed to marinate, cooking takes 30-35 minutes.

SERVING IDEAS Serve with Chapatties, Rotis or Cardamom Rice and a side dish such as Gobi Aloo or Spicy Channa Dhal.
Suitable for freezing.

WATCHPOINT Reduce cooking time if boneless chicken is used.

Chicken Tikka Masala

The delicate flavour of chicken smothered in almond and cream sauce makes this a wonderful choice for a dinner party or a special occasion menu.

SERVES 4

450g/1lb Chicken Tikka (see separate recipe)
½-inch cube of root ginger, peeled and coarsely chopped
2 cloves garlic, peeled and coarsely chopped
1 tsp salt or to taste
50g/2oz unsalted butter
1 small onion, finely chopped
¼ tsp ground turmeric
½ tsp ground cumin
½ tsp ground coriander
½ tsp garam masala
¼-½ tsp chilli powder
125ml/4fl oz liquid, made up of the reserved juice from the precooked Chicken Tikka and warm water
300ml/10fl oz double cream
2 heaped tbsps ground almonds

1. Mix together the ginger, garlic and ½ tsp salt from the specified amount and crush to a pulp. Keep the remaining salt aside for later use.

2. Melt the butter gently and fry the onions for 2-3 minutes.

3. Add the ginger/garlic paste and cook for 1 minute.

4. Stir in the turmeric and then the cumin, coriander, garam masala and chilli powder. Stir and cook for 2 minutes.

5. Add the liquid and stir gently.

6. Gradually add the cream and stir.

7. Add the remaining salt and simmer for 5 minutes and then add the chicken. Adjust heat to low, cover and cook for 10 minutes.

8. Stir in the ground almonds and simmer for 5-6 minutes.

9. Remove from heat.

TIME Preparation takes 10 minutes plus time needed to marinate the tikka, cooking takes 25 minutes plus time needed to cook the tikka.

SERVING IDEAS Serve with Saffron Rice and Spiced Green Beans. Suitable for freezing. Defrost thoroughly before reheating. Reheat gently in a covered pan; do not boil.

MURGHI JHAL FREZI

This delicious and relatively easy dish to cook, with thick spice paste clinging to the pieces of chicken, makes it an irresistible choice for entertaining.

SERVES 4-6

1kg/2.2lbs chicken joints
3 large onions, finely chopped
175ml/6fl oz water
1-inch cube of root ginger, peeled and grated
2-4 cloves garlic, peeled and crushed
1 tsp ground coriander
1 tsp ground cumin
1 tsp ground ajwain or caraway
½ tsp ground turmeric
½ chilli powder
2 cinnamon sticks, 2-inch long each, broken up
2 black cardamoms, split open the top of each pod
4 whole cloves
5 tbsps cooking oil
1¼ tsp salt or to taste
1 tbsp tomato purée
1-2 fresh green chillies, sliced lengthwise; seeded for a milder flavour
2 tbsps chopped coriander leaves

1. Skin and cut each joint into two, separate leg from thigh and cut each breast into two pieces, wash and dry on absorbent paper.

2. Put the chicken in a saucepan, add half the chopped onions, water, ginger, garlic, coriander, cumin, ajwain, turmeric, chilli powder, cinnamon, cardamom and cloves. Bring to the boil, stir and mix thoroughly. Cover and simmer for 20-25 minutes.

3. In a separate pan, heat the oil over medium heat and fry the rest of the onions until they are golden brown.

4. Remove each piece of chicken with a pair of tongs and add to the onions. Fry over medium heat until the chicken is brown (about 5 minutes).

5. Now add half the spiced liquid in which the chicken was cooked, stir and fry for 4-5 minutes. Add the rest of the liquid and fry for a further 4-5 minutes.

6. Add salt, tomato purée, green chillies and coriander leaves, stir and fry on low heat for 5-6 minutes. Remove from heat.

TIME Preparation takes 20-25 minutes, cooking takes 45-50 minutes.

SERVING IDEAS Serve with Chapattis, Puris or Parathas; or with Plain Boiled Rice and Tarka Dhal.
Suitable for freezing.

VARIATION Use lean pork instead of chicken.

WATCHPOINT Reduce the cooking time for boneless chicken and in stage 5, fry the chicken for a little longer to reach the paste-like consistency required.

Coriander Chicken

Coriander Chicken is quick and easy to make, it tastes wonderful and looks very impressive – a perfect choice for any dinner party menu.

SERVES 4-6

1kg/2.2lbs chicken joints, skinned
2-4 cloves garlic, peeled and crushed
125g/5oz thick set natural yogurt
5 tbsps cooking oil
1 large onion, finely sliced
2 tbsps ground coriander
½ tsp ground black pepper
1 tsp ground mixed spice
½ tsp ground turmeric
½ tsp cayenne pepper or chilli powder
125ml/4fl oz warm water
1 tsp salt or to taste
25g/1oz ground almonds
2 hard-boiled eggs, sliced
¼ tsp paprika

1. Cut each chicken joint into two, mix thoroughly with the crushed garlic and the yogurt. Cover the container and leave to marinate in a cool place for 2-4 hours or overnight in the refrigerator.

2. Heat the oil over medium heat and fry the onions until they are golden brown (6-8 minutes). Remove with a slotted spoon and keep aside.

3. In the same oil, fry the coriander, ground pepper, ground mixed spice and turmeric for 15 seconds and add the chicken along with all the marinade in the container.

4. Adjust heat to medium-high and fry the chicken until it changes colour (5-6 minutes).

5. Adjust the cayenne or chilli powder, water, salt, and the fried onion slices. Bring to the boil, cover the pan and simmer until the chicken is tender (about 30 minutes).

6. Stir in the ground almonds and remove from heat.

TIME Preparation takes 20 minutes plus time needed for marinating, cooking takes 45-50 minutes.

SERVING IDEAS Serve with Pilau Rice or Mushroom Pilau. Suitable for freezing.

WATCHPOINT Reduce cooking time if boneless chicken is used.

Chicken Dhansak

Dhansak is a combination of two or three types of lentils and meat or chicken.

SERVES 6-8

1kg/2.2lbs chicken joints, skinned
1 tsp salt or to taste
1-inch cube of root ginger, peeled and coarsely chopped
4-6 cloves garlic, peeled and chopped

Grind the following 10 ingredients in a coffee grinder
1 tsp coriander seeds
1 tsp cumin seeds
1 tsp fennel seeds
4 green cardamoms
1 cinnamon stick, 2-inches long, broken up
4-6 dried red chillies
10 black peppercorns
2 bay leaves
¼ tsp fenugreek seeds
½ tsp black mustard seeds

2 tbsps ghee or unsalted butter
125ml/4fl oz warm water

For the dhal
75g/3oz toor dhal (yellow split peas)
75g/3oz masoor dhal (red split lentils)
5 tbsps cooking oil
1 large onion, finely chopped
1 tsp ground turmeric
1 tsp garam masala
600ml/20fl oz warm water
1 tsp salt or to taste
1 tsp tamarind concentrate (available from Indian grocers) or 1½ tbsp lemon juice
1 tbsp chopped coriander leaves, optional

1. Wash and dry the chicken portions and cut each portion into two.

2. Add the salt to the ginger and garlic and crush to a pulp.

3. Make a paste of the ground ingredients and the ginger/garlic pulp by adding 6 tbsps water. Pour this mixture over the chicken and mix to coat thoroughly. Cover and set aside for 4-6 hours or overnight in the refrigerator.

4. Melt the ghee or butter over medium heat and fry chicken for 6-8 minutes, stirring frequently. Add the water, bring to the boil, cover and simmer for 20 minutes. Stir several times.

5. Meanwhile, mix together the toor and masoor dhals, wash and drain well.

6. Heat the oil over medium flame and fry onions for 5 minutes, stirring frequently. Add turmeric and garam masala, stir and fry for 1 minute. Add the dhal, adjust heat to low and fry for 5 minutes, stirring frequently. Add the water and salt, bring to the boil, cover and simmer for 30 minutes until soft, stirring occasionally. Remove from heat.

7. Using a metal spoon, push some of the cooked dhal through a sieve until there is a very dry and coarse mixture left. Discard the coarse mixture and sieve the rest of the dhal the same way.

8. Pour the sieved dhal over the chicken, cover and place the pan over medium heat. Bring to the boil, reduce heat and simmer for 20-25 minutes. Stir occasionally during the first half of the cooking time, but more frequently during the latter half, to ensure that the mixture does not stick to the bottom of the pan.

9. Dissolve the tamarind pulp in 3 tbsps boiling water. Add this to the chicken/dhal mixture, stir and mix thoroughly. Cover and simmer for 5 minutes. Stir in the coriander leaves and remove from heat. If using lemon juice, simply add this at the end of the cooking time.

Murghi Aur Palak

Murghi aur Palak is a delicious combination of chicken and spinach with fennel, coriander and chillies.

SERVES 4-6

1kg/2.2lbs chicken quarters, skinned
4 tbsps cooking oil
2 medium-sized onions, finely chopped
1-inch cube of root ginger, peeled and finely grated
2-3 cloves garlic, peeled and crushed

Make a paste of the following 4 ingredients by adding 3 tbsps water
1 tsp ground turmeric
1 tsp ground fennel
1 tsp ground coriander
½ tsp chilli powder

1½ tsps salt or to taste
90ml/3fl oz warm water
1 heaped tbsp ghee or unsalted butter
1-2 cloves garlic, peeled and finely chopped
6-8 curry leaves
½ tsp cumin seeds
½ tsp fennel seeds
1-2 dried red chillies, coarsely chopped
450g/1lb fresh or 225g/8oz frozen leaf spinach, (defrosted and drained) coarsely chopped
4 tbsps natural yogurt
½ tsp garam masala

1. Cut each chicken quarter into half, separating leg from thigh and cutting each breast into two, lengthwise.

2. Heat the oil over medium heat and fry the onions, ginger and garlic until the onions are lightly browned (6-8 minutes).

3. Adjust heat to low and add the spice paste, stir and fry for 4-5 minutes. Rinse out the bowl with 2 tbsps water and add to the spice mixture. Stir and fry for a further 2-3 minutes.

4. Add the chicken and adjust heat to medium-high. Stir and fry until chicken changes colour (about 3-4 minutes). Add 1 tsp salt and the water, bring to the boil, cover the pan and simmer for 15 minutes; stir once or twice during this time.

5. In a separate pan, melt ghee or butter over medium heat and add garlic and curry leaves followed by cumin, fennel and red chillies, stirring briskly. Wash fresh spinach thoroughly, remove any hard stalks and add the spinach and the remaining salt. Stir and fry for 5-6 minutes and mix spinach and chicken together, bring to the boil, cover the pan and simmer for 20 minutes, stirring occasionally.

6. Mix yogurt and garam masala together and beat until the yogurt is smooth. Add to the chicken/spinach mixture – stir and mix thoroughly. Cook uncovered for 6-8 minutes over medium heat, stirring frequently.

TIME Preparation takes 25-30 minutes, cooking takes 50-55 minutes.

SERVING IDEAS Serve with Fried Brown Rice and Potato Raita.

TO FREEZE Suitable for freezing, if fresh spinach is used.

VARIATION Use lamb, but replace fennel with cumin, both whole and ground.

Murghi Aur Aloo

This recipe is a fine example of the Persian influence in Indian cookery. Chicken and potatoes are cooked with saffron and a generous amount of fresh coriander.

SERVES 4-6

1kg/2.2lbs chicken joints, skinned
1½ tsps salt or to taste
1-inch cube of root ginger, peeled and coarsely chopped
4-6 cloves garlic, peeled and coarsely chopped

Grind the following ingredients in a coffee grinder
2 tsps cumin seeds
4-6 dried red chillies
2 black cardamoms; the inner seeds only or 4 green cardamoms with the skin
6 whole cloves
2 cinnamon sticks, each 2-inches long; broken up into 2-3 pieces
6 black peppercorns

Grind the following 2 ingredients separately
1 tbsp white poppy seeds
10 raw whole cashews

50g/2oz ghee or unsalted butter
25g/1oz fresh coriander leaves and stalks, finely chopped
1-2 fresh green chillies, cut into halves lengthwise; seed the chillies if a milder flavour is preferred
½ tsp ground turmeric
300ml/10fl oz warm water plus 4 tbsps cold water
½ tsp saffron strands
450g/1lb medium-sized potatotes, peeled and quartered
125g/5oz soured cream
2-3 hard-boild eggs, cut into quarters lengthwise

1. Wash the chicken and dry on absorbent paper. Cut each joint into two; separate leg from thigh and cut each breast into two pieces.

2. Add the salt to the ginger and garlic and crush them to a pulp.

3. Convert the ground ingredients, including the poppy seeds and the cashews, into a thick paste by adding the cold water. Break up any lumps with the back of a spoon and then set aside.

4. Melt the ghee or butter over low heat and add the ginger/garlic paste. Cook for 2-3 minutes stirring continuously.

5. Add the spice paste, stir and fry for 2-3 minutes.

6. Add chicken and adjust heat to medium-high. Fry the chicken until it changes colour (5-6 minutes).

7. Add the coriander leaves, green chillies and turmeric, stir and fry for a further 2-3 minutes.

8. Add the water, bring to the boil and add the saffron strands. Cover and simmer for 15 minutes.

9. Add the potatoes and cook for a further 20 minutes or until the chicken and the potatoes are tender and the gravy is fairly thick.

10. Beat the soured cream until smooth and stir into the chicken. Cook uncovered for 6-8 minutes stirring frequently. Remove from the heat.

11. Arrange the chicken curry in a serving dish and garnish with the quarters of hard-boiled eggs.

MAKKHANI MURGHI

Makkhani Murghi, or Chicken in a Butter Sauce, is rich, delicious and irresistible! It is bound to be an overwhelming success with your dinner guests!

SERVES 6-8

1kg/2.2lbs chicken breast, skinned
1¼ tsps salt or to taste
1-inch cube of root ginger, peeled and coarsely chopped
4-6 cloves garlic, peeled and coarsely chopped
125g/5oz thick set natural yogurt
The juice of 1 lemon

Grind the following 5 ingredients in a coffee grinder
1 cinnamon stick, 2-inches long; broken up
8 green cardamoms with the skin
6 whole cloves
8-10 red chillies
6-8 white peppercorns

2 tbsps cooking oil
2 tbsps tomato purée
225g/8oz butter
400g/14oz can of tomatoes
2 cinnamon sticks, each 2-inches long; broken up
150ml/5fl oz single cream

1. Wash and dry the chicken and cut into 4 × 2-inch strips.

2. Add the salt to the ginger and garlic and crush to a smooth pulp.

3. Combine the yogurt, lemon juice and the ground spices and beat until the mixture is smooth. Marinate the chicken in this mixture, cover the container and leave it in a cool place for 2-4 hours or overnight in the refrigerator.

4. Heat the oil over medium heat and add the ginger/garlic pulp, stir and fry for 1 minute. Add the chicken and stir and fry for 10 minutes.

5. Add the tomato purée and butter, cook on low heat, uncovered, for 10 minutes. Remove the pan from the heat, cover and keep aside.

6. Put the tomatoes and the cinnamon sticks in a separate pan, bring to the boil, cover and simmer for 10 minutes. Remove the lid and adjust heat to medium; cook uncovered until the liquid is reduced to half its original volume (6-8 minutes). Remove the pan from the heat and allow the tomato mixture to cool slightly.

7. Sieve the cooked tomatoes, discard the cinnamon sticks. Add the sieved tomatoes to the chicken and place the pan over medium heat. Bring the liquid to the boil, reduce heat to low and cook, uncovered, for 5-6 minutes.

8. Add the cream, stir and mix well, and simmer uncovered for about 5 minutes. Remove from the heat.

TIME Preparation takes 20-25 minutes plus time needed for marinating, cooking takes 40-45 minutes.

SERVING IDEAS Serve with Naan or Tandoori Roti or Plain Boiled Rice.

TO FREEZE Suitable for freezing, but reheat over very gentle heat. Simmer uncovered until heated through; do not boil.

Murghi Badami

Murghi Badami is a richer version of Chicken Korma, where the chicken is cooked entirely in natural yogurt and single cream. No water is added to the chicken and the result is a thick and silky gravy with a delightful taste.

SERVES 4-6

- 1kg/2.2lbs chicken joints, skinned
- 1 tsp salt or to taste
- 1-inch cube of root ginger, peeled and chopped
- 3-4 cloves garlic, peeled and chopped
- 1 tsp freshly ground black pepper
- 1 tbsp lemon juice
- 275g/10oz thick set natural yogurt
- 50g/2oz ghee or unsalted butter
- 2 medium-sized onions, finely sliced
- 6 green cardamoms, split open the top of each pod
- 1 tbsp ground coriander
- 1 tsp ground turmeric
- 150ml/5fl oz single cream
- ¼-½ tsp chilli powder
- 50g/2oz flaked almonds
- 1 heaped tbsp ground almonds

1. Cut each chicken joint into two – separating leg from thigh and cutting each breast into two pieces. Wash the chicken and dry with a cloth or absorbent paper. Make small incisions on both sides of the pieces of chicken with a sharp knife. This is to allow the spices to penetrate deep inside.

2. Add the salt to the ginger and garlic and crush to a fine pulp. Mix with the pepper and lemon juice. Rub this mixture into the chicken, cover it and keep aside for ½-1 hour.

3. Beat the yogurt until smooth and keep aside.

4. Melt the ghee or butter over medium heat and fry the onions until well browned (10-12 minutes). Remove pan from heat and squeeze out excess fat by pressing the onions to the side of the pan. Transfer the onions to a plate.

5. Return pan to heat and add cardamoms and coriander, stir and fry for 30 seconds. Add the chicken, adjust heat to medium-high and fry the chicken until it changes colour (5-6 minutes) stirring continuously.

6. Stir in the turmeric and the yogurt and simmer; cover the pan and cook for 15 minutes, stirring occasionally.

7. Reserve 2 tbsps of the fried onions and add the rest to the chicken along with the cream, chilli powder and the almonds, stir and mix well. Cover and simmer for a further 15-20 minutes stirring occasionally.

8. Sprinkle the ground almonds and mix well, cover and simmer for 6-8 minutes. Remove from the heat.

9. Put the chicken in a serving dish and garnish with the remaining fried onions.

TIME Preparation takes 25-30 minutes plus time needed for marinating, cooking takes 55-60 minutes.

SERVING IDEAS Serve with any Indian bread, Saffron Rice or Pilau Rice.

MURGH DILKUSH

Chicken is still regarded as a bit special in India as it is more expensive than other meats. This is a wonderfully aromatic chicken dish which is ideally suited for a special occasion.

SERVES 6-8

1.2kg/2½lbs chicken joints, skin removed
4 tbsps ghee or unsalted butter
2 medium-sized onions, finely chopped
1-inch cube of root ginger, peeled and coarsely chopped
4-6 cloves garlic, peeled and coarsely chopped
125g/5oz thick set natural yogurt

Roast the following ingredients gently over low heat until the spices release their aroma, cool and grind in a coffee grinder.

2-inch piece cinnamon stick, broken up
6 green cardamoms, skin left on
6 whole cloves
1 tsp cumin seeds
2-3 dried red chillies
1 tbsp channa dhal or yellow split peas

Similarly, roast the following 2 ingredients until they are lightly browned, cool and grind separately from the above ingredients, in a coffee grinder.

25g/1oz raw cashews
1 tbsp white poppy seeds

1 tsp garam masala
150ml/5fl oz warm water
1¼ tsps salt or to taste
25g/1 oz fresh coriander leaves, finely chopped
1 tbsp fresh mint leaves, finely chopped or 1 tsp dried or bottled mint
1-2 fresh green chillies, seeded and coarsely chopped

1. Cut each chicken joint into two (separate leg from thigh and cut each breast into two).

2. Melt 2 tbsps ghee, from the specified amount, over medium heat and fry the onions, ginger and garlic for 4-5 minutes. Squeeze out excess ghee by pressing the onion mixture onto the side of the pan with a wooden spoon and transfer them to another plate. Allow to cool slightly.

3. Put the yogurt into an electric blender or food processor and add all the roasted and ground ingredients and the fried onions. Blend until smooth.

4. Rub this marinade into the chicken and pour over any remaining marinade – mix thoroughly and leave to marinate for 4-6 hours or overnight in the refrigerator.

5. Melt the remaining 2 tbsps ghee over low heat and add the garam masala, stir and fry for 30 seconds.

6. Add the marinated chicken, adjust heat to medium-high and fry for 5-6 minutes, stirring frequently.

7. Add the water and salt, bring to the boil, cover and simmer until the chicken is tender (35-40 minutes).

8. Adjust heat to medium, add the fresh coriander, mint and green chillies – stir and fry for 5 minutes and remove from heat.

Murgh Musallam

SERVES 4-6

2 spring chickens or poussin, each weighing about 450g/1lb

Grind together the following 5 ingredients
2 tbsps white poppy seeds
2 tbsps sesame seeds
10 black peppercorns
4 green cardamoms
2-4 dried red chillies

125g/5oz thick set natural yogurt
2½ tsps salt or to taste
½ tsp ground turmeric
1 tbsp ground coriander
75g/3oz ghee or unsalted butter
2 medium-sized onions, finely sliced
2-3 cloves garlic, peeled and finely chopped
2 cinnamon sticks, 2-inches each; broken up
6 green cardamoms, split open the top of each pod
4 whole cloves
275g/10oz basmati rice, washed and soaked in cold water for 30 minutes
570ml/20fl oz water
½ tsp saffron strands
2 tbsps ghee or unsalted butter
1 medium-sized onion, finely chopped
2-4 cloves garlic, peeled and crushed

---

1. Remove the skin and the giblets from the chicken. With a sharp knife, make several slits all over each chicken (do not forget the thighs and the back).
2. Mix the ground ingredients with the yogurt and add 1 tsp salt, turmeric and coriander. Rub half of this mixture into the chickens, making sure that the spices are rubbed deep into the slits. Put the chickens in a deep container, cover and keep aside for 1 hour.
3. Meanwhile cook the pilau rice. Melt the 75g/3oz ghee or butter over medium heat and fry the sliced onions, chopped garlic, cinnamon, cardamom and cloves, until the onions are lightly browned (6-7 minutes).
4. Add the rice, stir and fry until all the moisture evaporates (4-5 minutes). Add the remaining salt, water and saffron strands. Bring to the boil, cover the pan and simmer until the rice has absorbed all the water (12-14 minutes). Do not lift the lid or stir the rice during cooking. Remove the pan from the heat and leave it undisturbed for about 10 minutes.
5. Using a metal spoon, carefully transfer about a quarter of the cooked rice to a plate and allow it to cool. Keep the remaining rice covered.
6. Stuff each chicken with as much of the cooled pilau rice as the stomach cavity will hold. Truss it up as for roasting, using trussing needles or a similar object to secure it so that the rice stays in tact while the stuffed chicken is being braised.
7. Melt the 2 tbsps ghee or butter in a cast iron or nonstick pan. Add the chopped onions and the crushed garlic, stir and fry for 2-3 minutes.
8. Place the chicken on the bed of onions, on their backs, along with any marinade left in the container, but not the other half of the marinade which has been reserved. Cover the pan and cook for 10 minutes; turn the chicken over, breast side down, cover and cook for a further 10 minutes.
9. Turn the chickens on their backs again and spread the remaining marinade evenly on each chicken. Cover the pan and cook for 30 minutes turning the chicken over every 10 minutes.

10. Put the chicken onto a serving dish and spread a little gravy evenly over the breast. Spoon the remaining gravy round the chicken.
11. Serve the remaining pilau rice separately.

CHICKEN LIVER MASALA

Curried liver is quite a popular item in India, particularly with Muslims. This recipe is made more interesting by adding diced potatoes and frozen garden peas.

SERVES 4

450g/1lb chicken liver
4 tbsps cooking oil
1 large onion finely chopped
1 cinnamon stick, 2-inches long, broken up
225g/8oz potatoes, peeled and diced
1¼ tsps salt or to taste
90ml/3fl oz warm water
3-4 cloves garlic, peeled and crushed

Make a paste of the following 4 ingredients by adding 2 tsps water
2 tsps ground coriander
1 tsp ground cumin
1 tsp ground turmeric
½ tsp chilli powder

1 small tin of tomatoes
100g/4oz frozen garden peas
2-3 fresh green chillies, whole
½ tsp garam masala

1. Clean the liver, remove all skin and gristle and cut roughly into ½-inch pieces.

2. Heat 2 tbsps oil over medium heat and fry the onions and cinnamon stick until the onions are soft.

3. Add the potatoes and ¼ tsp salt and stir fry the potatoes for about 2 minutes.

4. Add the water, cover the pan and simmer until the potatoes are tender.

5. Meanwhile, heat the remaining oil over medium heat in a heavy-based, wide pan. A nonstick or cast iron pan is ideal as the liver needs to be stir-fried over high heat.

6. Add the garlic and stir fry for 30 seconds.

7. Add the spice paste, reduce heat to low, and stir and fry for about 2 minutes.

8. Add half the tomatoes, along with some of the juice, stir and cook for a further 2-3 minutes, breaking the tomatoes with the spoon.

9. When the mixture is fairly dry, add the liver and adjust heat to medium-high. Stir-fry the liver for 3-4 minutes.

10. Add the remaining tomatoes and the juice, stir and fry for 5-6 minutes.

11. Cover the pan and simmer for 6-8 minutes.

12. Add the potatoes, peas, green chillies and the remaining salt and cook for 1-2 minutes. Adjust heat to medium and cook, uncovered, for a further 4-5 minutes.

13. Stir in the garam masala and remove from heat.

TIME Preparation takes 20-25 minutes, cooking takes 36-40 minutes.

SERVING IDEAS Serve with Plain Fried Rice or Chapatties or Rotis and Saagwalla Dhal.

Chicken Liver with Spinach

An unusual and interesting combination which is high in vitamins and iron. Do be careful while browning the liver, keep the pan covered and keep your face averted while stirring the liver as it tends to pop in hot oil.

SERVES 4-6

450g/1lb chicken liver
1¼ tsps salt or to taste
2-3 cloves garlic, peeled
100g/4oz frozen leaf spinach (defrosted and drained), or 325g/12oz fresh spinach coarsely chopped
5 tbsps cooking oil
1 tsp ground turmeric
1½ tsps ground coriander
1 tsp ground cumin
¼-½ tsp chilli powder
¼ tsp black mustard seeds
1 tsp cumin seeds
1 large onion, finely sliced
½ tsp garam masala
½ a small red pepper, white pith removed and cut into match stick strips

1. Clean the liver, remove skin and gristle and cut roughly into 1-inch pieces. Wash and drain thoroughly, and dry on absorbent paper.

2. Add the salt to the garlic and crush to a pulp, using a wooden pestle or pestle and mortar.

3. Heat 2 tbsps oil over medium heat, when the oil is smoking hot, put in the chicken liver, spread it quickly and cover the pan. Cook for 6-8 minutes, stir once or twice. Now remove the lid and dry off any excess liquid.

4. Add the garlic pulp, lower heat and stir fry the garlic for 2-3 minutes.

5. Add the turmeric, coriander, cumin and chilli powder; stir and mix well. Let the liver cook, uncovered, over low heat for 4-5 minutes, stirring occasionally.

6. In a separate pan, heat the remaining oil over medium heat and add the mustard seeds. As soon as they pop, add the cumin seeds followed by the onions. Stir and fry the onions until they are golden brown (6-8 minutes).

7. Add the garam masala and the red pepper and stir fry for 1-2 minutes.

8. Add the spinach, adjust heat to medium-high and stir fry the spinach for 2-3 minutes.

9. Add the spinach to the liver along with any juice/oil that is left in the pan. Adjust heat to low, stir and fry the spinach and the liver for 1-2 minutes. Cook, uncovered, for 6-8 minutes, stirring occasionally. Remove from heat.

TIME Preparation takes 15-20 minutes, cooking takes 35-40 minutes.

SERVING IDEAS Serve with Puris, Loochis or Plain Boiled Rice and Spicy Channa Dhal.
Suitable for freezing.

TANDOORI CHICKEN MASALA

The word masala means a combination of spices. In this recipe the chicken is simmered gently in a smooth velvety sauce flavoured with saffron, ground cardamom and cinnamon.

SERVES 4-6

1kg/2.2lbs cooked Tandoori Chicken (see separate recipe)
50g/2oz ghee or unsalted butter
1 large onion, finely chopped
½-inch cube of root ginger, peeled and crushed
2 cloves garlic, peeled and crushed
1 tsp ground cardamom
1 tsp ground cinnamon
¼ tsp chilli powder
1 tsp salt or to taste
125g/5oz soured cream
225ml/8fl oz warm stock; (made up of the reserved cooking liquid and warm water)
4 level tbsps ground almonds
2 tbsps milk
½ tsp saffron strands
25g/1oz toasted flaked almonds

1. Heat the ghee or butter over low heat and fry the onions until they are just soft, but not brown.

2. Add the ginger and garlic and fry for two minutes, stirring constantly.

3. Add the cardamom, cinnamon, chilli powder and salt and fry for 1 minute, stirring constantly.

4. Beat the soured cream with a fork until smooth, add half the stock while still beating. Add this mixture to the onions and bring the liquid to a slow simmer.

5. Add the remaining stock, cover the pan and simmer for 10 minutes.

6. Sprinkle the ground almonds evenly, stir and mix well and remove the pan from heat.

7. Heat the milk and soak the saffron strands in it for 10-15 minutes.

8. Arrange the tandoori chicken in a wide shallow pan. Hold a sieve over the pan and pour the sauce into it. Press with the back of a metal spoon to extract as much of the spiced mixture as possible as the onion pulp is necessary to add to the thickness of the gravy. Alternatively, liquidise the mixture until smooth and then pour over the chicken.

9. Sprinkle the saffron milk and all the saffron strands evenly over the chicken.

10. Place the pan back over gentle heat and bring the liquid to the boiling point. Cover the pan and simmer for 10 minutes, turning the chicken once or twice.

11. Put the chicken in a serving dish and garnish with the toasted almonds.

TIME Preparation takes 25-30 minutes plus time needed for marinating, cooking takes 25-30 minutes for the chicken and 20-25 minutes for the sauce.

SERVING IDEAS Serve with Pilau Rice and Mixed Vegetable Bhaji or Bhindi (Okra) with Coconut and/or Carrot & Peanut Raita.

Cauliflower Surprise

Here is an imaginative way to serve cauliflower which also looks attractive. The cauliflower is first blanched, then stuffed with spicy lean mince.

SERVES 4

1 medium-sized cauliflower
4 tbsps cooking oil
1 tsp cumin seeds
1 large onion, finely chopped
1-inch cube of root ginger, peeled and grated
3-4 cloves garlic, peeled and crushed
450g/1lb lean mince, lamb or beef
1 tsp ground turmeric
1 tbsp ground coriander
1 tsp ground cinnamon
1 tsp ground cardamom
½ tsp chilli powder
1 small tin of tomatoes, drained
1 tsp salt or to taste
¼ tsp black mustard seeds
½ tsp cumin seeds
8-10 curry leaves

To garnish
2 small tomatoes, quartered
1 tbsp chopped coriander leaves

1. Blanch the cauliflower in boiling salted water, then drain and cool.

2. Heat 3 tbsps oil over medium heat and add the cumin seeds; as soon as the seeds start popping, add the onions and fry for 3-4 minutes, stirring frequently.

3. Add the ginger and garlic, stir and fry for 1 minute.

4. Add the mince, adjust heat to medium-high, stir and fry the mince until it is crumbly and all the liquid evaporates.

5. Adjust heat to low and add the turmeric, coriander, cinnamon, cardamom and chilli powder. Stir and fry until the spices are well-blended (3-4 minutes).

6. Add the tomatoes and salt, stir and cook for 1-2 minutes. Cover the pan and simmer for 10-15 minutes. Remove the pan from heat and allow the mince to cool.

7. Place the cauliflower on a board, stem side up. Fill all the cavity between the stems with the cooked mince; this should be as tightly packed as possible.

8. Turn the cauliflower over and gently pull the florets apart and fill with as much mince as possible.

9. Heat the remaining oil over medium heat and add the mustard seeds. As soon as the seeds pop, add the cumin and the curry leaves.

10. Place the cauliflower on the seasoned oil, the right way up, and let it cook, uncovered for 2-3 minutes. Turn it over and cook the other side for 2-3 minutes.

11. Turn the cauliflower over again and arrange the remaining mince round it. Cover the pan and adjust heat to the minimum setting. Cook for 10-15 minutes or until the cauliflower is tender.

12. Put the cauliflower on a serving dish and spread some of the mince on it and arrange any remaining mince round it. Garnish with the tomatoes and the coriander leaves.

TIME Preparation takes 20 minutes plus cooling time, cooking takes 55-60 minutes.

ROGAN JOSH

Rogan Josh finds its origin in Kashmir, the northern-most state in India. In the recipe below, more than the usual quantity of spices are used, but these are toned down by using a large quantity of tomatoes and a little double cream.

SERVES 4-6

3 tbsps ghee or unsalted butter
1kg/2.2lbs leg of lamb, without bones, cut into 1½-inch cubes
1 tbsp ground cumin
1 tbsp ground coriander
1 tsp ground turmeric
1 tsp chilli powder
1-inch cube of root ginger, peeled and grated
2-4 cloves garlic, peeled and crushed
225g-275g/8-10oz onions, finely sliced
400g/14oz tin of tomatoes, chopped or whole
1 tbsp tomato purée
125ml/4fl oz warm water
1¼ tsps salt or to taste
90ml/3fl oz double cream
2 tsps garam masala
2 tbsps chopped coriander leaves

1. Melt 2 tbsps ghee or butter, from the specified amount, over medium heat and fry the meat in 2-3 batches until it changes colour. Remove each batch with a slotted spoon and keep aside.

2. Lower heat to minimum and add the cumin, coriander, turmeric, chilli powder, ginger and garlic. Stir and fry for 30 seconds.

3. Adjust heat to medium and add the meat along with all the ghee and juice in the container. Stir and fry for 3-4 minutes and add the onions. Fry for 5-6 minutes stirring frequently.

4. Now add the tomatoes and tomato purée – stir and cook for 2-3 minutes.

5. Add the water and salt, bring to the boil, cover and simmer until the meat is tender (about 60 minutes).

6. Stir in the cream and remove from heat.

7. In a separate pan melt the remaining ghee over medium heat and add the garam masala, stir briskly and add to the meat.

8. Transfer a little meat gravy to the pan in which the garam masala was fried – stir thoroughly to ensure that any remaining garam masala and ghee mixture is fully incorporated into the gravy and add this to the meat. Mix well.

9. Stir in the coriander leaves.

TIME Preparation takes 20 minutes, cooking takes 1 hour 30 minutes.

SERVING IDEAS Serve with plain boiled rice or plain fried rice and Cabbage with Cinnamon. If you are entertaining, add Naan or Tandoori Roti and Aubergine Raita.

TO FREEZE Freeze before adding cream, garam masala and coriander leaves. Defrost thoroughly before reheating. Bring to the boil, add the cream and remove from heat. Add garam masala and coriander leaves.

VARIATION Use braising steak, but increase cooking time.

Sikandari Raan

SERVES 6-8

1½-2kg/3½-4lbs leg of lamb

Put the following ingredients into an electric food processor or liquidiser and blend until smooth

300ml/10fl oz thick set natural yogurt

1-inch cube of root ginger, peeled and coarsely chopped

4-6 cloves garlic, peeled and coarsely chopped

1 medium-sized onion, coarsely chopped

1 fresh green chilli

2 tbsps fresh mint or 1 tsp dried or bottled mint

Add the following ingredients and blend for a few seconds longer

1 tbsp ground coriander

1 tsp ground cumin

1 tsp garam masala

1 tsp ground turmeric

1¼ tsps salt or to taste

Grind the following 3 ingredients in a coffee grinder

2 tbsps white poppy seeds

1 tbsp sesame seeds

2 tbsps desiccated coconut

25g/1oz ghee or unsalted butter

450g/1lb medium-sized potatoes, peeled and halved

Liquidise to a smooth paste

125g/5fl oz thick set natural yogurt

50g/2oz raw cashews

50g/2oz seedless raisins, soaked in a little warm water for 30 minutes

1. Remove as much fat as possible from the meat and lay it flat on a board. Make deep incisions from top to bottom at about ¼ -inch intervals. These incisions should be as deep as possible, almost down to the bone. Turn the leg over and repeat the process.

2. Mix the yogurt-based mixture with the ground spices. Rub this marinade into each incision, and then fill the incisions with it. Rub the remaining marinade all over the surface of the leg of lamb on both sides. Place in a covered container and leave to marinate in the refrigerator for 48 hours. Turn it over about every 12 hours.

3. Preheat the oven to 230°C/450°F/Gas Mark 8. Place the leg of lamb on a roasting tin, melt the ghee or butter and pour it over the meat. Cover the meat with aluminium foil or use a covered roasting dish and cook in the centre of the oven for 20 minutes. Reduce heat to 190°C/375°F/Gas Mark 5 and cook for 30 minutes. Now add the potatoes and spoon some of the spiced liquid over them as well as over the meat. Cover and cook for a further 35-40 minutes, basting the meat and the potatoes occasionally.

4. Now pour the liquidised nut mixture over the meat, cover and return the meat to the oven for about 30 minutes, basting the meat and the potatoes as before.

5. Transfer the meat onto a serving dish and arrange the potatoes around it. Spoon any remaining liquid over the meat and the potatoes. The meat is served cut into chunky pieces rather than thin slices.

TIME Preparation takes 25-30 minutes plus time needed for marinating, cooking takes 1 hour 45 minutes – 2 hours.

Kofta (Meatball) Curry

Koftas are popular throughout India, and they are made using fine lean mince which is blended with herbs and spices.

SERVES 4

For the koftas

450g/1lb lean minced lamb
2 cloves garlic, peeled and chopped
½-inch cube of root ginger, peeled and coarsely chopped
1 small onion, coarsely chopped
55ml/2fl oz water
1 fresh green chilli, seeded and chopped
2 tbsps chopped coriander leaves
1 tbsp fresh mint leaves, chopped
1 tsp salt or to taste

For the gravy

5 tbsps cooking oil
2 medium-sized onions, finely chopped
½-inch cube of root ginger, peeled and grated
2 cloves garlic, peeled and crushed
2 tsps ground coriander
1½ tsps ground cumin
½ tsp ground turmeric
¼-½ tsp chilli powder
1 small tin of tomatoes
150ml/5fl oz warm water
½ tsp salt or to taste
2 black cardamom pods, opened
4 whole cloves
2-inch piece of cinnamon stick, broken up
2 bay leaves, crumpled
2 tbsps thick set natural yogurt
2 tbsps ground almonds
1 tbsp chopped coriander leaves

1. Put half the mince, all the garlic, ginger, onion and the water into a saucepan and place over medium heat. Stir until the mince is heated through.

2. Cover and simmer until all liquid evaporates (30-35 minutes) then cook uncovered if necessary, to dry out excess liquid.

3. Combine the cooked mince with the rest of the ingredients, including the raw mince.

4. Put the mixture into a food processor or liquidiser and blend until smooth. Chill the mixture for 30 minutes.

5. Divide the mixture into approximately 20 balls, each slightly bigger than a walnut.

6. Rotate each ball between your palms to make neat round koftas.

7. Heat the oil over medium heat and fry the onions until they are just soft.

8. Add the ginger and garlic and fry for 1 minute.

9. Add the coriander, cumin, turmeric and chilli powder and stir quickly.

10. Add one tomato at a time, along with a little juice to the spice mixture, stirring until mixture begins to look dry.

11. Now add the water, salt, cardamom, cloves, cinnamon and the bay leaves.

12. Stir once and add the koftas. Bring to the boil, cover and simmer for 5 minutes.

13. Beat the yogurt with a fork until smooth, add the ground almonds and beat again – stir GENTLY into the curry. Cover and simmer until the koftas are firm.

14. Stir the curry GENTLY, cover again, and simmer for a further 10-15 minutes, stirring occasionally to ensure that the thickened gravy does not stick to the pan.

15. Stir in half the coriander leaves and remove from heat.

KHEEMA-SALI-MATTAR

This superb mince dish is another contribution from the ancient Persians, who have settled in India and have come to be known as the Parsis.

SERVES 4-6

5 tbsps cooking oil
1 tsp cumin seeds
1 large onion, finely chopped
½-inch cube of root ginger, peeled and finely grated
3-4 cloves garlic, peeled and crushed
½ tsp ground turmeric
1 tsp ground cinnamon
½ tsp ground nutmeg
1 tsp ground mixed spice
2 tsps ground coriander
½ tsp chilli powder
450g/1lb lean coarse mince, lamb or beef
1 small tin of tomatoes
1 tsp salt or to taste
150ml/5fl oz warm water
2 tbsps natural yogurt
150g/6oz frozen garden peas or shelled fresh peas, boiled until tender
2 tbsps chopped coriander leaves
2 tbsps ghee or unsalted butter
325g/12oz potatoes, peeled and cut into matchstick strips
¼ tsp salt
¼ tsp chilli powder

1. Heat the oil over medium heat and fry the cumin seeds until they pop, add the onions, ginger and garlic, fry until the onions are golden brown (6-7 minutes).

2. Add the turmeric, cinnamon, nutmeg, mixed spice, coriander and chilli powder, stir and fry on low heat for 2-3 minutes.

3. Add the mince, stir and fry until the mince is brown and all the liquid evaporates.

4. Add the tomatoes and cook for 2-3 minutes stirring frequently.

5. Add the salt and water, bring to the boil, cover and cook on low heat for 15-20 minutes.

6. Beat the yogurt until it is smooth and add this to the mince along with the peas, bring to the boil again, cover and simmer for 5 minutes.

7. Stir in half the coriander leaves and remove from heat.

8. Melt the ghee or butter over medium heat in a non-stick or cast iron pan and fry the potato sticks in a single layer until they are well browned and tender (5-6 minutes), reducing heat towards the end of the cooking time. You will need to do this in 2-3 batches. Drain the potato sticks on absorbent paper.

9. Season the potato sticks with the salt and chilli powder.

10. Put the mince in the middle of a serving dish and arrange the potato sticks around it. Garnish with the remaining coriander leaves.

TIME Preparation takes 15 minutes, cooking takes 55 minutes.

SERVING IDEAS Serve with any Indian bread and Bhindi (Okra) Raita.

Meat Maharaja

A rich lamb curry cooked in the style favoured by the great Maharajas of India. Ground poppy seeds and almonds are used to thicken the gravy and also to add a nutty flavour.

SERVES 4-6

---

4 tbsps ghee or unsalted butter
2 large onions, coarsely chopped
1-inch cube of root ginger, peeled and coarsely chopped
4-6 cloves garlic, peeled and coarsely chopped
1 fresh green chilli, seeded and chopped
1-2 dried red chillies, chopped
125g/5oz thick set natural yogurt
1 tsp black cumin seeds or caraway seeds

Mix the following 4 ingredients in a small bowl

3 tsps ground coriander
1 tsp garam masala
1 tsp ground turmeric
¼ tsp ground black pepper

2 tbsps white poppy seeds, ground in a coffee grinder
1kg/2.2lbs leg of lamb, cut into 1-inch cubes
1¼ tsps salt or to taste
2 tbsps ground almonds
2 tbsps chopped coriander leaves
1 tbsp lemon juice
25g/2oz unsalted pistachio nuts, lightly crushed

1. Melt 2 tbsps ghee from the specified amount over medium heat and fry the onions, ginger, garlic, green and red chillies until the onions are just soft (3-4 minutes). Remove from heat and allow to cool slightly.

2. Put the yogurt into an electric blender or food processor, add the onion mixture and blend to a purée. Keep aside.

3. Heat the remaining ghee or butter over low heat (do not overheat ghee) and add the black cumin or caraway seeds followed by the spice mixture and the ground poppy seeds. Stir and fry for 1 minute.

4. Add the meat, adjust heat to medium-high, stir and fry until meat changes colour (4-5 minutes). Cover the pan and let the meat cook in its own juice for 15 minutes. Stir occasionally during this time.

5. Add the blended ingredients and mix thoroughly. Rinse out blender container with 175ml/6fl oz warm water and add this to the meat. Stir in the salt and bring the liquid to the boil, cover the pan and simmer until the meat is tender. Stir occasionally during the first half of cooking time, but more frequently towards the end to ensure that the thickened gravy does not stick to the bottom of the pan.

6. Stir in the ground almonds and half the coriander leaves, cook, uncovered for 2-3 minutes.

7. Remove the pan from heat and add the lemon juice, mix well. Garnish with the remaining coriander leaves and sprinkle the crushed pistachio nuts on top.

Meat Dilruba

This delicious meat curry is in a class of its own. It is cooked in two stages making it easier to get much of the preparation and cooking out of the way in advance.

SERVES 4-6

1kg/2.2lbs boned leg of lamb
1¼ tsps salt or to taste
½-inch cube of root ginger, peeled and finely chopped
3-4 cloves garlic, peeled and finely chopped
1 tsp ground turmeric
125g/5oz thick set natural yogurt
1 large onion, finely sliced
3-4 dried red chillies, coarsely chopped
150ml/5fl oz water

Grind together in a coffee grinder
1 tbsp white poppy seeds
1 tsp fenugreek seeds

50g/2oz desiccated coconut, grind separately in a coffee grinder, about 15g/½oz at a time

2 tbsps ghee or unsalted butter
2 tbsps ground coriander
150ml/5fl oz milk
15g/½oz finely chopped coriander leaves
1 fresh green chilli, cut lengthwise into thin strips; remove seeds if preferred

1. Trim off excess fat from the meat, wash and pat dry, and cut into 1-inch cubes.

2. Put the ginger, garlic and salt in a pestle and mortar and crush them to a pulp. Alternatively, use a chopping board and crush them with the end of a wooden rolling pin.

3. Mix together the ginger/garlic pulp, turmeric and the yogurt and beat until the yogurt is smooth. Add this to the meat, mix thoroughly, cover the container and leave to marinate for 4-6 hours or overnight in the refrigerator.

4. Put the marinated meat into a heavy-based saucepan, add the onions, red chillies and the water. Bring to a slow simmer over gentle heat. Cover the pan and simmer for 50-60 minutes or until the meat is tender. Remove from the heat.

5. Melt the ghee over medium heat and add the ground coriander, stir and fry for 30 seconds. Add the ground poppy and fenugreek seeds and fry until the mixture is lightly browned, stirring constantly (1-2 minutes).

6. Lift the meat with a slotted spoon and add to the poppy/fenugreek mixture. Stir and fry over medium-high heat until all the moisture evaporates (6-7 minutes). Add the ground coconut, stir and fry for 2 minutes. Now add the milk and the liquid in which the meat was cooked. Stir and mix thoroughly. Cook, uncovered, over low heat for 4-5 minutes, stirring frequently.

7. Stir in the coriander leaves and the green chilli and remove from the heat.

TIME Preparation takes 25-30 minutes plus time needed for marinating, cooking takes 1 hour 15 minutes.

NAWABI KHEEMA PILAU

A rich rice dish in which mince is transformed into a wonderfully fragrant pilau by the addition of saffron, rose water and fried nuts.

SERVES 4-6

275g/10oz basmati rice
50g/2oz ghee or unsalted butter
1 tbsp extra ghee or unsalted butter
25g/1oz sultanas
25g/1oz raw cashews, split into halves
2 tbsps milk
1 tsp saffron strands
6 green cardamons, split open the top of each pod
4 whole cloves
1 tsp cumin seeds
2 bay leaves, crumpled
1-inch cube of root ginger, peeled and grated
2-3 cloves garlic, peeled and crushed
1-2 fresh green chillies, finely chopped and seeded if a milder flavour is preferred
1 tsp ground nutmeg
1 tsp ground cinnamon
1 tsp ground cumin
1 tbsp ground coriander
450g/1lb lean minced lamb
570ml/1 pint water
1½ tsps salt or to taste
150ml/5fl oz single cream
2 tbsps rosewater
2 hard-boiled eggs, sliced

1. Wash and soak basmati rice in cold water for ½ hour, then drain.

2. Melt the 1 tbsp ghee or butter over low heat and fry the sultanas until they swell up, then remove with a slotted spoon and keep aside.

3. In the same fat, fry the cashews until they are lightly browned, remove with a slotted spoon and keep aside.

4. Boil the milk, add the saffron strands and put aside. Alternatively, put the milk and the saffron strands in the microwave and boil on full power or about 45 seconds. Set aside.

5. Melt the remaining ghee or butter gently over low heat and fry the cardamoms, cloves, cumin seeds and the bay leaves for 1 minute.

6. Add the ginger, garlic and green chillies and stir fry for 30 seconds.

7. Add all the nutmeg, ground cinnamon, cumin and coriander and fry for 1 minute.

8. Add the mince and adjust heat to medium. Stir and fry the mince until all liquid dries up and it is lightly browned. This will take about 5 minutes.

9. Add the rice, stir and fry for about 5 minutes.

10. Add the water, salt, cream and the steeped saffron. Stir and mix well. Bring the liquid to the boil, cover the pan and simmer for 12-15 minutes without lifting the lid. Remove the pan from the heat and keep it undisturbed for a further 10-15 minutes.

11. Add half the nuts and raisins to the rice, then sprinkle the rosewater evenly on top. Using a fork, stir and mix in the ingredients gently.

12. Put the pilau in a serving dish and garnish with the remaining nuts and raisins and the sliced hard-boiled eggs.

TIME Preparation takes 20-25 minutes, cooking takes 40-45 minutes.

KOFTA BHOONA

Kofta Bhoona consists of tiny meatballs the size of marbles which are coated with a delicious spice paste.

SERVES 4-6

450g/1lb fine lean mince, lamb or beef
1 large clove of garlic, peeled and crushed
1 tsp garam masala
1-2 fresh green chillies, seeded and minced
2 tbsps fresh coriander leaves, minced
1½ tsps salt or to taste
3 tbsps cooking oil
1 large onion, finely chopped
¼-inch cube of root ginger, peeled and grated
2 tsps ground coriander
1 tsp ground cumin

Make a paste of the following 5 ingredients
½-1 tsp chilli powder
2 cloves garlic, peeled and crushed
½ tsp ground turmeric
2 tbsps tomato purée
125ml/4fl oz cold water

225ml/8fl oz warm water
50g/2oz frozen garden peas
¼ tsp garam masala
2 tbsps chopped coriander leaves

---

1. Put the mince in a large bowl and add the garlic, garam masala, green chillies, 1 tsp salt and the coriander leaves. Mix the ingredients thoroughly and knead the mince until it is smooth.

2. Divide the mixture into about 28-30 marble-sized balls (koftas). Make the koftas by rolling the balls between the palms in a circular motion until they are smooth and round.

3. Heat the oil over medium heat, preferably in a nonstick or cast iron pan, and fry the koftas in 2-3 batches. Turn the koftas as they brown and when they are brown all over, remove with a slotted spoon and drain on absorbent paper.

4. In the same oil, fry the onions and ginger until the onions are golden brown (6-8 minutes), stirring frequently.

5. Adjust heat to low and add the ground coriander, stir and fry for 30 seconds. Now add the ground cumin and fry for 30 seconds.

6. Adjust heat to medium and add 2 tbsps of the tomato purée mixture. Stir and fry until it dries up. Repeat the process until all the tomato purée mixture is used up.

7. Add the warm water and the remaining salt and bring to the boil.

8. Add the koftas, cover the pan and simmer for 10 minutes.

9. Now adjust heat to medium, bring the liquid to the boil, stir and cook for 4-5 minutes.

10. Add the peas and the garam masala and continue to cook, uncovered, until the gravy is fairly thick, stirring frequently.

11. Stir in the coriander leaves and remove from heat.

TIME Preparation takes 25-30 minutes, cooking takes 50-55 minutes.

SERVING IDEAS Serve with Mushroom Pilau or Parathas and a Raita or salad.

MEAT VINDALOO

Vindaloo is made by marinating the meat in vinegar and spices. It is traditionally a hot curry, but the quantity of chillies can be adjusted to suit individual taste.

SERVES 4-6

Grind the following 5 ingredients in a coffee grinder
2 tbsps coriander seeds
1 tbsp cumin seeds
6-8 dried red chillies
1 tbsps mustard seeds
½ tsp fenugreek seeds

3-4 tbsps cider or white wine vinegar
1 tsp ground turmeric
1-inch cube of root ginger, peeled and finely grated
3-4 cloves garlic, peeled and crushed
1kg/2.2lbs shoulder of lamb or stewing steak
4 tbsps cooking oil
1 large onion, finely chopped
1-2 tsps chilli powder
1 tsp paprika
1¼ tsps salt or to taste
450ml/15fl oz warm water
2-3 medium-sized potatoes
1 tbsp chopped coriander leaves, (optional)

1. In a large bowl, make a thick paste out of the ground spices, by adding the vinegar.

2. Add the turmeric, ginger and garlic. Mix thoroughly.

3. Trim off excess fat from the meat and cut into 1-inch cubes.

4. Add the meat and mix it well so that all the pieces are fully coated with the paste. Cover the bowl with cling film and leave to marinate for 4-6 hours or overnight in the refrigerator.

5. Put the meat in a pan and place this over medium heat, allow the meat to heat through, stirring occasionally; this will take about 5 minutes. Cover the pan, and cook the meat in its own juice for 15-20 minutes or until the liquid is reduced to a thick paste. Stir occasionally during this time to ensure that the meat does not stick to the bottom of the pan. Remove from heat and keep aside.

6. Heat the oil over medium heat and fry the onions until they are soft (about 5 minutes).

7. Add the meat and fry for 6-8 minutes stirring frequently.

8. Add the chilli powder, paprika and salt. Stir and fry for a further 2-3 minutes.

9. Add the water, bring to the boil, cover and simmer for 40-45 minutes or until the meat is nearly tender (beef will take longer to cook, check water level and add more water if necessary).

10. Meanwhile, peel and wash the potatoes. Cut them into approximately 1½-inch cubes. Add this to the meat and bring to the boil again. Cover the pan and simmer until the potatoes are cooked (15-20 minutes).

11. Turn the vindaloo on to a serving dish and sprinkle the coriander leaves on top.

TIME Preparation takes 10-15 minutes plus time needed for marinating, cooking takes 1 hour 15 minutes.

MARINATED LAMB CHOPS

This is an excellent way to cook lamb chops though a little unusual. The chops are tender and juicy and the gravy, thickened with a leaf spinach, is delicious.

SERVES 4-6

1kg/2.2lbs lamb chump chops
125g/5oz thick set natural yogurt
1-inch cube of root ginger, peeled and coarsely chopped
2-3 cloves garlic, peeled and coarsely chopped
1-2 fresh green chillies, seeded and coarsely chopped
2 tbsps cooking oil
6 green cardamoms, split open the top of each pod

Combine the following 5 ingredients in a bowl
1 tbsp ground coriander
1 tsp ground cinnamon
1 tsp ground turmeric
¼ tsp chilli powder
1 tsp paprika

175ml/6fl oz warm water
1¼ tsps salt or to taste

1. Trim off excess fat from the chops, wash and pat them dry. Flatten the chops slightly by beating them with a meat mallet. This will help tenderise and absorb the spices better.

2. Put the yogurt, ginger, garlic and green chillies in an electric liquidiser and blend until smooth.

3. Pour the yogurt marinade over the chops and mix thoroughly. Cover the container and allow the chops to marinate in a cool place for 4-6 hours or overnight in the refrigerator.

4. Heat the oil over medium heat, when the oil is hot, remove the pan from heat and add the cardamoms and the combined spices. Stir the ingredients once and place the pan back on heat.

5. Add the chops, adjust heat to high and stir and fry the chops for 4-5 minutes.

6. Add the water and salt, bring to the boil, cover the pan and simmer until the chops are nearly tender (35-40 minutes).

7. Meanwhile, prepare the spinach

---

2 tbsps cooking oil
1 tsp cumin seeds
2-3 cloves garlic, peeled and finely chopped
1 tsp ground cumin
1 large onion, finely sliced
450g/1lb leaf spinach; or 225g/8oz frozen (defrosted and drained) chopped

1. Heat the oil over medium heat and fry the cumin seeds until they start popping.

2. Add the garlic and ground cumin and immediately follow with the onions. Fry until the onions are lightly browned (8-10 minutes), stirring frequently.

3. Add the spinach and stir fry over medium-high heat for 1-2 minutes, then stir it into the chops.

4. Cover the pan and simmer for 20-25 minutes. Remove from heat.

ALOO GOSHT

A well-known north-Indian lamb curry with a distinctive flavour imparted by the ghee which is used to brown the potatoes before being added to the curry.

SERVES 4-6

1kg/2.2lbs leg or shoulder of lamb
1¼ tsps salt or to taste
1-inch cube of root ginger, peeled and coarsely chopped
3-4 cloves garlic, peeled and coarsely chopped
2 tbsps ghee or unsalted butter
450g/1lb medium-sized potatoes, peeled and cut into 1½-inch cubes
3 tbsps cooking oil
1 large onion, finely chopped
3-4 dried red chillies
2 cinnamon sticks, 2-inch long each, broken up

Make a paste of the following 5 spices by adding 3 tbsps water
1 tbsp ground coriander
1 tsp ground allspice
1 tsp paprika
1 tsp ground turmeric
¼-½ tsp chilli powder

1 tbsp tomato purée
2 black cardamoms, split open the top of each pod
4-6 whole cloves
450ml/15fl oz warm water
1 tbsp lemon juice
2 tbsps chopped coriander leaves

1. Trim off excess fat from the meat and cut it into 1½-inch cubes.

2. Add the salt to the ginger and garlic and crush to a pulp.

3. Melt the ghee or butter over medium heat in a non-stick or cast iron pan and fry the potatoes until they are well-browned on all sides (about 10 minutes). Remove the potatoes with a slotted spoon and keep aside.

4. Add the oil to any remaining ghee in the pan and when hot, fry the onions, red chillies and cinnamon sticks until the onions are soft (about 5 minutes).

5. Add the ginger and garlic pulp, and fry for a further 2-3 minutes stirring frequently.

6. Adjust heat to low and add the spice paste, stir and fry for 3-4 minutes.

7. Add the meat, adjust heat to medium-high, stir and fry until the meat changes colour (5-6 minutes), then stir in the tomato purée.

8. Now add the cardamoms, cloves and the water. Bring to the boil, cover and simmer for 45-50 minutes or 20 minutes in the pressure cooker with the 15lbs weight on.

9. Add the potatoes, bring to the boil again, cover and simmer for 15-20 minutes or until the potatoes are tender; if using pressure cooker, bring pressure down first, remove lid and add the potatoes. Cover and cook the potatoes without the weight.

10. Remove from heat and add the lemon juice and coriander leaves.

TIME Preparation takes 20-25 minutes, cooking takes 1 hour 30 minutes.

SHAHI KORMA

The word 'Shahi' means royal, so the title itself is evidence that this particular korma was created in the royal kitchens of the great Maharajas of India. The dish is rich and creamy and is a perfect choice for a special occasion.

SERVES 4-6

1kg/2.2lbs boned leg of lamb, fat trimmed and cut into 1½-inch cubes
125g/5oz thick set natural yogurt
½-inch cube of root ginger, peeled and grated
3-4 cloves of garlic, peeled and crushed
50g/2oz ghee or unsalted butter
2 medium-sized onions, finely chopped

Grind the following ingredients in a coffee grinder
2 tbsps coriander seeds
8 green cardamoms with the skin on
10 whole black peppercorns
3-4 dried red chillies

Mix the following 2 spices with the above ground ingredients
1 tsp ground cinnamon
1 tsp ground mace

3-4 tbsps chopped fresh mint or 1½ tsps dried or bottled mint
50g/2oz ground almonds
300ml/10fl oz warm water
½ tsp saffron strands, crushed
1½ tsp salt or to taste
50g/2oz raw split cashews
150ml/5fl oz single cream
1 tbsp rosewater

1. Put the meat into a bowl and add the yogurt, ginger and garlic. Mix thoroughly, cover the bowl with cling film and leave to marinate for 2-4 hours or overnight in the refrigerator.

2. Put the marinated meat, along with any remaining marinade in the container, in a heavy-based saucepan and place it over medium-low heat. Bring to a slow simmer, cover and cook the meat in its own juice for 45-50 minutes stirring occasionally. Remove the pan from the heat and lift the meat with a slotted spoon. Transfer the meat to another container and keep hot.

3. Melt the ghee over medium heat and fry the onions until they are lightly browned (8-9 minutes).

4. Adjust heat to low and add the ground ingredients and the mint; stir and fry for 2-3 minutes. Add the half of the liquid in which the meat was cooked, stir and cook for 1-2 minutes. Add the ground almonds and mix thoroughly; add the remaining meat stock, stir and cook for a further 1-2 minutes.

5. Adjust heat to medium and add the meat, stir and fry the meat for 5-6 minutes.

6. Add the water, saffron strands, salt and cashews, bring the liquid to a slow boil, cover and simmer for 20 minutes.

7. Add the cream, stir and mix well, simmer uncovered for 6-8 minutes.

8. Stir in the rosewater and remove from the heat.

TIME Preparation takes 20-25 minutes, cooking takes 1 hour 30 minutes.

SERVING IDEAS Serve with Naan or Plain Fried Rice and Green Beans in Garlic Butter.

KHEEMA MATTAR

A popular dish all over India, especially in the north. Lean mince is combined with garden peas and ground almonds and garnished with sliced hard-boiled eggs to make an attractive and delicious dish.

SERVES 4

6 tbsps cooking oil
1 tsp cumin seeds
2 dried red chillies
450g/1lb lean mince, lamb or beef
1 large onion, finely chopped
1-inch cube of root ginger, peeled and finely grated
4 cloves garlic, peeled and crushed
½ tsp ground turmeric
2 tsps ground coriander
1½ tsps ground cumin
½ tsp chilli powder
1 small tin of tomatoes or 3-4 fresh tomatoes, skinned and chopped
1 tsp salt or to taste
1 tbsp natural yogurt
175ml/6fl oz warm water
100g/4oz fresh or frozen garden peas; shelled weight
1 tbsp ground almonds
½ tsp garam masala
2 hard-boiled eggs, sliced
2 tbsps chopped coriander leaves

1. Heat 1 tbsp oil over medium heat and add the cumin seeds, as soon as they pop add the red chillies and then the mince. Stir and cook until the mince is evenly browned.

2. Meanwhile, heat the remaining oil over medium heat and add the onions. Stir and fry until the onions are soft, add the ginger and garlic and stir and fry for a further 2-3 minutes.

3. Stir in the turmeric and then the coriander, cumin and chilli powder.

4. Add the tomatoes along with all the juice, stir and cook for 3-4 minutes.

5. Add the mince and cook for 6-8 minutes, stirring frequently.

6. Add the salt and water and stir in the yogurt.

7. Cover the pan and simmer for 20 minutes.

8. Add the frozen peas and simmer for a further 10 minutes. If using fresh peas, boil until tender before adding to the mince.

9. Stir in the ground almonds and simmer for 2-3 minutes.

10. Remove from heat and stir in the garam masala.

11. Transfer onto a serving dish and arrange the sliced eggs on top. Garnish with the coriander leaves.

TIME Preparation takes 15 minutes, cooking takes 50 minutes.

SERVING IDEAS Serve with Chapatties, Parathas and/or Fried Brown Rice and Potato Raita
Suitable for freezing if fresh peas are used.

VARIATION Add peeled and diced potatoes in stage 7.

Lamb with Butterbeans

Adding beans or pulses to meat not only makes a more interesting and wholesome dish, but also makes it go further. The lamb and the buttery taste of the beans make an excellent combination.

SERVES 6-8

150g/6oz butter beans, washed and soaked overnight in plenty of cold water
600ml/20fl oz cold water
1¼ tsps salt or to taste
1-inch cube of root ginger, peeled and coarsely chopped
2-4 cloves garlic, peeled and coarsely chopped
5 tbsps cooking oil
2 medium-sized onions, finely chopped
2-3 dried red chillies
2 cinnamon sticks, each 2-inches long, broken up

Make a paste of the following 4 spices by adding 3 tbsps water
1½ tsps ground coriander
2½ tsps ground cumin
1 tsp ground turmeric
¼ tsp chilli powder (optional)

1kg/2.2lbs leg or shoulder of lamb, fat trimmed and cut into 1½-inch cubes
2 tbsps tomato purée
2-3 black cardamoms, split open the top of each pod
6 whole cloves
175ml/6fl oz warm water
Juice of half a lemon
2 tbsps chopped coriander leaves

1. Put the cold water and the butter beans in a saucepan and bring the liquid to the boil.

2. Partially cover the pan and cook over low heat for 15 minutes.

3. Now cover the pan tightly and simmer the beans for about 20 minutes. Remove the pan from heat and keep aside.

4. Add the salt to the ginger and garlic and crush to a pulp.

5. Heat the oil over medium heat and add the onions, red chillies and cinnamon sticks. Stir and fry until the onions are soft (about 5 minutes).

6. Add the ginger and garlic pulp and stir and fry for 2-3 minutes. Add the spice paste, adjust heat to low, stir and fry for a further 3-4 minutes.

7. Add the meat, turn heat up to medium-high and fry for 5-6 minutes, stirring frequently.

8. Stir in the tomato purée, then add the cardamoms, cloves and warm water. Bring to the boil, cover and simmer until the meat is tender, about 55-60 minutes.

9. Add the butter beans and the liquid in which they were cooked. Bring the liquid to the boil, cover the pan and simmer for 15 minutes.

10. Remove the pan from heat and add the lemon juice and coriander leaves.

TIME Preparation takes 20-25 minutes, cooking takes 1 hour 30 minutes.

SERVING IDEAS Serve with Plain Boiled Rice or Plain Fried Rice, or Naan. Suitable for freezing.

MEAT MADRAS

This hot, but delicious curry is named after Madras, the major city in southern India, perhaps because in the humid south, people eat rather hot food. Strange though it may seem, this is because hot and spicy food makes one perspire, thereby cooling the body.

SERVES 4-6

6 tbsps cooking oil
2 medium-sized onions, coarsely chopped
1-inch cube of root ginger, peeled and coarsely chopped
3-4 cloves garlic, peeled and coarsely chopped
4-6 dried red chillies
2 large cloves garlic, peeled and crushed
1-2 fresh green chillies, sliced lengthwise
1 small tin of tomatoes
3 tsps ground cumin
1 tsp ground coriander
½-1 tsp chilli powder
1 tsp ground turmeric
1kg/2.2lbs leg or shoulder of lamb, fat removed and cut into 1½-inch cubes
175ml/6fl oz warm water
1¼ tsps salt or to taste
1 tsp garam masala

1. Heat 3 tbsps oil from the specified amount over medium heat and fry the onions, coarsely chopped ginger, garlic and red chillies until the onions are soft (8-10 minutes), stirring frequently. Remove from heat and allow to cool.

2. Meanwhile, heat the remaining oil over medium heat and fry the crushed garlic and green chillies until the garlic is lightly browned.

3. Add half the tomatoes, along with the juice; stir and cook for 1-2 minutes.

4. Add the cumin, coriander, chilli powder and turmeric, adjust heat to low and cook for 6-8 minutes, stirring frequently.

5. Add the meat and adjust heat to medium-high. Stir and fry until meat changes colour (5-6 minutes).

6. Add the water, bring to the boil, cover and simmer for 30 minutes.

7. Place the fried onion mixture in an electric blender or food processor and add the remaining tomatoes. Blend until smooth and add this to the meat – bring to the boil, add salt and mix well. Cover the pan and simmer for a further 35-40 minutes or until the meat is tender.

8. Stir in the garam masala and remove from heat.

TIME Preparation takes 25-30 minutes, cooking takes 1 hour 20 minutes.

SERVING IDEAS Serve with Plain Boiled Rice or any Indian bread accompanied by Saag Bhaji and/or a Raita.
Suitable for freezing.

WATCHPOINT Meat Madras is meant to be hot, but if you do not like it hot, omit the chilli powder and seed the green chillies.

Kheema Shahzada

Kheema, or mince is not at all an under-rated item in Indian cookery and in fact, the recipe below elevates mince to gourmet status. Do make sure that the mince is lean and that it is not too fine.

SERVES 4

4 heaped tbsps ghee or unsalted butter
1 large onion, coarsely chopped
1-inch cube of root ginger, peeled and coarsely chopped
2-4 cloves garlic, peeled and coarsely chopped

Grind the following ingredients in a coffee grinder
1 cinnamon stick, 2-inches long; broken up
4 green cardamoms
4 whole cloves
4-6 dried red chillies
1 tbsp coriander seeds

Grind the following 2 ingredients separately
1 tbsp white poppy seeds
1 tbsp sesame seeds

450g/1lb lean coarse mince
½ tsp ground turmeric
50g/2oz raw cashews, split into halves
1 tsp salt or to taste
300ml/10fl oz warm water
150ml/5fl oz milk
2 hard-boiled eggs, quartered lengthwise
A few sprigs of fresh coriander

1. Melt 2 tbsps ghee or butter from the specified amount, over medium heat and fry the onions, ginger and garlic until the onions are soft (about 5 minutes). Squeeze out excess fat by pressing the fried ingredients onto the side of the pan with a wooden spatula and transfer them to a plate. Allow to cool.

2. Add the remaining ghee or butter to the pan and fry the ground ingredients, including the poppy and sesame seeds, for 1 minute, stirring constantly.

3. Add the mince and fry until all the liquid evaporates (about 10 minutes), stirring frequently.

4. Add the turmeric, stir and fry for 30 seconds.

5. Add the salt, cashews and the water, bring to the boil, cover the pan and cook over low heat for 15 minutes, stirring occasionally.

6. Meanwhile, put the milk into an electric liquidiser followed by the fried onions, garlic and ginger. Blend until the ingredients are smooth and stir into the mince. Bring to the boil again, cover the pan and simmer for 10-15 minutes or until the gravy is thick.

7. Put the mince onto a serving dish and garnish with the hard-boiled eggs and the coriander leaves.

TIME Preparation takes 25-30 minutes, cooking takes 40-45 minutes.

SERVING IDEAS Serve with Naan or Plain Pilau and Tomato & Cucumber Salad.

Suitable for freezing.

LAMB WITH MUNG BEANS

Mung beans are available from Indian grocers and health food shops. Do prepare this dish a day in advance because the flavour improves significantly when it is left to stand.

SERVES 6-8

150g/6oz whole mung beans
1¼ tsp salt or to taste
1-inch cube of root ginger, peeled and coarsely chopped
2-4 cloves garlic, peeled and coarsely chopped
700g/1½lbs leg or shoulder of lamb, cut into 1-inch cubes
450ml/15fl oz water
1 large onion, finely chopped

Grind the 6 following ingredients in a coffee grinder

2 dried red chillies
1½ tsps cumin seeds
2 tsps coriander seeds
4 whole cloves
1 cinnamon stick, 2-inches long; broken up
4 black peppercorns

1 tsp ground turmeric
1 small tin of tomatoes or 4 ripe tomatoes, skinned and chopped
2 tbsps chopped coriander leaves

1. Soak the mung beans overnight in plenty of cold water and drain well. Pulses usually contain a certain amount of grit and sand; make sure you clean the beans and wash them several times before soaking.

2. Add the salt to the ginger and garlic and crush them to a smooth pulp.

3. Place the meat and water in a large pan and bring the liquid to the boil. Cover the pan and simmer for 45 minutes.

4. Add the mung beans along with the onions. Bring back to the boil, cover the pan and cook on low heat for 25 minutes.

5. Add the ginger/garlic pulp, the ground spices, turmeric and the tomatoes. Simmer for 10 minutes, uncovered.

6. Remove from heat and stand aside for several hours before serving. The longer you let it stand, the better.

7. Reheat the curry and stir in the coriander leaves and simmer for 5 minutes before serving.

TIME Preparation takes 15-20 minutes plus time needed to soak the beans, cooking takes 1 hour 20 minutes.

SERVING IDEAS Serve with Plain Boiled Rice and Tomato and Cucumber Salad.
Suitable for freezing.

VARIATION Add 100g/4oz aubergines, cut into chunky pieces, along with the mung beans.

BHOONA GOSHT

The word 'Bhoon' means to fry and 'Gosht' means meat; Bhoona Gosht, therefore, means fried meat. This dish needs particular care and attention during frying. It is important to follow carefully the different level of temperature during the different stages of frying.

SERVES 4-6

1kg/2.2lbs leg or shoulder of lamb
5 tbsps cooking oil
3 large onions, finely chopped
1-inch cube of root ginger, peeled and grated or finely chopped
3-4 cloves garlic, peeled and crushed
1 tsp ground turmeric
2 tsps ground cumin
1 tbsp ground coriander
½-1 tsp chilli powder
200ml/7fl oz warm water
1¼ tsps salt or to taste
2 medium-sized ripe tomatoes, skinned and chopped; tinned tomatoes can be used
4-5 whole fresh green chillies
1 tsp garam masala
1 tbsps chopped coriander leaves
2 small ripe tomatoes, sliced

1. Trim off excess fat from the meat, wash and cut into 1-inch cubes. Drain on absorbent paper.

2. Heat the oil over medium heat and add the onions, ginger and garlic. Fry until the onions are just soft (about 5 minutes).

3. Lower heat and add the turmeric, cumin, coriander and chilli powder. Stir and fry for 2-3 minutes.

4. Add the meat, turn heat to medium and fry for 5 minutes stirring frequently. Cover the pan and cook on medium heat until all the liquid dries out (15-20 minutes). Stir frequently.

5. Turn heat to high and fry the meat for 2-3 minutes stirring continuously. Reduce heat to medium and fry for a further 7-8 minutes stirring frequently. The meat should now look fairly dry and the fat should be floating on the surface. Some of the fat can be drained off at this stage, but be careful not to drain off any of the spices.

6. Add the water and salt, bring to the boil, cover and simmer for 50-60 minutes or until the meat is tender. Add more water if necessary. At the end of the cooking time, the thick spice paste should be clinging to the pieces of meat.

7. Add the chopped tomatoes and the whole green chillies. Stir and fry for 3-4 minutes.

8. Stir in the garam masala and half the coriander leaves and remove from heat.

9. Put the bhoona gosht into a serving dish and arrange the sliced tomatoes round the meat. Sprinkle the remaining coriander leaves on top.

TIME Preparation takes 25-30 minutes, cooking takes 1 hour 45 minutes.

SERVING IDEAS Serve with Plain Boiled or Plain Fried Rice or with Parathas or Rotis. Mushroom Bhaji, Cauliflower Masala or Aloo Mattar also make an excellent accompaniment.

MEAT DILPASAND

A delectable lamb dish with a slightly creamy texture and a wonderfully nutty flavour derived from roasted and ground poppy seeds.

SERVES 4-6

1kg/2.2lbs leg of lamb
125g/5oz thick set natural yogurt
1 tsp ground turmeric
2 tbsps white poppy seeds
1-inch cube of root ginger, peeled and coarsely chopped
4-5 cloves garlic, peeled and coarsely chopped
1-2 fresh green chillies, seed them if a milder flavour is preferred
450g/1lb onions
3 tbsps ghee or unsalted butter
½ tsp chilli powder
1 tsp paprika
1 tbsp ground cumin
1 tsp garam masala
1 tbsp tomato purée
1¼ tsps salt or to taste
175ml/6fl oz warm water
25g/1oz creamed coconut or 2 tbsps desiccated coconut
2 tbsps chopped coriander leaves

1. Trim off any fat from the meat, wash and dry on absorbent paper and cut into 1½-inch cubes.

2. Add yogurt and turmeric, mix thoroughly, cover the container and leave to marinate for 4-6 hours or overnight in the refrigerator.

3. Roast the poppy seeds without fat over gentle heat until they are a shade darker – allow to cool.

4. Place the ginger, garlic and green chillies in an electric blender or food processor. Chop one onion, from the specified amount, and add to the ginger and garlic mixture. Blend until fairly smooth.

5. Chop the remaining onions finely.

6. Melt the ghee or butter over medium heat and fry onions until golden brown. This will take 10 to 12 minutes.

7. Adjust heat to low and add chilli powder, paprika, cumin and ½ tsp garam masala from the specified amount. Stir and fry for 2-3 minutes.

8. Now add the liquidised ingredients and fry for 10 to 12 minutes, stirring frequently. If during this time the spices tend to stick to the bottom of the pan, sprinkle with about 1 tbsp of water at a time as and when necessary.

9. Add the meat and adjust heat to medium-high. Fry for 4-5 minutes stirring constantly.

10. Add the tomato purée, salt and water, stir and mix, bring to the boil, cover and simmer for 45 minutes or until the meat is tender. Stir occasionally during the first half of cooking, but more frequently towards the end to ensure that the thickened gravy does not stick to the bottom of the pan.

11. If you are using creamed coconut, cut into small pieces with a sharp knife. Desiccated coconut should be ground in the coffee grinder before use to ensure that the necessary fine texture is achieved in making the curry. Finish off the cooking process in the same way as for creamed coconut.

12. Grind the poppy seeds in a coffee grinder and stir into the meat along with the creamed coconut. Stir until coconut is dissolved. Cover and simmer for 15 minutes.

13. Stir in the coriander leaves and the remaining garam masala. Remove from heat.

PASANDA BADAM CURRY

Pasanda is a classic north Indian dish where the meat is cut into thin slices and cooked in a rich sauce containing saffron, yogurt and cream.

SERVES 4-6

900g/2lbs boned leg of lamb
1-inch cube of root ginger, peeled and coarsely chopped
4-6 cloves garlic, peeled and coarsely chopped
2 fresh green chillies, seeded and coarsely chopped
4 tbsps natural yogurt
50g/2oz ghee or unsalted butter
3 medium-sized onions, finely sliced
½ tsp ground turmeric
1 tsp ground cumin
2 tsps ground coriander
½ tsp ground nutmeg
¼-½ tsp chilli powder
225ml/8fl oz warm water
1¼ tsps salt or to taste
150ml/5fl oz single cream
25g/1oz ground almonds
1 tsp garam masala or ground mixed spice
2 tbsps rosewater
½ tsp paprika

1. Beat the meat with a meat mallet to flatten it to ¼-inch thickness, then cut into thin slices (about 1½-inch long and ½-inch wide).

2. Put the ginger, garlic, green chillies and yogurt into an electric liquidiser or food processor and blend until smooth.

3. Melt the ghee or butter over medium heat and fry the onions until they are lightly browned (6-8 minutes).

4. Add the turmeric, cumin, coriander, nutmeg and chilli powder; adjust heat to low, stir and fry for 2-3 minutes.

5. Add the meat and fry it over high heat for 3-4 minutes or until it changes colour.

6. Add about 2 tbsps of the liquidised ingredients and cook for 1-2 minutes, stirring frequently. Repeat this process until all the yogurt mixture is used up.

7. Now fry the meat over medium heat for 4-5 minutes stirring frequently. When the fat begins to seep through the thick spice paste and floats on the surface, add the water, bring to the boil, cover the pan and simmer until the meat is tender (about 60 minutes), stirring occasionally.

8. Add the salt, cream and ground almonds and let it simmer without the lid for 5-6 minutes.

9. Stir in the garam masala and rosewater and remove from heat.

10. Put the pasanda into a serving dish and sprinkle the paprika on top.

TIME Preparation takes 30 minutes, cooking takes 1 hour 20 minutes.

SERVING IDEAS Serve with Mattar Pilau and Cabbage and Mint Salad.

VARIATION Use braising steak.

MEAT DURBARI

The word 'Durbar' means forum or formal gathering. This wonderful lamb dish originated in the royal kitchens and was served at special gatherings held by the great Mughal Emperors.

SERVES 4

1kg/2.2lbs leg of lamb

Grind the following 9 ingredients in a coffee grinder and make a paste by adding the vinegar

1 tbsp mustard seeds
1 tbsp sesame seeds
2 tbsps white poppy seeds
10 black peppercorns
2-4 dried red chillies
1 bay leaf
2-inch piece of cinnamon stick, broken up
4 whole cloves

The inner seeds of 2 black cardamoms
3 tbsps white wine vinegar
1¼ tsp salt or to taste
3-4 cloves garlic, peeled and coarsely chopped
3 tbsps ghee or unsalted butter
1 large onion, finely chopped
1-inch cube of root ginger, peeled and finely grated
175ml/6fl oz warm water
1 tbsp tomato purée
2 fresh green chillies, slit lengthwise into halves, seeded for a milder flavour
2 tbsps chopped coriander leaves

1. Trim off excess fat from the meat and cut into 2-inch cubes.

2. Rub the spice paste well into the meat and leave to marinate for 4-6 hours, or overnight in the refrigerator.

3. Add the salt to the garlic and crush to a smooth pulp.

4. Melt the ghee or butter gently over low heat, add the onions and ginger, adjust heat to medium and fry them until the onions are soft (3-4 minutes).

5. Add the garlic paste and fry for a further 2-3 minutes stirring frequently.

6. Add the meat and cook in the onion mixture untill all sides of meat are sealed and brown.

7. Add the water, bring to the boil, cover and simmer until the meat is tender.

8. Add the tomato purée, green chillies and coriander leaves – adjust heat to medium and cook for 3-4 minutes stirring continuously. Remove the pan from the heat.

TIME Preparation takes 20-25 minutes plus time needed to marinate, cooking takes 1 hour 10 minutes.

SERVING IDEAS Serve with Mushroom Pillau and Saagwalla Dhal; with Parathas or Rotis and Cauliflower with Gram Flour. Serve any chutney or relish for a traditional touch.
Suitable for freezing.

KHEEMA-PALAK (MINCE WITH SPINACH)

In India, mince is rarely cooked on its own. Various combinations are used to make it more interesting, and mince and spinach is one of the most popular.

SERVES 4-6

4 tbsps cooking oil
½ tsp black mustard seeds
1 tsp cumin seeds
1 fresh green chilli, finely chopped and seeded if a milder flavour is preferred
1-inch cube of root ginger, peeled and finely grated
6 cloves garlic, peeled and crushed
450g/1lb lean mince, lamb or beef
1 large onion, finely sliced
2 cinnamon sticks, 2-inches long each, broken up
½ tsp ground turmeric
1 tbsp ground cumin
½ tsp ground black pepper
325g/12oz fresh spinach leaves, chopped or 225g/8oz frozen spinach, defrosted and drained
1 tsp salt or to taste
1 small tin of tomatoes, drained and chopped or 3-4 medium sized ripe tomatoes, skinned and chopped
1 tsp garam masala

1. Heat half the oil in a wide shallow pan over medium heat and fry the mustard seeds until they crackle. Add the cumin seeds and immediately follow with the green chilli, ginger and half the garlic. Stir and fry for 30 seconds.

2. Add the mince, stir and fry until all the liquid evaporates – this will take 8-10 minutes. Remove the pan from the heat and keep aside.

3. In a separate pan, heat the remaining oil over medium heat and stir in the rest of the garlic. Add the onions and cinnamon sticks and fry until the onions are lightly browned (6-8 minutes), stirring frequently.

4. Adjust heat to low and add the turmeric, cumin and black pepper. Stir and fry for 1 minute. Add the spinach and mix thoroughly.

5. Add the mince and stir until the spinach and the mince are thoroughly mixed. Cover the pan and simmer for 15 minutes.

6. Adjust heat to medium, add salt and the tomatoes, stir and cook for 2-3 minutes.

7. Add the garam masala, stir and cook for a further 2-3 minutes. Remove the pan from heat.

TIME Preparation takes 15-20 minutes, cooking takes 40 minutes.

SERVING IDEAS Serve with Loochis or Rotis and Sour-hot Potatoes. With Plain Boiled Rice, Spicy Channa Dhal and Cucumber and Onion Raita.

TO FREEZE Suitable for freezing if fresh spinach is used.

Savoury Mince & Eggs

A very attractive and unusual way to present mince which also makes an economical and filling family meal.

SERVES 4-6

4 tbsps cooking oil
1 large onion, coarsely chopped
1-inch cube of root ginger, peeled and coarsely chopped
4-6 cloves garlic, peeled and coarsely chopped
125g/5oz thick set natural yogurt
1 tsp cumin seeds
1 tsp ground turmeric
1 tsp ground coriander
450g/1lb lean coarse mince, lamb or beef
1 tsp paprika
300ml/10fl oz warm water
1 tsp salt or to taste
1 tbsp tomato purée
½ tsp garam masala
2 tbsps chopped coriander leaves
4-6 small eggs (1 per person)

1. Heat 2 tbsps of oil from the specified amount over medium heat and fry onion, ginger and garlic for 3-4 minutes stirring frequently. Remove from heat and allow to cool slightly.

2. Put the yogurt and fried onion mixture into a liquidiser or food processor and blend until smooth. Set aside.

3. Heat the remaining oil and fry the cumin seeds until they pop.

4. To prevent the spices from burning, remove the pan from the heat and add the turmeric and coriander, stir and mix thoroughly.

5. Place the pan back on the heat and add the mince. Fry the mince over medium heat until it is lightly browned and completely dry.

6. Add the paprika, water and salt, bring to the boil, cover and simmer for 15 minutes. Stir occasionally.

7. Add the blended ingredients and tomato purée, bring to the boil again, cover and simmer for a further 15 minutes. Stir occasionally.

8. Stir in the garam masala and the coriander leaves. Remove from heat.

9. Preheat oven to 190°C/375°F/Gas Mark 5.

10. Put the mince into an ovenproof dish. Make 4-6 hollows, according to the number of eggs used, about 1-inch apart. Break an egg into each hollow; do not worry about the egg white spilling over the hollow. Bake in the centre of the oven for 30 minutes or until the eggs are set. Bake for a few minutes longer if you like the yolks hard.

11. Garnish with the remaining coriander leaves.

TIME Preparation takes 10-15 minutes, cooking takes 55 minutes.

SERVING IDEAS Serve with Parathas or Rotis. Aloo ki Bhaji makes a good accompaniment. It is also excellent with garlic bread.

TO FREEZE Freeze before adding the eggs.

VARIATION Add 100g/4oz frozen garden peas in stage 7.

microwave

Prawns in Garlic and Tamarind

A quick and tasty dish using frozen prawns and boiled, diced potatoes. The potatoes help to thicken the gravy and add an extra dimension to the dish.

SERVES 4

225g/8oz old potatoes
2 tsps ground coriander
1 tsp chilli powder or to taste
1 tsp paprika
3 tbsps cooking oil
4-5 cloves garlic, peeled and crushed
225g/8oz onions, finely chopped
90ml/3fl oz hot water
1 level tsp tamarind concentrate or 1½ tbsps lemon juice
1 tsp salt or to taste
450g/1lb frozen peeled prawns, defrosted and drained
1 tbsp besan (chick pea flour), sieved

1. Put the potatoes in a 2-3 pint dish and add 4 tbsps hot water. Cover and cook on high for 2½ minutes. Turn the potatoes over, re-cover and cook on high for a further 2 minutes.

2. Stand the potatoes aside for 8 minutes then immerse them in cold water until they are completely cold. Peel and dice them evenly.

3. Put the coriander, chilli powder and paprika in small glass bowl and heat on high for 1½ minutes. Stir and stand aside.

4. Mix 2 tbsps oil from the specified amount, half the garlic and all the onions in a 3-pint casserole, cover and cook on high for 5 minutes, stirring every 1½ minutes.

5. Add the spice mixture and cook, uncovered, on high for 2 minutes, stirring halfway through.

6. Add the water, tamarind, salt and the prawns. Stir and mix well. Cover and cook on high for 4 minutes, stirring every 2 minutes.

7. Add the potatoes, re-cover and cook on high for 2 minutes.

8. Preheat a browning dish on high for 4-5 minutes, add the remaining oil and cook on high for 1 minute. Add the garlic and cook on high for 30 seconds to 1 minute until golden brown. Stir the garlic oil into the prawns.

9. Sprinkle the besan evenly on the prawns, stir and mix thoroughly. Cook, uncovered, on high for 2 minutes, stirring halfway through.

10. If you are using lemon juice, simply add this with the besan and mix well, then cook for specified time.

TIME Preparation takes 15-20 minutes, cooking takes 20 minutes.

SERVING IDEAS Serve with Plain Boiled Rice or Cinnamon Rice and Cauliflower Upkari.

AUBERGINE CURRY

The tangy, slightly hot taste of this dish enhances the natural flavour of the aubergine. The sliced aubergines absorb the coconut sauce beautifully and every bite tastes delicious.

SERVES 4-6

325g/12oz aubergine
1½ tsp ground cumin
½ tsp garam masala
¼-½ tsp chilli powder
400g/14oz tin of tomatoes
4 fresh green chillies, sliced lengthwise and seeded for a milder flavour
10-12 curry leaves
1¼ tsps salt or to taste
90ml/3fl oz hot water
75g/3oz creamed coconut, cut into small pieces

1. Quarter the aubergine lengthwise and cut each quarter into ¼-inch thick slices. Soak in salted cold water for 15 minutes and drain. Rinse well.

2. Mix the cumin, garam masala and chilli powder in a small glass bowl and heat on high for 2 minutes. Stir and stand aside.

3. Put the tomatoes, along with all the juice, and the green chillies in a 4-pint casserole or bowl. Cover with a lid or cling film, puncture cling film and cook on high for 3 minutes.

4. Stir the tomatoes and add the aubergine, curry leaves, salt and water. Re-cover and cook on high for 6 minutes, stirring every 2 minutes.

5. Stir in the heated spices and mix thoroughly. Cover and cook on high for 5 minutes, stirring as before.

6. Add the coconut, cover and cook on high for 5 minutes, stirring and re-positioning the aubergine halfway through cooking time.

7. Stand the dish aside for 10 minutes before serving.

TIME Preparation takes 22 minutes including soaking the aubergine, cooking takes 21 minutes.

SERVING IDEAS Serve with Plain Boiled Rice and Seekh Kababs.

MUSTARD FISH

A traditional dish from Assam and Bengal, the two eastern states of India. For speed and convenience, mustard powder and desiccated coconut have been used in this recipe, with a delightfully satisfying result.

SERVES 4

700g/1½lbs skinned fillet of cod or haddock
40g/1½ oz desiccated coconut
1½ tbsps mustard powder
4 fresh green chillies
125ml/4fl oz water
1 tsp salt or to taste
1 tomato, cut into 8 pieces
2 tbsps finely chopped coriander leaves

1. Wash the fish gently in cold water and pat dry.

2. Cut each fillet into ½-inch thick and 2-inch long pieces.

3. Grind the desiccated coconut in a coffee grinder until it is smooth.

4. Slice two chillies lengthwise and leave the other two whole. Seed the sliced chillies if a milder flavour is preferred.

5. Put the coconut in a bowl and add the rest of the ingredients except chillies, tomatoes and coriander. Stir and mix until a thick batter-like mixture is formed.

6. Pour this mixture over the fish and mix thoroughly, but gently with a metal spoon.

7. Place the whole chillies at the bottom of a 3-pint casserole and arrange half the fish on top.

8. Place the sliced chillies and half the coriander leaves on the layer of fish and cover with the remaining fish. Arrange the tomatoes on top.

9. Cover the dish with a lid or cling film; puncture cling film and cook on medium for 5 minutes, then stir and continue cooking for a further 5 minutes on medium.

10. Allow to stand for 8 minutes and garnish with the remaining coriander leaves.

TIME Preparation takes 15-20 minutes, cooking takes 10 minutes.

SERVING IDEAS Serve with Plain Boiled Rice and Mixed Vegetable Bhaji. Suitable for freezing.

Chicken Korma

In addition to being quick, the microwave oven method retains all the delicious and distinctive flavour of Chicken Korma.

SERVES 4

700g/1½lbs chicken breast, skinned and boned
125g/5oz thick set natural yogurt
2 cloves garlic, peeled and crushed
¼-inch cube of root ginger, peeled and crushed or grated

Mix together the following 5 ingredients
2 tsps ground coriander
½ tsp freshly ground black pepper
½ tsp ground cinnamon
½ tsp ground cardamom
¼ tsp ground turmeric

15g/½oz ghee or unsalted butter
1 medium-sized onion, finely sliced
75ml/2½fl oz single cream
¾ tsp salt or to taste
50g/2oz ground almonds
15g/½oz flaked almonds, toasted

1. Cut the chicken breast into 1-inch cubes.

2. Mix the yogurt, garlic and ginger together, add the chicken and mix until the chicken pieces are fully coated. Cover the container and leave to marinate in a cool place for 2 hours.

3. Put the bowl containing the ground spices in the microwave and heat on high for 2 minutes. Stir and keep aside.

4. Put the ghee in a 3-pint casserole and melt on high for 45 seconds.

5. Stir in the onions, cover and cook on high for 4 minutes, stirring halfway through.

6. Stir in the heated spices and cook, uncovered, on high for 1½ minutes.

7. Stir the spices, then add the chicken. Stir and mix well. Cover and cook on high for 4 minutes, stirring after 2 minutes, then on medium for 4 minutes.

8. Add the cream, cover and cook on medium for 4 minutes.

9. Stir in the salt and ground almonds; mix thoroughly. Cook, uncovered, on medium for 3 minutes. Stir halfway through.

10. Stand for 6 minutes and garnish with the toasted almonds.

TIME Preparation takes 20-25 minutes plus marinating time, cooking takes 15½ minutes.

SERVING IDEAS Serve with Pilau Rice or Cinnamon Rice. Suitable for freezing.

Marinated Trout

A delicately flavoured dish with a slightly hot and tangy taste. Do cook it a few hours in advance and reheat as the flavour improves if allowed to stand for some time.

SERVES 4

2 trout (total weight 700g/1½lbs)
2-3 cloves garlic, peeled and coarsely chopped
1 tsp salt or to taste
½ tsp chilli powder
½ tsp tamarind concentrate or 1 tbsp lemon juice
1 tbsp water
1 tbsp olive oil

1. Scale the fish, remove the heads and slit along the belly right down to the tail. Gut the fish and wash inside and out gently in cold water.

2. Put the fish on a board, on its stomach and gently but firmly run your fingers along the centre bone. This will loosen the bone, turn the fish over and gently pull out the centre bone. If it does not come away in one piece, simply pull away the remaining pieces in exactly the same way.

3. Now cut the fish lengthwise into half. Cut each half into 3 pieces.

4. Crush the garlic and salt together to a smooth pulp. Add the rest of the ingredients and mix thoroughly.

5. Put 1 tsp of the marinade over each piece of fish and spread it so that it coats the entire surface. Place any remaining marinade on the fish and place the fish in a covered container. Leave to marinate in the refrigerator for 3-4 hours. Remove from the refrigerator 30 minutes before cooking.

6. Arrange the fish, skin side down, in a shallow dish, with the thin end towards the centre of the dish. Cover with cling film and puncture the film. Cook on medium for 4 minutes.

7. Turn the fish over (skin side up), and cook, covered on medium for a further 2 minutes.

8. Allow to stand for several hours, then reheat on medium setting and serve.

TIME Preparation takes 20-25 minutes plus time for marinating, cooking takes 6 minutes.

SERVING IDEAS Serve with Tarka Dhal and Plain Boiled Rice. Suitable for freezing.

Mackerel in Coconut Milk

A popular Saraswat recipe converted for the microwave. It is traditionally known as 'Amshi-Tikshi' meaning sour-hot. The quantity of chilli powder, however, can be adjusted to suit individual taste.

SERVES 4

700g/1½lbs mackerel
3-4 cloves garlic, peeled and coarsely chopped
1¼ tsps salt or to taste

Mix together the following 4 ingredients
1½ tsps ground coriander
¼ tsp ground turmeric
1 tsp paprika
1-1½ tsps chilli powder

225ml/8fl oz warm water
75g/3oz creamed coconut, cut into small pieces
1 level tsp tamarind concentrate or 2 tbsps lemon juice

1. Remove the head from the fish, and cut the fish into about 2-inch wide pieces; do not cut along the belly.

2. Wash each piece of fish gently in cold water inside and out.

3. Add the salt to the garlic and crush it to a pulp.

4. Heat the spice mixture on high for 1½ minutes, stir and stand aside.

5. Put the water, coconut and tamarind into a 3-pint casserole, cover and cook on high for 6 minutes, stirring halfway through.

6. Add the spice mixture and the garlic to the coconut milk, stir and mix thoroughly.

7. Arrange the pieces of fish in the coconut milk in a single layer and spoon some of it over the fish. Cover as before and cook on medium for 6 minutes, reposition pieces in dish after every 2 minutes. Add lemon juice during this time and mix gently.

8. Stand dish aside for 5 minutes before serving.

TIME Preparation takes 10-15 minutes, cooking takes 13 minutes.

SERVING IDEAS Serve with Plain Boiled Rice and Cauliflower Upkari. Suitable for freezing.

Chicken with Cashews

This Mughlai-style recipe has a rich and creamy sauce which is made by blending raw cashews with milk. Diced, pre-boiled potatoes are added towards the end, which also helps to thicken the gravy.

SERVES 4

275g/10oz old potatoes

Mix together the following 7 ingredients in a glass bowl

½ tsp ground cinnamon

½ tsp ground cardamom

½ tsp ground allspice

1 tsp ground coriander

½ tsp freshly ground black pepper

1 tsp paprika

¼ tsp ground turmeric

50g/2oz raw cashews

125ml/4fl oz milk

1 fresh green chilli, chopped

1 medium-sized onion, finely chopped

½-inch cube of root ginger, peeled and grated

2 tbsps oil

2 cloves garlic, peeled and crushed

175ml/6fl oz hot water

700g/1½lbs boned chicken breast, skinned and cut into 1-inch cubes

1 tsp salt or to taste

1. Put the potatoes in a 2-3 pint casserole and add 4 tbsps hot water. Cover and cook on high for 3 minutes. Turn the potatoes over, re-cover and cook on high for 2 minutes.

2. Stand the potatoes for 6-8 minutes, then immerse them in cold water until they are completely cold. Peel and dice the potatoes evenly.

3. Heat the spice mixture on high for 2 minutes. Stir and stand aside.

4. Put the cashews, milk and green chilli in an electric liquidiser and blend until smooth.

5. In a 4-pint casserole, mix the oil, onions, ginger and garlic. Cover with a lid or cling film, puncture cling film and cook on high for 4½ minutes, stirring halfway through.

6. Add the spice mixture, stir and mix thoroughly. Cook, uncovered, on high for 2 minutes and stir.

7. Now add the water and chicken, stir and mix well. Cover and cook on high for 4 minutes, stirring after 2 minutes. Cook for a further 4-6 minutes on medium, stirring after every two minutes.

8. Add the salt and the cashew paste, cover and cook on high for 2 minutes.

9. Add the potatoes, stir and mix well. Cook, uncovered, on medium for 3 minutes, stirring halfway through.

TIME Preparation takes 10-15 minutes, cooking takes 20 minutes.

SERVING IDEAS Serve with Cinnamon Rice and Green Beans in Garlic Butter.

TO FREEZE Suitable for freezing, but freeze before adding the potatoes.

Prawn Curry

A north-Indian style prawn curry adapted for the microwave with amazingly delicious result! Use fresh or frozen prawns but make sure that frozen praws are defrosted and drained before use.

SERVES 4

Mix together the following 5 ingredients in a small glass bowl
2 tsps ground coriander
½ tsp garam masala
½-1 tsp chilli powder
1 tsp paprika
¼ tsp ground turmeric

225ml/8fl oz water
2 cloves garlic, peeled and crushed
1 tsp salt or to taste
75g/3oz creamed coconut, cut into small pieces
450g/1lb peeled prawns
3 tbsps cooking oil
1 medium-sized onion, finely chopped
2 fresh green chillies, seeded and sliced lengthwise
Juice of half a lemon
2 tbsps chopped coriander leaves

1. Put the bowl of spice mixture in the microwave and heat, uncovered, on high for 2 minutes. Stir and keep aside.

2. Put the water, garlic, salt, coconut and spice mixture in a 3-pint casserole and mix thoroughly.

3. Add the prawns and mix. Cover with a lid or cling film, puncture cling film and cook on medium for 6-8 minutes. Stir halfway through.

4. Preheat the browning dish on high for 4-5 minutes. Add the oil and heat on high for 1 minute. Add the onions to the hot oil and fry on high for 4-5 minutes until they are lightly browned, stirring frequently. Stir the onions into the prawns along with the green chillies and half the coriander leaves. Cover and cook on high for 1½ minutes.

5. Remove from the oven, stir in the lemon juice and stand for 5 minutes.

6. Garnish with the coriander leaves.

TIME Preparation takes 10 minutes, cooking takes 14 minutes.

SERVING IDEAS Serve with plain boiled rice and Caulilower Upkari. Suitable for freezing, if fresh prawns are used.

COOK'S TIP If you do not have a browning dish heat the oil over a medium heat on a conventional cooker until they are lightly browned. Stir the onions into the prawns along with the green chillies and half the coriander leaves. Cover and cook on high for 1½ minutes.

Chicken and Mushroom Curry

The combination of chicken and mushroom is delicious. Here, the traditional garam masala is replaced with allspice which has the flavour of cardamom, cinnamon and nutmeg.

SERVES 4

1 tsp ground coriander
½ tsp ground cumin
½ tsp ground turmeric
½ tsp chilli powder
½ tsp ground allspice
2 tbsps cooking oil
1 medium-sized onion, finely chopped
½-inch cube of root ginger, peeled and finely chopped or grated
1-2 cloves garlic, peeled and crushed
700g/1½lbs chicken thighs, skinned and boned
1½ tbsps tomato purée
90ml/3fl oz hot water
225g/8oz closed cup mushrooms, thickly sliced
1 tsp salt or to taste
25g/1oz ground almonds
2 tbsps chopped coriander leaves

1. Put the ground coriander, cumin, turmeric, chilli powder and allspice in a small glass bowl and heat, uncovered, on high for 2 minutes. Stir and stand aside.

2. Put the oil, onion, ginger and garlic in a 3-pint casserole or bowl, cover with a lid or cling film; puncture cling film and cook on high for 2½ minutes.

3. Stir in the spice mixture and cook, uncovered, on high for 2 minutes.

4. Add the chicken, tomato purée and water, and stir and mix thoroughly. Cover as before and cook on high for 4 minutes. Stir every 2 minutes. Reduce temperature setting to medium and cook for 6 minutes. Stir after 3 minutes.

5. Add the mushrooms and salt, stir and mix well. Cover again and cook on medium for 4 minutes, stir after 2 minutes.

6. Stir in the ground almonds and cook, uncovered, on low for 3 minutes. Stir halfway through.

7. Remove and stir in half the coriander leaves. Use the remaining coriander leaves to garnish the curry.

8. Allow the dish to stand for 6 minutes before serving.

TIME Preparation takes 15 minutes, cooking takes 23 minutes.

SERVING IDEAS Serve with Cardamom Rice or Plain Boiled Rice. Suitable for freezing.

Prawns in Coconut Milk

Adapted for the microwave, this is a speciality from the coastal region of India where large prawns are found. The gravy is enriched with fresh coconut milk, but in this recipe, creamed coconut and standard frozen prawns are used.

SERVES 4

75g/3oz creamed coconut, cut into small pieces
1 fresh green chilli, chopped and seeded if a milder flavour is liked
½-inch cube of root ginger, peeled and finely grated
1 tsp salt or to taste
150ml/5fl oz hot water
450g/1lb peeled frozen prawns, defrosted and drained
100g/4oz frozen garden peas
2 tsps ground coriander
½-1 tsp chilli powder
2 tbsps cooking oil
1 medium-sized onion, finely chopped
1½ tbsps lemon juice

1. Put the coconut, green chilli, ginger, salt and water into a 2-pint casserole or bowl, cover with a lid or cling film. Puncture the cling film and cook on high for 2 minutes.

2. Stir and mix the ingredients thoroughly, re-cover and cook on high for a further 2 minutes or until the coconut is fully dissolved.

3. Add the prawns and mix well, cover and cook on high for 2 minutes.

4. Add the peas, cover as before and cook on high for 1½ minutes. Stir the contents and stand for 5 minutes.

5. Put the coriander and chilli powder in a small glass bowl and heat on high for 1½ minutes when the spices will release their aroma. Let the mixture stand for 45 seconds then stir into the prawns.

6. Preheat a microwave browning dish on high for 4-5 minutes. Add the oil and heat on high for 1 minute. Add the onion and 'fry' in the oil on high for 5-6 minutes until lightly browned, stirring frequently. Stir the onions into the prawns.

7. Add the lemon juice and mix thoroughly.

TIME Preparation takes 10 minutes, cooking takes 9 minutes plus 5 minutes 45 seconds standing time.

SERVING IDEAS Serve with Plain Boiled Rice and Cauliflower Upkari.

COOK'S TIP If you do not have a microwave browning dish, use the conventional cooker. Heat the oil over a medium heat and fry the onions until they are lightly browned, stirring frequently. Stir the onions into the prawns.

Saffron Rice

A wonderfully fragrant rice cooked in a full-flavoured stock prepared with a few whole spices and saffron strands. A pinch of powdered saffron can be used instead of the strands, though the strands have more flavour and colour.

SERVES 4

225g/8oz basmati rice
480ml/16fl oz water
1 cinnamon stick, 2-inches long, broken up into 2-3 pieces
3 green cardamoms, bruised
3 whole cloves
2 bay leaves, crumpled
⅛ tsp saffron strands
1 tsp salt or to taste
1 tsp butter

1. Wash the rice and soak it in cold water for 30 minutes. Drain well.

2. Put the water, cinnamon, cardamom, cloves, bay leaves and saffron in a 2-pint jug and cover with cling film. Puncture the film and cook on high for 5 minutes. Stand aside for 5 minutes.

3. Put the rice, salt and butter in a 4-5 pint dish (be sure to use the correct sized dish to avoid spillage during cooking).

4. Strain the spiced liquid over the rice, stir and mix well. Cook on high for 8 minutes, then cook on medium for 2 minutes.

5. Stand aside for 5 minutes. Fork through the rice before serving.

TIME Preparation takes 30 minutes to soak the rice, cooking takes 15 minutes plus 10 minutes standing time.

SERVING IDEAS Serve with Chicken Tikka Masala or Tandoori Chicken Masala.
Suitable for freezing.

Plain Boiled Rice

Cooking rice in the microwave is a delight as it does not need the slightest attention. The best result is achieved by using two levels of power control rather than cooking the rice on high throughout.

SERVES 4-6

275g/10oz basmati rice, washed and soaked in cold water for 30 minutes
570ml/20fl oz hot water
1 tsp butter
1 tsp salt

1. Drain the rice thoroughly.

2. Put all the ingredients in a 5-pint casserole or other dish, cover with a lid or cling film; puncture cling film and cook on high for 6 minutes, then on medium for 4 minutes.

3. Stand for 6-8 minutes. Fork through the rice before serving.

TIME Preparation takes 30 minutes to soak the rice, cooking takes 10 minutes.

SERVING IDEAS Plain Boiled Rice can be served with almost any curry, but it tastes particularly good with dishes like Bhoona Gosht, Chicken Kohlapuri and Mustard Fish.

Suitable for freezing.

Cinnamon Rice

A delicious boiled rice, flavoured with cinnamon and bay leaves. Frozen garden peas are added to enhance appearance.

SERVES 4

225g/8oz basmati rice, washed and soaked in cold water for 30 minutes
100g/4oz frozen garden peas or pre-cooked fresh peas
475ml/16fl oz hot water
2 cinnamon sticks, 2-inches long each, broken up
2 bay leaves, crumpled
1 tsp butter
½ tsp salt

1. Drain the rice thoroughly.

2. Put all the ingredients together in a 5-pint casserole or bowl and mix well. Cover with a lid or cling film; puncture cling film and cook on high for 8 minutes, then on medium for 4 minutes.

3. Stand aside for 10 minutes. Fork through the rice before serving. Remove cinnamon and bay leaves if liked.

TIME Preparation takes 30 minutes to soak the rice, cooking takes 12 minutes.

SERVING IDEAS Serve with Chicken Korma or Chicken with Cashews. Suitable for freezing if fresh peas are used.

Tomato Rice

In this delicious recipe basmati rice is cooked with cinnamon, bay leaves and tinned tomatoes. The soft red colour of the rice, when garnished with tender, fresh coriander leaves, looks most attractive.

SERVES 4

225g/8oz basmati rice
Small tin of tomatoes
1 cinnamon stick, 2-inches long; broken up into 2-3 pieces
1 bay leaf, crumpled
1-2 fresh green chillies, seeded and sliced lengthwise
1 tsp salt or to taste
1 tsp butter
A few sprigs of fresh coriander leaves

1. Wash the rice, soak in cold water for 30 minutes and drain well.

2. Sieve the tomatoes and mix the pulp with hot water to make up to 500ml/18fl oz.

3. Put the tomato flavoured water into a jug or bowl and add the cinnamon and bay leaf. Cover and cook on high for 3½ minutes. Stir and stand aside, covered, for 15-20 minutes.

4. Put the rice in a 5-pint casserole or bowl and add the spiced liquid, green chillies, salt and butter. Cover with cling film and puncture film; cook on high for 12 minutes.

5. Stand for 5-6 minutes.

6. Fork through the rice, remove cinnamon, bay leaf and chillies and garnish with the sprigs of fresh coriander.

TIME Preparation takes 30 minutes to soak the rice, cooking takes 15 minutes.

SERVING IDEAS Serve with Bhoona Gosht, Fish Bhoona or Tarka Dhal, Saagwalla Dhal and Kababs.
Suitable for freezing.

Tarka Dhal

This delicious tarka dhal recipe requires less than half the time used for the conventional method of cooking.

SERVES 4

225g/8oz masoor dhal (red split lentils), cleaned and washed
570ml/20fl oz hot water
½-inch cube of root ginger, peeled and finely chopped or grated
¼ tsp ground turmeric
2 ripe tomatoes, skinned and chopped
4 fresh green chillies, whole
¾ tsp salt or to taste
2 tbsps oil or ghee
1 tsp black mustard seeds
10-12 curry leaves
10-12 fenugreek seeds
3-4 dried red chillies, whole
1 tbsp chopped coriander leaves

1. Put the dhal, water, ginger and turmeric in 4-5 pint casserole or bowl, cover with a lid or cling film, puncture cling film and cook on high for 5 minutes.

2. Stir the dhal, re-cover and cook on medium for 10 minutes, stirring every 3 minutes.

3. Add the tomatoes, green chillies and salt; stir and mix well. Cover and cook on high for 2½ minutes.

4. Preheat a browning dish on high for 4-5 minutes, add the oil and heat for 1 minute on high. Add the mustard seeds, cook on high for 30 seconds-1 minute until they pop. Now add the curry leaves, fenugreek and red chillies.

5. Stir the hot oil seasoning into the dhal and garnish with the coriander leaves.

TIME Preparation takes 10 minutes, cooking takes 18 minutes.

SERVING IDEAS Serve with Cinnamon Rice and Marinated Trout. Suitable for freezing.

VARIATION If you do not have a browning dish, use a conventional cooker. Heat the oil and add the mustard seeds. As soon as the seeds begin to pop, add the curry leaves, fenugreek and red chillies. Remove from heat and stir the hot oil seasoning into the dhal.

Cauliflower Upkari

The microwave has transformed the taste of this traditional recipe. The pieces of cauliflower remain firm yet tender and succulent and the flavour of the whole spices comes through beautifully.

SERVES 4-6

700g/1½lbs cauliflower florets
1 tbsp cooking oil
½ tsp black mustard seeds
8-10 curry leaves
2-4 dried red chillies, whole
¾ tsp salt or to taste

1. Cut the cauliflower florets into ½-inch pieces and soak in plenty of lightly salted water for 30 minutes. Drain and rinse well.

2. Spread the oil on the base of a 4-5 pint casserole or basin and sprinkle the mustard, curry leaves and chillies.

3. Arrange the cauliflower evenly on the spices, cover with a lid or cling film. Puncture cling film and cook on high for 5 minutes without stirring.

4. Sprinkle the salt evenly on the cauliflower, then stir and mix well. Cover again and cook on high for 7 minutes, stirring every 2 minutes.

5. Stand for 5-7 minutes.

TIME Preparation takes 10 minutes, cooking takes 12 minutes.

SERVING IDEAS Serve with Prawns or Mackerels in Coconut Milk and Plain Boiled Rice.

Aloo Mattar

This potato and peas curry can be cooked in the microwave with great success. Tomato purée is used to thicken the gravy and fewer spices than in the conventional recipe are used, as spices tend to taste much stronger when used in the microwave.

SERVES 4-6

550g/1¼lbs new potatoes
225ml/8fl oz hot water
½ tsp garam masala
1 tsp ground cumin
¼ tsp ground turmeric
½ tsp chilli powder
2 tbsps cooking oil
100g/4oz onions, finely chopped
8-10 curry leaves
100g/4oz frozen garden peas
¾ tsp salt or to taste
1 tbsp tomato purée

1. Put the water and the potatoes in a casserole or basin, cover and cook on high for 4½ minutes.

2. Turn the potatoes over, cover again and cook on high for 4 minutes. Stand for 6-8 minutes. Allow the potatoes to cool thoroughly.

3. Peel and dice the potatoes evenly.

4. Put the garam masala, cumin, turmeric and chilli powder in a small glass bowl and heat on high for 1 minute. Stir and stand aside for 5 minutes.

5. Put the oil, onions and curry leaves in a 3-pint casserole or basin and mix well. Cover with a lid or cling flim, puncture cling film and cook on high for 3½ minutes. Stir halfway through cooking time.

6. Add the heated spice mixture and mix thoroughly. Cook, uncovered, on high for 3 minutes, stir after 1 minute.

7. Add the peas, potatoes, salt, tomato purée and the remaining water and mix thoroughly. Cover and cook on high for 2½ minutes. Stir the contents, re-cover and cook or medium for 3½ minutes.

8. Stir the curry, cover and stand for 6-8 minutes.

TIME Preparation takes 15 minutes, cooking takes 20 minutes.

SERVING IDEAS Serve with Loochis or Puris accompanied by Kababs or Tandoori Chicken.

Mixed Vegetables with Cinnamon

A colourful and attractive combination of vegetables which is delicious served with roast lamb or beef.

SERVES 4-6

2 tbsps cooking oil
1-2 fresh green chillies, seeded and sliced lengthwise
2 cinnamon sticks, 2-inches long each, broken up into 2-3 pieces
1 tsp cumin seeds
100g/4oz finely sliced onions
450g/1lb green cabbage, finely shredded
100g/4oz carrots, scraped and coarsely grated
50g/2oz frozen garden peas or pre-cooked fresh peas
1¼ tsp salt or to taste
¼ tsp chilli powder (optional)

1. In a large bowl or casserole put the oil, green chillies, cinnamon sticks and cumin seeds. Cover the ingredients with the sliced onions.

2. Cover the dish with a lid or cling film, puncture cling film and cook on high for 2½ minutes, stirring after 1 minute.

3. Add the vegetables and sprinkle with the salt and chilli powder (if used). Stir and mix well then cover the dish as before and cook on high for 8 minutes, stirring every two minutes.

4. Uncover the dish and cook on medium for 2 minutes. Stir and let it stand for 5 minutes.

TIME Preparation takes 15 minutes, cooking takes 12 minutes.

SERVING IDEAS Serve as an accompaniment with rice or chapatties and Aloo Gosht or Bhoona Gosht.

Potato Gushi

A delicious potato curry adapted for the microwave from the fascinating range of Saraswat cookery. Their cooking methods are simple and health-conscious. The art of mixing only two or three spices in different combinations and creating a numerous range of delicious flavours is unique to this style of cooking.

SERVES 4-6

450g/1lb medium-sized old potatoes
4 tbsps hot water
225ml/8fl oz warm water

Grind the following 2 ingredients in a coffee grinder
4 tbsps desiccated coconut
3-4 dried red chillies

¾ tsp salt or to taste
2 tbsps cooking oil
2-3 cloves garlic, peeled and crushed
1 tsp ground coriander
1 tbsp lemon juice

1. Put the potatoes in a 3-pint dish and add the hot water. Cover and cook on high for 4 minutes.

2. Turn the potatoes over, re-cover and cook on high for a further 4 minutes. Stand for 10 minutes, then keep them immersed in cold water until they are completely cold.

3. Peel and dice the potatoes evenly.

4. Put the potatoes in a 2-pint casserole and pour over the warm water. Add the ground coconut mixture and salt. Stir and mix thoroughly. Cover and cook on high for 2 minutes.

5. Stir the potatoes, cover again and cook on medium for 4 minutes.

6. Preheat a browning dish for 4 minutes on high. Add the oil and heat for 1 minute, remove and add the garlic. Cook for 30 seconds to 1 minute on high until golden brown. Stir in the ground coriander.

7. Stir the hot oil seasoning into the potatoes and mix thoroughly.

8. Add the lemon juice and mix well.

TIME Preparation takes 15 minutes plus cooling time for the potatoes, cooking takes 15 minutes.

SERVING IDEAS Serve with Mackerels in Coconut Milk and Plain Boiled Rice or with Puris/Loochis and Kababs or Masala Machchi.

COOK'S TIP If you do not have a browning dish, heat the oil on a conventional cooker, add the garlic and when it turns slightly brown stir in the ground coriander and remove from heat.

Mixed Vegetable Bhaji

A combination of fresh and frozen vegetables is used to make this delicious side dish. The flavour of the dish will blend well with almost any meat, fish or chicken curry.

SERVES 4

3 medium-sized new potatoes
2 tbsps cooking oil
½ tsp black mustard seeds
3-4 dried red chillies, whole
1 fresh green chilli, seeded and coarsely chopped
10-12 curry leaves
1 medium-sized onion, finely sliced
150g/6oz fresh carrots, scraped or peeled and cut into matchstick strips
100g/4oz frozen sliced green beans, defrosted and drained
¾ tsp salt or to taste

1. Put the potatoes in a 1-pint dish or bowl and add 4 tbsps hot water. Cover and cook on high for 3 minutes. Turn them over, re-cover and cook on high for a further 2 minutes. Stand potatoes aside for 8 minutes, then keep them immersed in cold water until they are completely cold.

2. Peel and dice the potatoes evenly.

3. Put the oil, mustard seeds, red and green chillies and curry leaves in a 4-pint casserole. Spread the onions on top, cover and cook on high for 5 minutes without stirring.

4. Spread the carrots over the onions and add 1 tbsp hot water. Cover and cook on high for 3 minutes, stirring halfway through.

5. Add the beans, cover and cook on high for 4 minutes, stirring halfway through.

6. Add the potatoes and salt, stir and mix well. Cook, uncovered on high, for 1½ minutes.

7. Stir and stand aside for 5 minutes before serving.

TIME Preparation takes 10-15 minutes, cooking takes 18 minutes.

SERVING IDEAS Serve as an accompaniment with any meat, fish or chicken curry and Chapatties, Rotis, Parathas or rice.

Cabbage Bhaji

A simple, tasty way to cook cabbage. The natural juice secreted by the cabbage during cooking is soaked up by the ground desiccated coconut, creating a wonderful flavour and texture.

SERVES 4-6

2 tbsps cooking oil
½ tsp black mustard seeds
8-10 fenugreek seeds (optional)
10-12 curry leaves
2-4 dried red chillies
2 fresh green chillies, seeded and sliced lengthwise
600g/1¼lbs green or white cabbage, finely shredded
1 tsp salt or to taste
25g/1oz desiccated coconut, ground in a coffee grinder
1 ripe tomato, sliced
1 tbsp desiccated coconut

1. Put the oil, mustard, fenugreek, (if used) curry leaves and chillies in a 4-pint casserole and cover with the cabbage.

2. Cover the casserole with a lid or cling film, puncture cling film and cook on high for 6 minutes, stirring halfway through cooking time.

3. Add the salt and the ground coconut; stir and mix well. Re-cover and cook on high for a further 6 minutes, stirring every 2 minutes.

4. Arrange the sliced tomato on the cabbage and sprinkle with the extra 1 tbsp of coconut. Cover and cook on high for 1½ minutes. Stand for 5 minutes before serving.

TIME Preparation takes 10 minutes, cooking takes 13 minutes.

SERVING IDEAS Serve accompanied by Prawns in Garlic, and Tamarind and Plain Boiled Rice.

Sour-Hot Potatoes

The tangy taste in this dish comes from tamarind. Ready-to-use tamarind concentrate is available from Indian grocers. If it is difficult to obtain, use lemon juice.

SERVES 4

450g/1lb old potatoes
¾ tsp tamarind concentrate or 1½ tbsps lemon juice
150ml/5fl oz hot water
2 cloves garlic, peeled and crushed
1 tsp salt or to taste
½ tsp chilli powder
1 tsp paprika
4 tbsps cooking oil
1 tsp black mustard seeds
1 large onion, finely chopped
1½ tsps ground coriander

1. Put the potatoes in a 2-pint bowl or casserole and add 4-5 tbsps hot water. Cover with a lid or cling film, puncture the cling film and cook on high for 3 minutes.

2. Turn the potatoes over, re-cover and cook on high for a further 3½ minutes. Stand for 5 minutes.

3. Immerse the potatoes in cold water and allow them to cool completely; or cook the potatoes in advance and leave them in the refrigerator.

4. Peel and cut the potatoes into 1-inch cubes.

5. Put the tamarind and the water into a 2-pint bowl or casserole and cook, uncovered, on high for 50 seconds.

6. Stir and mix thoroughly then add the garlic, salt, chilli powder and paprika. Cover and cook on high for 45 seconds.

7. Add the potatoes and cook, uncovered, on full power for 3 minutes, stirring halfway through.

8. Preheat a microwave browning dish for 4-5 minutes on high. Add the oil and heat on high for 1 minute.

9. Add the mustard seeds. Cook on high until they start popping – 30 seconds-1 minute. Add the onions.

10. Cook on high for 4-6 minutes until golden brown, stirring after each minute add the coriander, stir and cook on high for 30 seconds. Stir this mixture into the potatoes.

TIME Preparation takes 10-15 minutes plus cooling time for the potatoes, cooking takes 15 minutes.

SERVING IDEAS Serve with Puris or Loochis or as a side dish with rice, Tarka Dhal and Kababs.

COOK'S TIP If you do not have a microwave browning dish, use a conventional cooker. Heat the oil over medium heat and fry the mustard seeds until they crackle. Add the onions and fry until they are golden brown, stirring frequently. Add the ground coriander, stir and fry for 1 minute. Stir this mixture into the potatoes.

Cauliflower with Cashews

An interesting combination of texture and flavour and a speedy preparation and cooking method, make this dish the perfect choice for entertaining.

SERVES 4

1 tsp ground coriander
½ tsp garam masala
¼ tsp ground turmeric
½-1 tsp chilli powder or cayenne pepper
150ml/5fl oz milk
75g/3oz raw cashews, split into halves
450g/1lb cauliflower florets, cut into ½-inch pieces
¾ tsp salt or to taste
25g/1oz ground almonds
1 tbsp chopped coriander leaves

1. Put the coriander, garam masala, turmeric and chilli or cayenne in small glass bowl and heat on high for 1½ minutes. Stir and stand aside for 5 minutes.

2. Put the milk, cashews and the heated spices into a 3-pint casserole, cover with a lid or cling film; puncture cling film and cook on high for 3 minutes, stirring halfway through cooking time.

3. Add the cauliflower and salt, re-cover and cook on high for 6 minutes, stirring every 2 minutes.

4. Stir in the ground almonds and cook, uncovered, on high for 3 minutes, stirring every minute.

5. Garnish with the fresh coriander leaves.

TIME Preparation takes 10 minutes, cooking takes 13 minutes.

SERVING IDEAS Serve with Chicken Korma, Meat Durbari, Shahi Korma and rice or bread.

Courgettes with Coconut & Green Chillies

An unusual but delightful way to cook courgettes which tastes good with grilled fish and poultry. Do make sure that the desiccated coconut is first ground in a coffee grinder to obtain the fine texture needed.

SERVES 2-4

1 tbsp cooking oil
4-6 fresh green chillies, seeded and sliced lengthwise
1 clove garlic, peeled and crushed
2 ripe tomatoes, skinned and chopped
225g/8oz courgettes, cut into ¼-inch thick slices
½ tsp salt or to taste
4 tbsps chopped coriander leaves
2 tbsps desiccated coconut, ground in a coffee grinder

1. Put the oil, green chillies, garlic and tomatoes into a 2-pint casserole. Cover with cling film or a lid; puncture cling film and cook on high for 3 minutes, stirring halfway through cooking time.

2. Add the courgettes, salt and coriander leaves. Stir and mix well. Re-cover and cook on high for 3 minutes, stirring halfway through cooking time.

3. Stir in the coconut, cover as before and cook on high for 3 minutes, stirring as before.

4. Allow the dish to stand for 4 minutes before serving.

TIME Preparation takes 5-10 minutes, cooking takes 9 minutes.

SERVING IDEAS Serve with Chicken & Mushroom Curry and Plain Boiled Rice.

Lettuce and Coconut Chutney

Here is a very tasty way to use up lettuce leaves which are not fresh enough to use in a salad.

SERVES 8-10

50g/2oz desiccated coconut
300ml/10fl oz hot water
150g/6oz lettuce leaves, washed and coarsely chopped
1-2 fresh green chillies, seeded and chopped
1 level tsp tamarind concentrate or 1½ tbsps lemon juice
½ tsp salt or to taste
½ tsp ground cumin

1. Put half the water and all the coconut in a 4-pint bowl or casserole. Cover and cook on high for 2 minutes.

2. Stir the coconut and add the remaining water. Spread the lettuce leaves on top evenly, re-cover and cook on high for 2 minutes.

3. Stir the contents, cover and let it stand for 5 minutes, then uncover and allow it to cool for 15-20 minutes.

4. Put the coconut and lettuce mixture, green chillies and tamarind in an electric liquidiser and blend until smooth.

5. Add the salt and cumin and blend for a few seconds longer.

TIME Preparation takes 10-15 minutes, cooking takes 4 minutes.

SERVING IDEAS Serve with Kababs and Pakoras or as a relish with a main meal.

Suitable for freezing.

Tomato Chutney

The prominent flavour in this chutney is green chilli and cinnamon, together, they create an unusual and mouth-watering aroma. Fresh tomatoes were used for this recipe, but tinned tomatoes can be used if they are drained well.

SERVES 8-10

450g/1lb ripe tomatoes, coarsely chopped
225g/8oz onions, peeled and finely chopped
½-inch cube of root ginger, peeled and finely sliced
2-3 cloves garlic, peeled and crushed
1-2 fresh green chillies, seeded and chopped
1 cinnamon stick; 2-inches long, broken up
2 tsps caster sugar
1 tsp salt or to taste

1. Put all the ingredients, except sugar and salt, in a bowl, cover and cook on high for 4 minutes, stirring the contents halfway through. Uncover, add sugar and salt and cook on high for a further 4 minutes.

2. Allow to cool, then put into a liquidiser or food processor and blend until smooth.

3. Pass the entire contents through a sieve, discard all residue left in the sieve.

4. Store in a moisture-free jar in the refrigerator for up to 10 days.

TIME Preparation takes 5-10 minutes, cooking takes 8 minutes.

SERVING IDEAS Serve with Onion Bhajiyas and Pakoras, or Kababs.

COURGETTE CHUTNEY

A rich tasting chutney, made by cooking the courgettes briefly and blending them with desiccated coconut and other ingredients. The flavour of root ginger and fresh green chillies blended with the creamy taste of the chutney is splendid.

SERVES 8-10

50g/2oz desiccated coconut
225g/8oz courgettes, washed and coarsely chopped
225ml/8fl oz water
¾ tsp salt or to taste
1 level tsp tamarind concentrate or 1 tbsp lemon juice
1-2 fresh green chillies, seeded and coarsely chopped
½-inch cube of root ginger, peeled and coarsely chopped
2-3 tbsps finely chopped onions

1. Put the coconut, courgette and water in a 3-pint bowl or casserole, cover and cook on high for 10 minutes. Stir every 2-3 minutes.

2. Let the ingredients stand for 5 minutes, then stir in the salt and the tamarind. Allow the mixture to cool.

3. Put the courgette and coconut mixture in an electric liquidiser and add the green chillies and ginger, blending until the ingredients are smooth.

4. If using lemon juice, add this to the rest of the ingredients in the blender.

5. Stir in the onions before serving.

TIME Preparation takes 5 minutes, cooking takes 10 minutes.

SERVING IDEAS Serve with any snacks or as a side dish with rice and Lamb with Mung Beans or Chicken Kohlapuri.
Suitable for freezing.

VARIATION Use tender marrow.

Savoury Rice Cake

A particular variety of lentil is required for this recipe known as 'urid dhal' or black gram. This is available from Indian grocers. The rice used can be of any type except brown rice.

SERVES 6-8

225g/8oz rice
100g/4oz Urid Dhal or black gram
300ml/10fl oz water
1 tsp salt or to taste
1 tsp ground cumin
1 tsp freshly milled black pepper
Oil or ghee for shallow frying

1. Wash and soak the rice and Urid Dhal separately overnight in cold water. Drain thoroughly.

2. Put the rice into an electric liquidiser and add 55ml/2fl oz water from the specified amount. Switch on for a few seconds or until it reaches a paste-like consistency. This should not be too fine.

3. Transfer the rice paste to a steel bowl or pan which has been rinsed in hot water.

4. Now put the Urid Dhal in the liquidiser and add 150ml/5fl oz water from the specified amount. Liquidise this to a smooth paste. Stir the contents once or twice to ensure even blending.

5. Add the dhal paste to the rice and stir in the remaining water, mix thoroughly, cover the container and leave to ferment in a warm place. The airing cupboard or the top of the boiler is ideal.

6. When fermented, the mixture will look light and frothy. It can take between 6 and 8 hours to ferment.

7. Add the salt, cumin and pepper, mix thoroughly.

8. Line a 6-8 inch souffle dish or similar container with a greaseproof paper or baking parchment. Spoon the mixture into the dish and put the dish on an inverted glass plate or flan dish.

9. Cook on high for 8 minutes, then on medium for 2½ minutes.

10. When cool, turn out the cake on a board, cut into about ¼-inch thick slices all across the cake and cut each slice into 2-3 pieces.

11. Preheat the browning dish for 4-5 minutes on high. Add the oil or ghee and heat for 1 minute on high, then the rice cake slices and cook on high for 5-6 minutes, turning frequently, until golden brown. They may have to be fried in batches.

TIME Preparation takes 6-8 hours or overnight for soaking, 6-8 hours for fermenting, cooking takes 10½ minutes, frying takes 8-10 minutes.

SERVING IDEAS Serve as a snack with Lettuce and Coconut Chutney or any other Chutney.
Suitable for freezing. Freeze before frying.

COOK'S TIP If you do not have a microwave browning dish – shallow fry on a conventional cooker in ghee or oil until golden brown on both sides. They will need to be fried in 2-3 batches.

bread and rice

NAAN

Naan is traditionally cooked in the Tandoor. It is not difficult to cook naan in a very hot oven, although the distinctive taste of clay cooking will be missing.

MAKES 8 Naan

450g/1lb plain flour
1 tsp salt
1 tsp Kalonji-onion seeds, (optional)
1 tsp sugar
1½ sachets fast action or easy dissolve yeast
50ml/3fl oz milk
125g/5oz natural yogurt
1 medium-sized egg, beaten
50g/2oz ghee or butter
2 tbsps sesame seeds or white poppy seeds

1. Put the flour, salt, kalonji, sugar and yeast into a large bowl and mix well.

2. Warm the milk until it is lukewarm, reserve 1 tbsp yogurt and add the rest to the milk and blend thoroughly.

3. Beat the egg and keep aside.

4. Melt the butter or ghee.

5. Add the milk and yogurt mixture, egg and ghee or butter to the flour, knead with your hands or in the food processor or mixer until a soft and springy dough is formed.

6. Place the dough in a large plastic food bag and tie up the uppermost part so that the dough has enough room for expansion.

7. Rinse a bowl (preferably steel, as this will retain heat better) with hot water and put the bag of dough in it. Put the bowl in a warm place, until risen to double the original quantity (½-1 hour)

8. Divide the dough into 8 balls, cover them and keep aside for 10-15 minutes.

9. Preheat over to 230°C/450°F/Gas Mark 8 and put an ungreased baking sheet into the over to preheat for about 10 minutes. Remove baking sheet from the oven and line with a greased greaseproof paper or baking parchment.

10. Take one of the balls and stretch it gently with both hands to make a teardrop shape. Lay this on the baking sheet and press it gently to stretch it to about 6-7-inches in length, maintaining the teardrop shape at all times. Make 2-3 similar shapes at a time and brush with the reserved yogurt, then sprinkle with the sesame or poppy seeds. Bake on the top rung of the oven for 10-12 minutes, or until puffed and browned.

TIME Preparation takes 10-15 minutes plus time needed to prove the dough, cooking takes 20-25 minutes.

SERVING IDEAS Serve with any meat, chicken or vegetable curry. Suitable for freezing.

VARIATION Use 1 tsp caraway or cumin seeds instead of the onion seeds while making the dough.

TANDOORI ROTI

Tandoori Rotis, like Naan, are cooked in the Tandoor – a barrel-shaped clay oven which distributes an even and fierce heat. Tandoori rotis can be cooked in a very hot conventional oven, they are equally delicious though the flavour is different.

MAKES 8 Rotis

125g/5oz natural yogurt
450g/1lb plain flour
1 tsp sugar
1 tsp baking powder
½ tsp salt
1½ sachets fast action yeast
1 level tbsp ghee or unsalted butter
1 medium egg, beaten
150ml/5fl oz warm milk

1. Beat the yogurt until smooth, and set aside.

2. In a large bowl, sift the flour with the sugar, baking powder, salt and yeast. Add ghee and mix thoroughly. Add yogurt and egg and knead well, use food mixer or food processor with dough hook, if preferred.

3. Gradually add the warm milk and keep kneading until a smooth and springy dough is formed.

4. Place the dough in a large plastic food bag and tie up the uppermost part of the bag so that the dough has enough room for expansion inside.

5. Rinse a large bowl with hot water and put the bag of dough in it. Use a steel, metal or enamel bowl as these will retain heat better, or use a saucepan if you do not have a suitable bowl. Place the bowl in a warm place (top of the boiler or airing cupboard is ideal) for ½-¾ hour when it will be almost double in volume.

6. Preheat oven to 225°C/450°F/Gas Mark 8.

7. Line a baking sheet with greased greaseproof paper or baking parchment.

8. Divide the dough into 8 equal-sized balls. Place a ball between your palms and flatten by pressing it down.

9. Dust the ball lightly in a little flour and roll it out gently to a 4-inch disc. Place in the prepared baking sheet. Make the rest of the rotis the same way.

10. Bake on the top rung of the oven for 10-12 minutes. Turn the rotis over and bake for a further 2 minutes.

TIME Preparation takes 10-15 minutes, cooking takes 25 minutes.

SERVING IDEAS Serve with any meat, chicken or vegetable curry. Suitable for freezing.

VARIATION Use wholemeal flour.

CHAPATTIES

A Chapattie is a dry roasted unleavened bread best eaten as soon as it is cooked. They are not as filling as Rotis or Parathas, so 2-3 chapatties per person is quite normal.

MAKES 14 Chapatties

325g/12oz fine wholemeal flour or Atta/ Chapatti flour
½ tsp salt
1 tbsp butter, or ghee
170ml-280ml/6-10fl oz warm water (quantity depends on the texture of the flour)
1 tbsp extra flour in a shallow bowl or plate

1. Food Mixer Method: Place the flour, salt and fat together in the bowl and mix thoroughly at the medium-to-low speed taking care to see that all the fat has been broken up and well incorporated into the flour. Turn speed down to minimum and gradually add the water. When the dough is formed, knead it until it is soft and pliable. Cover the dough with a well-moistened cloth and keep aside for ½-1 hour.

2. Hand Method: Put the flour and salt in a large bowl and rub in the fat. Gradually add the water and keep mixing and kneading until a soft and pliable dough is formed. Cover the dough as above and keep aside.

3. Divide the dough into 14 walnut-sized portions. Roll each portion in a circular motion between the palms to make a smooth round ball, then flatten the ball to make a round cake. Dip each cake into the dry flour and roll the chapatti into a disc of about 6-inch diameter.

4. An iron griddle is normally used for cooking chapattis, but if you do not have one, then make sure you use a heavy-based frying pan as the chapatties need even distribution of heat during cooking. Overheating of the pan will cause the chapatties to stick to the pan and burn.

5. Heat the griddle or frying pan over medium heat and place a chapatti on it, cook for 30 seconds and turn the chapatti over. Cook until brown spots appear on both sides, turning it over frequently.

6. To keep the chapatties warm, line a piece of aluminium foil with absorbent paper and place the chapatties on one end, cover with the other end and seal the edges.

TIME Preparation takes 20-25 minutes, cooking takes 35-40 minutes.

SERVING IDEAS Serve with any meat, chicken or vegetable curry
Suitable for freezing.

Puris

This deep-fried unleavened bread is one of those items which needs last minute preparation. The dough can be made in advance, but rolling out and frying should be done simultaneously and once fried, they should be served immediately.

MAKES 14-15 Puris

275g/10oz fine wholemeal flour or atta or chapatti flour
½ tsp salt
¼ tsp sugar
1 tbsp margarine or oil
150-275ml/5-10fl oz warm water (quantity of water will depend on the texture of the flour – fine textured flour will absorb less water than the coarser variety)
Oil for deep frying

1. In a bowl, mix flour, salt and sugar. Rub in the margarine or oil. Now add the water very slowly and keep mixing and kneading until a stiff dough has formed. Alternatively, put the flour, salt, sugar and fat in a food processor or food mixer with a dough hook and switch on. When the fat is well incorporated into the flour, gradually add the water. Once the dough has been formed and kneaded for a few seconds, switch off the machine.

2. Divide the dough into 14-15 equal portions, each about 1½-inch diameter. Make the balls by rolling a portion of the dough between your palms in a circular motion. Have a little dry flour ready in a bowl or a plate. Dust each ball lightly in this and flatten the ball into a round cake. Treat all the balls the same way and cover them with a damp cloth.

3. Roll out the puris to about 3½-inch diameter discs. Rolling out should be done evenly to ensure tight edges which help the puris to puff up when they are dropped in hot oil. A flat perforated spoon is ideal for frying puris.

4. It is easier to roll and fry one puri at a time. If you wish to roll out all of them you will need a large work surface to keep them as they should not be piled together.

5. Careful handling is needed while rolling and frying the puris – if they are damaged or pierced, they will not puff up.

6. Heat the oil to 160°C in a deep fryer. Place one puri at a time in the oil and gently press it down – as soon as the puri puffs up turn it over and cook for about 30 seconds. Drain on absorbent paper. Fry the remaining puris in the same way.

7. Fried puris must not be heaped one on top of the other but placed on an open tray so as not to flatten or damage them (this stage is not important when the puris are made for the specific purpose of using with a filling).

TIME Preparation takes 5-10 minutes, cooking takes 15-20 minutes.

SERVING IDEAS Serve with Aloo Gosht or Murghi Jhal Frezi and Aloo ki Bhaji.

Loochis

Loochis are similar to puris – the main difference is that they are made with plain flour instead of the chapatti flour (atta) and with certain dishes they do taste better than puris.

MAKES 14-15 Loochis

275g/10oz plain flour plus 1 tbsp extra flour for dusting
½ tsp salt
¼ tsp sugar
1 tsp kalonji (onion seeds); optional
1 tbsp butter, margarine or ghee
150-175ml/5-6fl oz warm water (this will depend on the texture of the flour)
Oil for deep frying

1. In a large bowl, mix the flour, salt, sugar and kalonji. Rub in the fat and gradually add the water. Either knead with your hands or in the food processor until a stiff dough is formed.

2. Divide the dough into 14-15 walnut-sized balls. Take each ball between your palms and roll it in a circular motion. Press it down gently to make a flat, about ½-inch thick round cake. When you have made all the round cakes, cover them with a damp cloth.

3. Dust each flattened cake lightly with the extra flour and roll out to about 3½-inch discs. It is easier to roll out and fry one loochi at a time unless you have someone to help you. If you roll out all of them first, they need to be kept in a single layer – piling on each other may cause them to stick together.

4. Loochis puff up like balloons during frying. To ensure that the loochis are beautifully puffed, roll them out carefully and evenly without damaging or piercing them. Use a flat perforated spoon for frying.

5. Heat the oil to 160°C in a deep fryer. Place one loochi at a time in the hot oil – it will soon float to the surface and start puffing up. It helps to cook the loochis evenly if you press it down gently by touching the spoon only to the edge of the loochi. As soon as the loochi puffs up, turn it over gently and cook for about 30 seconds or until lightly browned. Drain on absorbent paper. Fry the rest of the loochis the same way.

6. Keep the fried loochis in a single layer, i.e. do not pile one on top of the other as this will damage them.

TIME Preparation takes 10-15 minutes, cooking takes 15-20 minutes.

SERVING IDEAS Serve with Bhoona Gosht accompanied by Aloo Mattar as an optional side dish. For entertaining, add a pilau or biriani with Raita and Popadoms.

TO RE-HEAT To enjoy them at their best, serve as soon as they are fried. They can be reheated, however, in a hot oven for 5-6 minutes; put them in a large tray in a single layer.

Batura

Batura is a leavened bread which is made of plain flour and then deep-fried. The dough is made with natural yogurt and has a soft, velvet-like texture.

SERVES 6

325g/12oz plain flour
1 tsp salt
2 tsps fast action or easy blend yeast
1 egg, beaten
125g/5oz natural yogurt
2-3 tbsps warm water
Oil for deep frying

1. Put the flour, salt and yeast in a bowl and mix well.

2. Add the egg, yogurt and water and knead until a soft and pliable dough is formed. Alternatively, put all the ingredients into the bowl of a food processor which has a dough hook, and switch on until the dough is formed.

3. Put the dough in a large plastic food bag and tie up the uppermost part of the bag, leaving room for the dough to expand.

4. Put the bag in a steel, metal or cast-iron bowl/saucepan which has been rinsed out in hot water. Leave the dough in a warm place for 3-4 hours for it to rise.

5. Remove the dough from the bag and divide it into 6 equal portions.

6. Roll each portion gently between your palms in a circular motion and flatten it to a round cake.

7. Dust the cake lightly in a little flour and roll it out gently to a large dish, about 6-inch diameter.

8. Heat the oil to 180°C; take care not to overheat the oil. Place a batura in the hot oil and fry it for 1 minute; turn it over and fry the other side for a further minute or until it is a rich creamy colour. Drain on absorbent paper.

9. Make and fry all the baturas the same way. It is easier to roll out and fry one batura at a time rather than rolling them all out first.

TIME Preparation takes 5-10 minutes plus 35-40 minutes for proving the dough, cooking takes 12-15 minutes.

SERVING IDEAS Serve with Marinated Lamb Chops, Kheema Mattar or Chicken Liver Masala.

VARIATION Use equal quantity of plain and wholemeal flour.

ROTIS

Rotis are a type of unleavened wholemeal bread. The dough is enriched with ghee or butter as for Parathas, but they are much easier to make. If you cannot get chapatti flour, use equal quantities of wholemeal flour and plain flour.

MAKES 8 Rotis

½ tsp salt
50g/2oz butter, or ghee
325g/12oz atta/chapatti flour or 160g/6oz each of wholemeal and plain flour
170ml-280ml/6-10fl oz warm water (quantity depends on the texture of the flour)
2 tbsps ghee or unsalted butter for frying

1. Hand Method: Rub the salt and fat into the flour until you reach a coarse breadcrumb consistency. Gradually add the water and knead until a soft and pliable dough is formed.

2. Food Mixer Method: Put the salt, fat and flour into the bowl and switch on to minimum speed. When the fat has completely broken up and incorporated well into the flour, gradually add the water and knead until the dough is soft and pliable.

3. Divide the dough into 8 balls. Hold each ball between your palms and rotate it in a circular motion until it is smooth and round, flatten the ball into a round cake and dust it very lightly in a little plain flour. Roll it out to about 6-inch diameter; cover the rest of the balls with a damp cloth while you are working on one.

4. Heat a heavy-based frying pan over medium heat; it is important to have a heavy-based pan as the rotis need even distribution of heat.

5. When the pan is hot, place a roti on it and flip it over after about 30 seconds. Spread 1 tsp ghee or butter over it and turn the roti over. Repeat the process for the other side. Brown both sides evenly and remove from heat.

6. Line a piece of aluminium foil with absorbent paper and put the cooked rotis on one end, cover with the other end and seal the edges. This will keep the rotis warm for 30-40 minutes.

TIME Preparation takes 15-30 minutes, cooking takes 25-30 minutes.

SERVING IDEAS Serve with any meat, chicken or vegetable curry.
Suitable for freezing.

PARATHAS

A Paratha is a crisp, rich unleavened bread. The dough is made with a fair amount of fat and each paratha is rolled out, spread with a little ghee or butter, folded and rolled out again to its final shape. It is rather like making flaky pastry but the method is simpler.

MAKES 4 Parathas

325g/12 oz wholemeal flour or chapatti flour (atta) plus 1 tbsp extra flour for dusting
½ tsp salt
125g/5oz ghee or unsalted butter
125-150ml/4-5fl oz warm water

---

1. Sift the flour and the salt together. Rub 50g/2oz fat from the specified amount into the flour until thoroughly mixed.

2. Gradually pour in the water and knead the mixture until you get a soft and pliable dough.

3. Divide the dough into 4 equal sized balls and flatten them by placing them between your palms and pressing gently.

4. Dust each flattened portion of dough with the flour and roll out to 8-inch diameter. On this spread about one tsp of fat evenly from the remaining 3oz portion.

5. With your hands, roll up the dough from the edge until you have a tube about an inch wide and 8 inches long. Gently stretch the dough lengthways and then curl each end inwards in an anti-clockwise direction to resemble a backwards S.

6. Now flip the upper half onto the lower half and flatten. Lightly dust this all over with flour and roll out again until the dough is about 8-inch diameter and one-eighth-of-an-inch in thickness.

7. Melt remaining fat and keep aside; heat the frying pan (preferably a cast iron one) over medium heat and place the paratha on it. Flip it over in about 30 seconds.

8. Spread 1 tbsp of the melted fat on the paratha. Flip it over again. Lower heat. Spread 1 tbsp of the melted fat on this side as well.

9. With a steel or a wooden spatula press the paratha gently into the frying pan, especially the edges. Flip it over after one minute and repeat the pressing action. Cook the second side for one minute.

10. Continue to cook both sides evenly till the paratha is uniformly light brown.

TIME Preparation takes 30 minutes, cooking takes 20 minutes.

SERVING IDEAS Serve with Chicken Do-Piaza, Kheema Mattar or Saagwalla Dhal. If there is rice on the menu, the parathas can be cut into halves or quarters.
Suitable for freezing.

VARIATION Use equal quantity of plain flour and wholemeal flour.

Plain Fried Rice

Plain fried rice is enjoyable with many dishes as the mild taste blends in happily with other flavours. The recipe below is perfect when you want to cook something quick, but a little more special than boiled rice.

SERVES 4-6

275g/10oz basmati or other long grain rice, washed and soaked in cold water for ½-1 hour
2 tbsps ghee or 3 tbsps cooking oil
1 tsp fennel seeds
1 tsp salt or to taste
500ml/18fl oz water for basmati rice or 600ml/20fl oz for other long grain rice.

1. Drain the rice and set aside.

2. Heat the oil or ghee over medium heat and fry the fennel seeds until they are brown. Add the rice and salt, stir and fry for 4-5 minutes then lower heat for the last 2-3 minutes of cooking.

3. Add the water and bring to the boil. Cover the pan and simmer for 12 minutes for basmati rice and 15-18 minutes for other long grain rice without lifting the lid.

TIME Preparation takes a few minutes plus time needed to soak the rice, cooking takes 20-25 minutes.

SERVING IDEAS Serve with Meat Madras, Meat Vindaloo, Bengal Fish Curry or Fish Bhoona. A complementary vegetable dish, such as Cabbage with gram flour or French Bean & Potato Bhaji is an excellent accompaniment. Suitable for freezing.

WATCHPOINT There is no need to lift the lid to check the rice during cooking. This will only result in the loss of vital steam which helps to cook the rice leaving each grain beautifully separate.

Plain Boiled Rice

Rice cookery needs no special technique, but a few simple rules will produce perfect results every time. Do not lift the lid while the rice is cooking. Do not stir the rice at any stage during cooking or immediately after it has been removed from the heat. This will ensure dry and separate grains every time.

SERVES 4-6

275g/10oz basmati or other long grain rice, washed and soaked in cold water for 30 minutes
1 tsp butter or ghee
½ tsp salt
500ml/18fl oz water

1. Drain the rice thoroughly and put into a saucepan with the water.

2. Bring to the boil, stir in the salt and the butter.

3. Place the lid on the saucepan and simmer: 12 minutes for basmati rice, 15 minutes for other long grain rice.

4. Remove from heat and keep the pot covered for a further 10-12 minutes.

5. Fork through the rice gently before serving. Use a metal serving spoon as wooden ones tend to squash the grains.

TIME Preparation takes 30 minutes, cooking takes 12-15 minutes.

SERVING IDEAS Plain Boiled Rice can be served with any curry. The rice can be garnished with fried onion rings or fresh coriander leaves. Suitable for freezing.

Fried Brown Rice

This is the traditional rice dish which accompanies chicken or meat dhansak. It can also be served with a host of other dishes.

SERVES 4-6

275g/10oz basmati or other long grain rice
4 tbsps cooking oil
4 tsps sugar
1 tsp cumin seeds
2 cinnamon sticks, 2-inches long each, broken up
6 whole cloves
6 black peppercorns
2 bay leaves, crumpled
570ml/20fl oz water
1 tsp salt

1. Wash the rice and soak in cold water for 30 minutes. Drain well.

2. In a heavy-based saucepan, heat the oil over medium heat and add the sugar.

3. The sugar will gradually begin to change colour to a dark brown. As soon as it does, add the cumin seeds, cinnamon, cloves, black peppercorns and bay leaves. Fry for 30 seconds.

4. Add the rice and fry for about 5 minutes, stirring frequently and lowering heat towards the last minute or two.

5. Add the water and salt. Bring to the boil, cover and simmer without lifting the lid: 12-15 minutes for basmati rice, 15-18 minutes for other long grain rice.

6. Remove the pan from heat and keep it undisturbed for a further 10-15 minutes before serving.

TIME Preparation takes a few minutes plus time needed to soak the rice, cooking takes 20-25 minutes.

SERVING IDEAS Serve with Chicken Dhansak, Meat Dilpasand or Kheema Mattar.
Suitable for freezing.

WATCHPOINT If the lid is lifted and the rice is stirred during cooking, the loss of steam will cause the rice to stick and turn soggy. Do not handle the rice immediately after it has been cooked to ensure dry and separate grains.

PILAU RICE

Pilau is usually a beautifully fragrant rice or a combination of rice and meat, poultry, fish or vegetables. It is always cooked in pure butterfat ghee, but unsalted butter is a good substitute.

SERVES 4-6

275g/10oz basmati rice
50g/2oz ghee or unsalted butter
1 large onion, finely sliced
2-4 cloves garlic, peeled and finely chopped
8 whole cloves
8 green cardamoms, split open the top of each pod
2 cinnamon sticks, 2-inches long each, broken up
8 whole peppercorns
1 tsp ground turmeric
570ml/20fl oz water
1¼ tsps salt or to taste
1 heaped tsp butter
25g/1oz seedless sultanas
25g/1oz flaked almonds

1. Wash the rice and soak in cold water for ½ an hour. Drain well.

2. In a heavy-based pan melt the ghee or butter over medium heat and fry onions until they are soft but not brown (about 5 minutes).

3. Add the garlic, cloves, cardamoms, cinnamon sticks and peppercorns. Stir and fry until the onions are golden brown (3-4 minutes).

4. Add the rice and turmeric, stir and fry for 1-2 minutes. Adjust heat to low, stir and fry the rice for a further 2-3 minutes.

5. Add the water and the salt, bring to the boil, cover and simmer for 15 minutes without lifting the lid.

6. Remove the pan from heat and keep it undisturbed for a further 10-12 minutes.

7. Melt the 1 tsp butter over gentle heat and fry sultanas until they change colour and swell up (1 minute). Transfer the sultanas onto a plate and in the same fat fry the almonds until they are lightly browned. Remove and put onto a separate plate.

8. Put the pilau rice into a serving dish and, using a fork, gently mix in the fried sultanas and almonds.

TIME Preparation takes 10 minutes plus time needed to soak the rice, cooking takes 25-30 minutes.

SERVING IDEAS Serve with Chicken Korma, Tandoori Chicken Masala, or Meat Maharaja.
Suitable for freezing.

VARIATION Omit the almonds and use a hard-boiled sliced egg to garnish.

Cardamom Rice

When time may be short to cook a Pilau Rice or when you may feel like having a milder flavoured rice, Cardamom Rice is the answer as it can be served with a whole host of dishes.

SERVES 4-6

175g/10oz basmati or other long grain rice
50g/2oz ghee or unsalted butter
6 green cardamoms; split open the top of each pod
1 tsp black cumin seeds or caraway seeds
1 tsp salt or to taste
500ml/18fl oz water for basmati rice or 600ml/20fl oz for other long grain rice

1. Wash the rice, soak in cold water for ½-1 hour and drain thoroughly.

2. Melt the ghee or butter over low heat and fry cardamom and caraway seeds for 1 minute.

3. Add the rice, stir and fry over medium heat for 2-3 minutes, adjust heat to low, stir and fry for a further 2-3 minutes.

4. Add salt and water and mix well. Bring to the boil, cover the pan and simmer for 12 minutes for basmati rice and 15-18 minutes for other long grain rice without lifting the lid.

5. Remove from heat and keep the pot undisturbed for 6-8 minutes.

TIME Preparation takes 5-10 minutes plus time needed to soak the rice, cooking takes 20-25 minutes.

SERVING IDEAS This rice can be served with almost any Indian dish. Suitable for freezing.

WATCHPOINT Do not lift the lid or stir the rice during cooking. Do not stir immediately after the rice has been cooked.

Carrot Pilau

An imaginative way to turn plain boiled rice, left over or freshly cooked, into a colourful and flavoursome pilau which can be served with meat, fish or chicken curry.

SERVES 4-6

275g/10oz basmati rice, washed and soaked in cold water for ½ hour
500ml/18fl oz water
1 tsp salt or to taste
1 tsp butter or ghee
2 tbsps ghee or unsalted butter
1 tsp cumin or caraway seeds
1 medium-sized onion, finely sliced
2 cinnamon sticks, each 2-inches long, broken up
4 green cardamoms, split open the top of each pod
1 tsp garam masala or ground mixed spice
150g/6oz coarsely grated carrots
100g/4oz frozen garden peas
½ tsp salt or to taste

1. Drain the rice thoroughly and put into a saucepan with the water.

2. Bring to the boil, stir in the salt and the butter.

3. Allow to boil steadily for 1 minute.

4. Place the lid on the saucepan and simmer for 12-15 minutes. Do not lift the lid during this time.

5. Remove the pan from heat and keep it covered for a further 10 minutes.

6. Meanwhile, prepare the rest of the ingredients.

7. Melt the ghee or butter over medium heat and fry cumin or caraway until they crackle.

8. Add the onions, cinnamon and cardamom. Fry until the onions are lightly browned (4-5 minutes), stirring frequently.

9. Add the garam masala or ground mixed spice, stir and cook for 30 seconds.

10. Add the carrots, peas and the salt, stir and cook for 1-2 minutes.

11. Now add the rice, stir and mix gently using a metal spoon or a fork as wooden spoon or spatula will squash the grains. Remove the pan from heat.

TIME Preparation takes 10-15 minutes plus time needed to soak the rice, cooking takes 25-30 minutes.

SERVING IDEAS Serve with Fish Bhoona, Chicken Kohlapuri or Bhoona Gosht. Mint and Onion Raita makes and excellent accompaniment. Suitable for freezing.

MIXED VEGETABLE PILAU

Vegetable lovers will adore this pilau; the rice and the vegetables are cooked together with a selection of spices and their individual flavours blend beautifully.

SERVES 6-8

50g/2oz ghee or unsalted butter
1 large onion, finely sliced
3-4 cloves garlic, peeled and finely chopped

Grind the following 7 ingredients in a coffee grinder
1 tsp black cumin seeds or caraway seeds
1 tsp coriander seeds
6 black peppercorns
1 bay leaf
2 dried red chillies
1 cinnamon stick, 2-inches long; broken up
6 green cardamoms

½ tsp ground turmeric
225g/8oz cauliflower florets, cut into ½-inch pieces
1 small green pepper, white pith removed and cut into 1-inch strips
100g/4oz carrots, scraped and thinly sliced
275g/10oz basmati rice, washed and soaked in cold water for 30 minutes and drained
50g/2oz frozen garden peas or fresh peas boiled until nearly tender
50g/2oz frozen sweetcorn
1½ tsp salt or to taste
570ml/20fl oz water

1. Melt the ghee or butter over medium heat and fry the onions and garlic until the onions are golden brown (6-8 minutes).

2. Add the ground spices and the turmeric and fry for 2 minutes over low heat, stirring frequently.

3. Add the cauliflower, green pepper and carrots, stir and fry for 2-3 minutes.

4. Add the rice and fry for a further 2-3 minutes stirring constantly.

5. Add the peas, sweetcorn and salt, and mix well. Now add the water, bring to the boil, cover the pan and simmer until the rice has absorbed all the water (12-15 minutes). Allow about 18 minutes for other types of long grain rice. Do not lift the lid or stir the rice during cooking.

6. Remove the pan from the heat, uncover and allow steam to escape for 2 minutes. Do not stir the rice immediately after cooking. Cover the pan and keep it undisturbed for 10 minutes before serving.

TIME Preparation takes 30 minutes, cooking takes 25-30 minutes.

SERVING IDEAS Serve with Barrah Kababs, Tandoori Chicken, Nargisi Kababs and a Raita or Chutney.

VARIATION Omit the cauliflower and use 225g/8oz button mushrooms, halved or quartered.

Mattar Pilau

An easy to prepare pilau rice which has an attractive look provided by the rich green colour of the garden peas.

SERVES 4-6

275g/10oz basmati rice
75g/3oz ghee or unsalted butter
2 tsp fennel seeds
2-3 dried red chillies
6 whole cloves
2 cinnamon sticks, 2-inches long each, broken up
6 green cardamoms, split open the top of each pod
2 bay leaves, crumpled
1 large onion, finely sliced
150g/6oz frozen garden peas
1 tsp ground turmeric
1¼ tsps salt or to taste
570ml/20fl oz water

1. Wash the rice and soak it in cold water for half an hour. Drain thoroughly.

2. Melt the butter over medium heat and fry the fennel seeds until they are brown.

3. Add the chillies, cloves, cinnamon, cardamom and bay leaves. Stir once and add the onions. Fry until the onions are lightly browned, stirring frequently.

4. Add the rice, peas, turmeric and salt. Stir and fry until the rice is fairly dry (4-5 minutes), lowering heat towards the last 1-2 minutes.

5. Add the water and bring to the boil. Cover the pan and simmer for 12-15 minutes without lifting the lid. Remove the pan from heat and leave it undisturbed for a further 10-15 minutes.

TIME Preparation takes 10 minutes plus time needed to soak the rice, cooking takes 25-30 minutes.

SERVING IDEAS Serve with Pasanda Badam Curry, Meat Maharaja or Murgh Dilkush.

VARIATION Use 75g/3oz frozen sweet corn and 75g/3oz garden peas.

MUSHROOM PILAU

The delicate flavour of the mushrooms blends happily with the distinctive flavour and aroma of basmati rice and the whole spices used in this pilau. Other long grain rice can be used, but the pilau will not be as fragrant and delicious as basmati rice.

SERVES 4-6

275g/10oz basmati rice
50g/2oz ghee or unsalted butter
1 tsp caraway seeds
1 large onion, finely sliced
2 cinnamon sticks, each 2-inches long; broken up
225g/8oz button mushrooms, thickly sliced
½ tsp ground turmeric
1¼ tsps salt or to taste
500ml/18fl oz water
6 green cardamoms, split open the top of each pod
6 whole cloves
2 bay leaves, crumpled

1. Wash and soak the rice in cold water for 30 minutes. Drain and keep aside.

2. Melt the ghee or butter over medium heat and fry the caraway seeds for 30 seconds.

3. Add the onions and cinnamon sticks, stir and fry until the onions are golden brown (6-8 minutes).

4. Add the rice and fry, stirring constantly, for 3-4 minutes. Add the mushrooms, turmeric and salt, stir and fry for a further 2-3 minutes over low heat.

5. Add the water, cardamoms, cloves and bay leaves; bring to the boil, cover the pan and simmer for 12-15 minutes. Do not lift the lid or stir the rice during cooking.

6. Remove from the heat, uncover and allow steam to escape for 1-2 minutes. Cover the pan and keep aside for 10-15 minutes before serving.

TIME Preparation takes 20-25 minutes plus time needed to soak the rice, cooking takes 25-30 minutes.

SERVING IDEAS Serve with Chicken Korma, Murghi Badami or Meat Maharaja.
Suitable for freezing.

side dishes

GREEN BEANS IN GARLIC BUTTER

Tender green beans, cooked in their own juice, make a mouth-watering accompaniment to any rich meat, fish or poultry dish.

SERVES 4-6

25g/1oz unsalted butter
½ tsp cumin seeds
3-4 cloves garlic, peeled and crushed or finely chopped
¼-½ tsp chilli powder
450g/1lb frozen whole green beans
½ tsp salt or to taste

1. Melt the butter over low heat and fry the cumin seeds for 30 seconds.

2. Add the garlic and fry for 1 minute.

3. Add the chilli powder and immediately follow with the beans. Stir and fry for 1-2 minutes.

4. Add the salt and mix thoroughly. Cover the pan and simmer the beans in their own juice until they are tender (10-12 minutes), stirring occasionally.

5. Remove from the heat.

TIME Preparation takes 5-10 minutes, cooking takes 15 minutes.

SERVING IDEAS Serve with Chicken Korma, Fish Shahjahani, or Murghi Badami.

VARIATION Use cauliflower cut into tiny pieces.

Potatoes with Poppy Seeds

This quick and easy, but thoroughly delicious, potato dish comes from Assam. Serve it as a side dish or as a snack with Puris – simply gorgeous!

SERVES 4-6

5 tbsps cooking oil
½ tsp Kalonji (onion seeds), optional
1 tsp cumin seeds
4-6 cloves garlic, peeled and crushed
1 tsp freshly ground black pepper
½ tsp ground turmeric
700g/1½lbs potatoes, peeled and diced
1 fresh green chilli, finely chopped
6 tbsps white poppy seeds
1 tsp salt or to taste

1. Heat the oil in a non-stick or cast iron pan until smoking. Remove the pan from heat and add the kalonji (if used) and cumin seeds.

2. As soon as the seeds start crackling, add the garlic and place the pan over medium heat.

3. Add the ground black pepper and turmeric, stir briskly and add the potatoes and the green chilli. Fry the potatoes for 2-3 minutes stirring constantly.

4. Reduce heat to low, cover the pan and cook until the potatoes are tender (12-15 minutes), stirring occasionally.

5. Meanwhile, grind the poppy seeds in a coffee grinder into a coarse mixture. Add this to the potatoes, adjust heat to medium and fry the potato and poppy seed mixture for 5-6 minutes, stirring frequently.

6. Stir in the salt and remove the pan from heat.

TIME Preparation takes 10 minutes, cooking takes 20 minutes.

SERVING IDEAS Serve with Puris or Loochis as a snack or make a meal by adding Seekh Kababs and Date Sauce to the menu.

WATCHPOINT Make sure the potatoes are cut into small cubes, if cut into chunky pieces it will be difficult to cook them thoroughly in the specified time.
Use a non-stick or cast iron pan, otherwise the potatoes will stick.

Cauliflower Masala

This dish, with potatoes and peas, is flavoured with a few basic ingredients and the finished dish is semi-dry, making it an ideal accompaniment to rice and curry or Indian bread.

SERVES 4-6

---

1 medium-sized cauliflower
2 medium-sized potatoes
4 tbsps cooking oil
1 tsp cumin seeds
1 large onion
½ tsp ground turmeric
1 tsp ground coriander
1 tsp ground cumin
¼-½ tsp chilli powder
2 ripe tomatoes, skinned and chopped
175ml/6fl oz warm water
100g/4oz shelled peas, fresh or frozen (cook fresh peas until they are tender before using)
1-2 fresh green chillies, seeded and slit lengthwise into halves
1 tsp salt or to taste
½ tsp garam masala
1 tbsp chopped coriander leaves

1. Cut the cauliflower into ½-inch diameter florets – wash and drain.

2. Peel and cut the potatoes lengthwise into thick strips about ½-inch.

3. Heat the oil over medium heat and add the cumin seeds. As soon as they start popping, add the onions and fry until they are soft (about 5 minutes).

4. Turn heat down to low and add the turmeric, coriander, cumin and chilli powder. Stir and fry for 2-3 minutes and add the chopped tomatoes. Fry for a further 2-3 minutes stirring continuously.

5. Add the potatoes and the water. Bring to the boil, cover the pan and simmer until the potatoes are half-cooked.

6. Add the cauliflower, cover the pan again and simmer until the potatoes are tender (about 10 minutes).

7. Stir in the peas, green chillies, salt and garam masala. Cover and cook for 5 minutes.

8. Remove from heat and stir in the coriander leaves.

TIME Preparation takes about 25 minutes, cooking takes 30-35 minutes.

SERVING IDEAS Serve with Kofta Pilau or Plain Boiled Rice accompanied by Meat Madras or Meat Bhoona. Also excellent with Puris or Loochis. Not suitable for freezing as the potatoes will turn mushy when defrosted and cauliflower does not freeze too well once cooked.

VARIATION Cook in 1½oz/45g ghee instead of oil for a richer flavour.

KHUMBI AUR BESAN KI BHAJI

The use of mushrooms is somewhat limited in Indian cooking. However, in the West the abundant supply of mushrooms throughout the year makes it possible to create mouthwatering dishes at any time.

SERVES 4

325g/12oz white mushrooms
2 tbsps cooking oil
2-3 cloves garlic, peeled and crushed
½ tsp salt or to taste
½ tsp chilli powder
2 tbsps finely chopped coriander leaves
1 tbsp lemon juice
2 tbsps besan (gram flour or chick pea flour), sieved

1. Wash the mushrooms and chop them coarsely.

2. Heat the oil over medium heat and add the garlic. Allow garlic to turn slightly brown and add the mushrooms, stir and cook for 2 minutes.

3. Add salt, chilli powder and coriander leaves, stir and cook for 1 minute.

4. Add the lemon juice and mix well.

5. Sprinkle the besan over the mushroom mixture, stir and mix immediately. Remove from heat.

TIME Preparation takes 15 minutes, cooking takes 6-8 minutes.

SERVING IDEAS Serve as a side dish.
Suitable for freezing.

Gobi Aloo

Gobi Aloo, or cauliflower with potatoes, is a classic north Indian dish. The potatoes are first boiled and the cauliflower is blanched. The two are then braised together gently with a few spices to give it a subtle but distinctive flavour.

SERVES 4-6

3 medium-sized potatoes
1 medium-sized cauliflower
5 tbsps cooking oil
½ tsp black mustard seeds
½ tsp cumin seeds
12-15 fenugreek seeds
1-2 dried red chillies, coarsely chopped
1 medium-sized onion, coarsely chopped
1 fresh green chilli, coarsely chopped
½ tsp ground turmeric
½ tsp ground cumin
1 tsp ground coriander
1¼ tsp salt or to taste
1 tbsp chopped coriander leaves (optional)

1. Boil the potatoes in their jacket and allow to cool thoroughly. The potatoes can be boiled and left in the refrigerator for 2-3 days.

2. Peel the potatoes and cut them into 2-inch squares.

3. Blanch the cauliflower in boiling water for 2 minutes, do not over-boil the cauliflower as it should remain firm after cooking. Allow the cauliflower to cool and cut it into ½-inch diameter florets.

4. Heat the oil over medium heat in a wide shallow pan, preferably non-stick or cast iron.

5. Add the mustard seeds, and as soon as they begin to pop, add the cumin and fenugreek seeds and then the red chillies.

6. Add the onions and the green chilli, stir and fry until the onions are golden brown (8-10 minutes).

7. Add the cauliflower, reduce heat to low, cover the pan and cook for 6-8 minutes.

8. Add the potatoes, turmeric, cumin, coriander and salt. Stir gently until all the ingredients are mixed thoroughly. Cover the pan and cook until the potatoes are heated through (6-8 minutes).

9. Stir in the coriander leaves (if used) and remove from the heat.

TIME Preparation takes 25-30 minutes, cooking takes 15-20 minutes.

SERVING IDEAS Serve as an accompaniment to any meat or chicken curry or Chapatties and Rotis. Excellent with Puris or Loochis.

TO FREEZE Freeze before adding the potatoes. Add the potatoes during reheating.

VARIATION Add 100g/4oz frozen garden peas with the cauliflower.

Cauliflower Cutlets

This unusual recipe is an excellent way of using up a cauliflower which is a few days old.

MAKES 10-12 Cutlets

1 small cauliflower
2 medium-sized potatoes
2 tbsps cooking oil plus oil for shallow frying
¼ tsp black mustard seeds
½ tsp cumin seeds
1 large onion, finely chopped
1 fresh green chilli, seeded and finely chopped
1 tsp ground fennel
1 tsp ground coriander
¼-½ tsp chilli powder or cayenne
½ tsp salt or to taste
50g/2oz plain flour
2 tbsps chopped coriander leaves

1. Cook the whole cauliflower in boiling water for 6-8 minutes, drain and cool.

2. Boil the potatoes in their jacket and peel them.

3. Chop the cauliflower coarsely and mash it with the potatoes

4. Heat the 2 tbsps oil over medium heat and fry mustard seeds until they crackle, then add the cumin seeds.

5. Add the onions and green chilli, stir and fry until the onions are soft (4-5 minutes).

6. Adjust heat to low, add the ground fennel, ground coriander, chilli powder or cayenne and salt, stir and cook for 2-3 minutes.

7. Remove the pan from heat and add the potatoes, cauliflower, flour and coriander leaves. Stir and mix thoroughly.

8. Allow the mixture to cool completely, then divide it into 10-12 portions.

9. Form each portion into a cutlet shape and flatten to about one eighth of an inch thickness.

10. Heat the oil over medium heat in a heavy-based frying pan, preferably cast iron or non-stick, and fry the cutlets in a single layer until they are golden brown on both sides.

11. Drain on absorbent paper.

TIME Preparation takes 30-35 minutes, cooking takes 15-20 minutes.

SERVING IDEAS Serving ideas: Serve with a pilau rice such as Nawabi Kheema Pilau, Kofta Pilau and Raita or a vegetable curry. Suitable for freezing.

Mixed Vegetable Bhaji

In this delicious dish all the vegetables are cooked in a tightly covered dish in their own juice until tender, but firm. The dish has no gravy and is a perfect partner for most curries.

SERVES 4

3 tbsps cooking oil
½ tsp black mustard seeds
½ tsp cumin seeds
2-4 dried red chillies, whole
3-4 cloves garlic, peeled and crushed
¼-½ tsp chilli powder
100g/4oz carrots, scraped and cut into match stick strips
100g/4oz French beans or dwarf beans, cut to the same length as the carrots
225g/8oz potatoes, peeled and cut into matchstick strips
100g/4oz finely shredded onions
¾ tsp salt or to taste
15g/½oz fresh coriander leaves, including the tender stalks, finely chopped

1. Heat the oil in a wide shallow pan over medium heat.

2. Add the mustard seeds and as soon as they begin to pop, add the cumin seeds and the red chillies.

3. Add the garlic and chilli powder and immediately follow with all the vegetables and the onions.

4. Add the salt, stir and cook for 2-3 minutes. Cover the pan tightly and reduce heat to minimum setting. Let the vegetables sweat for 20-25 minutes, stirring occasionally.

5. Add the coriander leaves and stir-fry the vegetables over medium heat for 1-2 minutes and remove from the heat.

TIME Preparation takes 25 minutes, cooking takes 30 minutes.

SERVING IDEAS Serve with any meat/chicken/fish curry.

TO FREEZE Suitable for freezing, but as cooked potatoes do not freeze well, they should be omitted. Alternatively, add pre-boiled potatoes during re-heating.

Gobi Mattar (Cabbage with Garden Peas)

A quick and easy side dish to prepare which not only tastes good, but also looks colourful and attractive.

SERVES 4-6

325g/12oz green cabbage
3 tbsps cooking oil
¼ tsp black mustard seeds
½ tsp cumin seeds
10-12 fenugreek seeds (optional)
2-4 dried red chillies, whole
1 small onion, finely sliced
½ tsp ground turmeric
100g/4oz frozen garden peas
¾ tsp salt or to taste
1 tsp ground coriander
¼-½ tsp chilli powder
2 small ripe tomatoes, skinned and chopped
1 tbsp chopped coriander leaves (optional)

1. Shred or chop the cabbage finely.

2. Heat the oil over medium heat and fry the mustard seeds until they pop.

3. Add the cumin seeds followed by the fenugreek (if used), red chillies and the onions. Stir and fry until the onions are soft (about 5 minutes).

4. Stir in the turmeric and add the cabbage. Stir and mix thoroughly.

5. Add the peas and salt, stir and cover the pan. Lower heat to minimum and cook for 5 minutes.

6. Add the ground coriander, the chilli powder and the chopped tomatoes. Stir until it is completely dry.

7. Remove from heat and stir in half the coriander leaves.

8. Put the cabbage into a serving dish and sprinkle the remaining coriander leaves on top (if used).

TIME Preparation takes 15 minutes, cooking takes 10-15 minutes.

SERVING IDEAS Serve as an accompaniment with Meat Madras, Murghi Jhal Frezi or Lamb with Butterbeans.

TO FREEZE Suitable for freezing if pre-boiled fresh peas are used.

ALOO CHOLE

Chick peas are delicious cooked with spices and diced potatoes. They do need prolonged cooking before they are tender. If you have one it is worth cooking them in the pressure cooker which will only take 20 minutes with the 15lbs pressure on.

SERVES 4-6

225g/8oz chick peas, picked over and washed
900ml/30fl oz water
½-inch cube of root ginger, peeled and grated
1 large potato, peeled and cut into 1½-inch cubes
1 tsp ground cumin
½ tsp ground turmeric
¼-½ tsp chilli powder, optional
1-2 fresh green chillies, slit lengthwise into halves; seeded for a milder flavour
25g/1oz ghee or unsalted butter
1 large onion, finely chopped
1¼ tsp salt or to taste
½ tsp garam masala
1 tbsp lemon juice
1 tbsp chopped fresh mint or 1 tsp dried mint

1. Soak the chick peas overnight in plenty of cold water. Rinse several times and drain well.

2. Put the chick peas, water and ginger into a saucepan and place over a high heat, bring to the boil, cover the pan and simmer for 1¼-1½ hours or until the peas are tender. Alternatively, put the peas and the ginger in a pressure cooker and add 450ml/15fl oz water. Bring to the boil, then following the usual method for pressure cooking, cook under pressure for 20 minutes. Stand the pressure cooker aside until pressure is reduced.

3. Add the potatoes, cumin, turmeric, chilli powder and the green chillies, and the mint, if you are using it dried. Bring to the boil again, cover the pan and simmer for a further 15-20 minutes or until the potatoes are tender.

4. Melt the ghee over medium heat and fry the onions until they are lightly browned (6-8 minutes). Stir this into the chick peas along with the salt and garam masala.

5. Remove the pan from heat and stir in the lemon juice and fresh mint.

TIME Preparation takes 10-15 minutes plus time needed to soak the peas, cooking takes 1½-1¾ hours.

SERVING IDEAS Serve with Puris or Loochis or as a side dish with meat/fish/chicken curry. Avoid serving with Mughlai dishes (rich and creamy curries).

TO FREEZE Suitable for freezing, but freeze before adding the potatoes.

Saag Bhaji

Spinach simmered in spices and combined with diced, fried potatoes.

SERVES 4-6

6 tbsps cooking oil
½ tsp black mustard seeds
1 tsp cumin seeds
8-10 fenugreek seeds (optional)
1 tbsp curry leaves
2-3 cloves garlic, peeled and finely chopped
2-4 dried red chillies, coarsely chopped
450g/1lb fresh leaf spinach or 225g/8oz frozen leaf spinach finely chopped
1 tbsp ghee or unsalted butter
1 large potato, peeled and diced
1 large onion, finely sliced
½ tsp ground turmeric
1 tsp ground cumin
½ tsp garam masala
¼-½ tsp chilli powder
2-3 ripe tomatoes, skinned and chopped
1 tsp salt or to taste

1. Heat 2 tbsps oil from the specified amount over medium heat and fry mustard seeds until they pop.

2. Add the cumin seeds, fenugreek (if used) and curry leaves and immediately follow with the garlic and red chillies. Allow garlic to turn slighly brown.

3. Add the spinach, stir and mix thoroughly. Cover and simmer for 15 minutes stirring occasionally.

4. Melt the ghee or butter over medium heat and brown the diced potatoes. Remove from heat and keep aside.

5. Heat the remaining oil over medium heat and fry onions until well browned (about 10 minutes), take care not to burn the onions or they will taste bitter.

6. Adjust heat to minimum and add turmeric, cumin, garam masala and chilli powder, stir and fry for 2-3 minutes.

7. Add the spinach, potatoes, tomatoes and salt, cover and simmer for 10 minutes or until the potatoes are tender, stirring occasionally. Remove from heat.

TIME Preparation takes 25-30 minutes, cooking takes 50 minutes.

SERVING IDEAS Serve with Dahl Gosht and Plain Boiled Rice or Murghi Jhal Frezi and Parathas/Rotis/Chapatties.

TO FREEZE Freeze before adding the potatoes.

Aloo Ki Bhaji

Boiled potatoes, diced and braised with a few whole spices and onions make a quick and easy side dish.

SERVES 4-6

700g/1½lbs potatoes
5-6 tbsps cooking oil
½ tsp black mustard seeds
2-3 dried red chillies
⅛ tsp fenugreek (methi) seeds
225g/8oz onions, finely sliced
1-2 fresh green chillies, sliced lengthwise and seeded if a milder flavour is preferred
1 tsp ground turmeric
1 tsp salt or to taste
25g/1oz chopped coriander leaves

1. Boil the potatoes in their jackets and allow to cool thoroughly. Boiled potatoes can be left for a day or two in the refrigerator.

2. Peel the potatoes and dice them evenly.

3. Heat the oil over medium heat in a wide shallow pan and fry the mustard seeds until they pop.

4. Add the red chillies and the fenugreek seeds; immediately follow with the onions and green chillies.

5. Fry the onions until they are golden brown (8-10 minutes).

6. Add the turmeric, potatoes and salt. Stir and fry gently until the potatoes are heated through (8-10 minutes).

7. Remove from heat and stir in the coriander leaves.

TIME Preparation takes 15-20 minutes plus time needed to boil and cool the potatoes, cooking takes 20 minutes.

SERVING IDEAS Serve with Puris or Loochis to make a substantial snack or as a side dish with rice, chicken or meat curry.

Cabbage with Cinnamon

Cinnamon fried with onions has a rather distinctive and delicious flavour. The dish is not particularly spicy, but this combination gives it a special touch.

SERVES 4-6

4 tbsps cooking oil
1 large onion, finely sliced
2 fresh green chillies, sliced lengthwise; seeds removed if a milder flavour is preferred
3 cinnamon sticks, each 2-inches long; broken up into 2-3 pieces
1 large potato, peeled and cut into 1-inch cubes
½ tsp ground turmeric
¼ tsp chilli powder
125ml/4fl oz warm water
1 small white cabbage, finely shredded
1 tsp salt or to taste
1 tbsp chopped coriander leaves

1. Heat the oil over medium heat and fry the onions, green chillies and cinnamon sticks until the onions are soft (about 5 minutes).

2. Add the potatoes, stir and fry on low heat for 6-8 minutes.

3. Stir in the turmeric and chilli powder.

4. Add the water and bring it to the boil, cover the pan and simmer until the potatoes are half cooked (6-8 minutes).

5. Add the cabbage and salt, stir and mix well. Lower the heat to minimum setting, cover the pan and cook until the vegetables are tender (the cabbage should not be mushy). The finished dish should be fairly moist but not runny. If there is too much liquid left in the pan, take the lid off and let the liquid evaporate.

6. Stir in the coriander leaves and remove the pan from heat.

TIME Preparation takes 25 minutes, cooking takes 25 minutes.

SERVING IDEAS Serve with any Indian bread or rice and Rogan Josh, Bhoona Gosht or Murgh Dilkush.

TO FREEZE If you wish to freeze it, cook the cabbage only and add pre-boiled diced potatoes during reheating.

VARIATION For a colourful look, add 50g/2oz frozen garden peas.

Potatoes with Garlic and Chillies

These are rather like spicy French fries, but they are not deep fried. A perfect alternative to chips or French fries when you want a touch of spice with plain meat, fish or chicken.

SERVES 4-6

450g/1lb potatoes, peeled and washed
3 tbsps cooking oil
½ tsp black mustard seeds
½ tsp cumin seeds
4 cloves garlic, peeled and crushed
¼-½ tsp chilli powder
½ tsp ground turmeric
1 tsp salt or to taste

1. Cut the potatoes to the thickness of French fries, but half their length.

2. In a wide, shallow non-stick or cast iron pan, heat the oil over medium heat.

3. Add the mustard seeds and then the cumin. When the seeds start popping, add the garlic and allow it to turn lightly brown.

4. Remove the pan from the heat and add the chilli powder and turmeric.

5. Add the potatoes and place the pan back on heat. Stir and turn heat up to medium.

6. Add the salt, stir and mix, cover the pan and cook for 3-4 minutes and stir again. Continue to do this until the potatoes are cooked and lightly browned. Remove from the heat.

TIME Preparation takes 15-20 minutes, cooking takes 15 minutes.

SERVING IDEAS Serve with any curry and rice or Chapatties/Rotis.

VARIATION Use cauliflower florets, cut into small pieces.

FRENCH BEAN & POTATO BHAJI

Sliced French beans and potatoes are braised together with a mixture of whole and powdered spices to make this quick side dish. A saucepan or frying pan with a tight-fitting lid enables the vegetables to cook in their own juice, producing a wonderful flavour.

SERVES 4-6

4-5 tbsps cooking oil
½ tsp black mustard seeds
½ tsp cumin seeds
1 large onion, finely sliced
3-4 dried red chillies, coarsely chopped
10-12 fenugreek seeds
15g/½oz coriander leaves, finely chopped
½ tsp ground turmeric
1 large potato, peeled and cut into matchstick strips
275g/10oz French beans, sliced
1 tsp salt or to taste
1 tsp ground cumin

1. Heat the oil over medium heat and add the mustard seeds. As soon as the seeds pop, add the cumin seeds, then the onions, red chillies and fenugreek. Fry the ingredients for 3-4 minutes, stirring frequently.

2. Add the coriander leaves and turmeric, stir and fry for 1 minute.

3. Add the potatoes, beans and salt. Stir until the ingredients are mixed thoroughly. Cover the pan and cook on lowest setting until the vegetables are tender (about 25 minutes), stirring occasionally.

4. Add the ground cumin, stir and cook for 2-3 minutes and remove from the heat.

TIME Preparation takes 15 minutes, cooking takes 30 minutes.

SERVING IDEAS Serve with Chicken Do-Piaza, Meat Vindaloo or Fish Bhoona.

Kashmiri Dum Aloo

This is a lovely way to serve new potatoes. The potatoes are boiled, then fried until they are golden brown, and finally simmered gently in natural yogurt and spices.

SERVES 4

550g/1¼lbs small new potatoes
2 tbsps ghee or unsalted butter
1 tsp fennel seeds

Mix the following 5 ingredients in a small bowl
½ tsp ground cumin
1 tsp ground coriander
¼ tsp freshly ground black pepper
½ tsp ground turmeric
½ tsp ground ginger

125g/5oz thick set natural yogurt
1 tsp salt or to taste
¼ tsp garam masala
1 tbsp chopped coriander leaves
1 fresh green chilli, seeded and finely chopped

1. Boil the potatoes in their jackets, cool and peel them. Prick the potatoes all over with a tooth pick to enable the spices to penetrate deep inside.

2. Melt the ghee over medium heat in a non-stick or cast iron pan (steel or enamel pans will cause the potatoes to stick and break up).

3. When the ghee is hot, fry the potatoes in a single layer until they are well browned (8-10 minutes), turning them over frequently. Remove them with a slotted spoon and set aside.

4. Remove the pan from the heat and stir in the fennel seeds followed by the spice mixture. Adjust heat to low and place the pan back on the heat, stir the spices and fry for 1 minute.

5. Add the yogurt and salt, and mix well. Add the potatoes, cover the pan and simmer for 10-12 minutes. Add the garam masala and remove the pan from the heat.

6. Stir in the coriander leaves and the green chilli.

TIME Preparation takes 30-35 minutes including boiling the potatoes, cooking takes 20-25 minutes.

SERVING IDEAS Serve as a side dish with Chicken Korma, Meat Maharaja or Murghi Badami.

Spiced Green Beans

Sliced green beans are braised with a few spices, then tossed in roasted, ground sesame seeds to create the unique flavour of this dish.

SERVES 4-6

2 tbsps sesame seeds
3 tbsps cooking oil
¼ tsp black mustard seeds
4-6 cloves garlic, peeled and finely chopped
1-2 dried red chillies, coarsely chopped
½ tsp ground turmeric
1 tsp ground coriander
450g/1lb frozen sliced green beans, defrosted and drained
¾ tsp salt or to taste
1 tbsp desiccated coconut

1. Heat an iron griddle or other heavy-based pan over medium heat and dry-roast the sesame seeds until they are lightly browned, stirring constantly. Transfer them to a plate and allow to cool.

2. Heat the oil over medium heat and add the mustard seeds. When they begin to pop, add the garlic and allow it to turn slightly brown.

3. Add the red chillies, turmeric and coriander, stir briskly and add the beans and salt. Mix thoroughly, lower heat to minimum setting, cover the pan tightly and cook until the beans are tender (15-20 minutes), stirring occasionally.

4. Grind the sesame seeds and the coconut in a coffee grinder and stir into the beans. Remove the pan from the heat.

TIME Preparation takes 10-15 minutes, cooking takes 25-30 minutes

SERVING IDEAS Serve with Chicken Tikka Masala, Murgh Musallam or Shahi Korma.

Bhindi (Okra) with Coconut

A quick and delicious way to cook okra. Roasted and ground poppy and sesame seeds with coconut coat the okra and add a very special flavour.

SERVES 4

225g/8oz bhindi (okra)
2 tbsps sesame seeds
1 tbsp white poppy seeds
1-2 dried red chillies
2 tbsps desiccated coconut
1 fresh green chilli, coarsely chopped
3 tbsps cooking oil
½ tsp black mustard seeds
¼ tsp fenugreek seeds
2 cloves garlic, peeled and finely chopped or crushed
½ tsp salt or to taste

1. Wash the bhindi, trim off head and cut each bhindi into two pieces.

2. Heat an iron griddle or other heavy-based pan over medium heat and dry-roast the sesame and poppy seeds until they are lightly browned. Transfer the seeds to a plate and allow them to cool.

3. Reheat the griddle and dry-roast the coconut until the coconut is lightly browned, stirring constantly. Transfer the coconut to a plate and allow it to cool.

4. Put the sesame and poppy seeds and the dried red chillies in a coffee grinder and switch on; when half done, add the coconut and the green chilli and grind until smooth.

5. Heat the oil over medium heat and add the mustard seeds, as soon as the seeds pop add the fenugreek followed by the garlic. Allow garlic to turn slightly brown and add the bhindi and salt; stir and mix thoroughly. Lower heat to the minimum setting, cover the pan and cook for about 10 minutes, stirring occasionally.

6. Stir in the ground ingredients and mix well. Remove from the heat.

TIME Preparation takes 15-20 minutes, cooking takes 12-15 minutes.

SERVING IDEAS Serve with Shahi Korma or Murghi Badami.

Aloo Mattar

In India, unlike in the west, potatoes are not eaten instead of rice, but as well as rice. The recipe below is a semi-moist dish which blends easily with meat, chicken or fish curries.

SERVES 4-6

4 tbsps cooking oil
1 medium-sized onion, finely chopped
2 cinnamon sticks, each 2-inches long, broken up
½-inch cube of root ginger, peeled and finely chopped
½ tsp ground turmeric
2 tsps ground cumin
¼ tsp chilli powder
¼ tsp freshly ground black pepper
450g/1lb potatoes, peeled and cut into 1-inch cubes
1-2 whole fresh green chillies
1 tbsp tomato purée
1 tsp salt or to taste
225ml/8fl oz warm water
100g/4oz frozen garden peas
1 tbsp chopped coriander leaves (optional)

1. Heat the oil over medium heat and fry the onion, cinnamon and ginger for 4-5 minutes, stirring frequently.

2. Reduce heat to low and add the turmeric, cumin, chilli powder and black pepper. Stir and fry for one minute.

3. Add the potatoes and the green chillies, stir and cook until the spices are blended thoroughly (2-3 minutes).

4. Stir in the tomato purée and salt.

5. Add the water, bring to the boil, cover the pan and cook over medium to low heat until the potatoes are half cooked (about 10 minutes).

6. Add the peas, cover the pan and cook until the potatoes are tender.

7. Remove the pan from the heat, stir in half the coriander leaves (if used) and sprinkle the remainder on top.

TIME Preparation takes 10-15 minutes, cooking takes 25-30 minutes.

SERVING IDEAS Serve with Puris or Loochis or with rice and any meat, fish or chicken curry.

Cabbage with Gram Flour

A truly delicious and very quick dish to prepare which is a distinctive feature of the Saraswat style of cooking.

SERVES 4-6

4 tbsps cooking oil
½ tsp black mustard seeds
½ tsp cumin seeds
8-10 fenugreek seeds
3-4 cloves garlic, peeled and crushed
Pinch of asaphoetida (optional)
1 medium-sized onion, finely shredded
¼ tsp ground turmeric
½ tsp chilli powder
275-325g/10-12oz white cabbage, finely shredded
1 tsp salt or to taste
55ml/2fl oz water
2 heaped tbsps besan (gram flour or chick pea flour), sieved

1. Heat the oil in a wide shallow pan over medium heat and fry mustard seeds until they pop.

2. Add the cumin seeds followed by the fenugreek.

3. Stir in the garlic and allow it to turn slightly brown

4. Add the asaphoetida (if used) and immediately follow with the onions, turmeric and chilli powder. Stir and fry for 1-2 minutes.

5. Add the cabbage and salt, stir and mix thoroughly. Reduce heat to low, cover the pan and cook for 8-10 minutes, stirring occasionally. The cabbage should be tender but firm.

6. Sprinkle the water evenly on the cabbage, then sprinkle the besan and cook for 1-2 minutes stirring continuously. Remove from heat.

TIME Preparation takes 10-15 minutes, cooking takes 15 minutes.

SERVING IDEAS Serve as an accompaniment to any meat, fish or chicken curry, but avoid serving with Mughlai dishes (rich and creamy curries).

VARIATION Omit the onion and use half green cabbage and half leek.

Bhindi (Okra) Masala

Okra is available from Indian grocers and most good supermarkets. Some greengrocers also sell okra nowadays.
For this recipe, choose the small tender ones, scrub each one gently and wash thoroughly.

SERVES 4

225g/8oz bhindi (okra)
2 tbsps cooking oil
1 tsp ground coriander
¼ tsp ground cumin
¼ tsp ground turmeric
Small tin of tomatoes
¼ tsp chilli powder
½ tsp salt or to taste
1 tbsp chopped coriander leaves

---

1. Scrub each bhindi gently, wash them and slice off the tops.

2. Heat the oil over medium heat in wide shallow pan. When hot, remove the pan from the heat and add the ground coriander, cumin, garam masala and turmeric. The pan is removed from the heat so as not to burn the spices.

3. Place the pan back on the heat and add the tomatoes and the chilli powder. Stir and cook for 2-3 minutes.

4. Add the whole bhindis and the salt. Stir and cover the pan. Lower heat to the minimum setting and cook for about 10 minutes. Stir once or twice during this time. When cooked, the bhindi should be tender but firm.

5. Put the bhindi onto a serving dish and sprinkle the coriander leaves on top.

TIME Preparation takes 10 minutes, cooking takes 12-15 minutes.

SERVING IDEAS Serve with Bhoona Gosht, Fish Bhoona or Chicken Kohlapuri.

AUBERGINE BHARTA

Bharta is a puréed or mashed vegetable which is flavoured with spices. Aubergine Bharta is traditionally made by roasting the aubergine over charcoal or burnt-down ashes of wood fire. For the recipe below, however, the aubergine has been grilled.

SERVES 4

---

1 large aubergine (450g/1lb)
4 tbsps cooking oil
½ tsp black mustard seeds
½ tsp fennel seeds
1-inch cube of root ginger, peeled and grated
2-3 cloves garlic, peeled and crushed
1 fresh green chilli, finely chopped
1 large onion, finely chopped
½ tsp ground turmeric
¼-½ tsp chilli powder (optional)
2 small ripe tomatoes, skinned and chopped
1 tsp salt or to taste
1 small tomato, sliced
15g/½oz fresh coriander leaves, finely chopped

---

1. Wash the aubergine and make 2-3 small incisions on it. This is to prevent the aubergine from bursting during cooking.

2. Preheat the grill to medium and cook the aubergine for 12-15 minutes or until tender to the touch. Turn it frequently during cooking. Remove the aubergine and allow it to cool.

3. Cut the aubergine lengthwise into two. Scrap the flesh off gently with a knife. Discard the skin.

4. Purée the flesh or mash it with a fork. Heat the oil over medium heat and add the mustard seeds; as soon as they begin to pop add the fennel seeds, then the ginger, garlic and green chilli. Stir fry the ingredients for 1 minute then add the onions. Stir and fry the onions until they are just soft.

5. Stir in the turmeric and chilli powder.

6. Add the tomatoes, stir and cook for 2 minutes.

7. Add the aubergine and salt, and stir and cook for 2-3 minutes.

8. Stir in half the coriander leaves and remove the pan from heat.

9. Put the aubergine in a serving dish and garnish with the sliced tomatoes. Sprinkle the remaining coriander leaves on top.

TIME Preparation takes 10-15 minutes, cooking takes 30-35 minutes.

SERVING IDEAS Serve with Chicken Pilau, Kofta Pilau or Chicken Do-Piaza, Bhoona Gosht, and rice.
Suitable for freezing.

Tarka Dhal (Spiced Lentils)

Dhal of some sort is always cooked as part of a meal in an Indian household. As a vast majority of the Indian population is vegetarian, dhal is a good source of protein.

SERVES 4

150g/6oz Masoor dhal (red split lentils)
750ml/1¼ pint water
1 tsp ground turmeric
1 tsp ground cumin
1 tsp salt or to taste
25g/1oz ghee or unsalted butter
1 medium-sized onion, finely chopped
2 cloves garlic, peeled and finely chopped
2 dried red chillies, coarsely chopped

1. Put the dhal, water, turmeric, cumin and salt into a saucepan and bring the liquid to the boil.

2. Reduce heat to medium and cook uncovered for 8-10 minutes, stirring frequently.

3. Now cover the pan and simmer for 30 minutes, stirring occasionally.

4. Remove the dhal from the heat, allow to cool slightly and mash through a sieve.

5. Melt the ghee or butter over medium heat and fry the onion, garlic and red chillies until the onions are well browned (8-10 minutes).

6. Stir in half the fried onion mixture to the dhal and put the dhal in a serving dish. Arrange the remaining fried onions on top.

TIME Preparation takes about 10 minutes, cooking takes about 50 minutes.

SERVING IDEAS Serve with Plain Boiled Rice and Murghi Jhal Frezi.

WATCHPOINT Pulses tend to froth and spill over. The initial cooking without the lid in stage 2 should help to eliminate this problem, but should you find that it is spilling over, then partially cover the pan until the froth settles down; this should take only a few minutes.

Spicy Channa Dhal

This is a speciality of the north-eastern region of India. In Assam and Bengal this dhal is invariably served during weddings and other special gatherings. Channa dhal is available from Indian grocers, but if it is difficult to get, yellow split peas can be used.

SERVES 4-6

225g/8oz channa dhal or yellow split peas
40g/1½oz ghee or unsalted butter
1 large onion, finely sliced
2 cinnamon sticks, each 2-inch long, broken up into 2-3 pieces
6 green cardamoms, split open the top of each pod
2-4 dried red chillies, coarsely chopped
½ tsp ground turmeric
¼-½ tsp chilli powder
1¼ tsps salt or to taste
600ml/20fl oz warm water
2 bay leaves, crumpled
40g/1½oz desiccated coconut
2 ripe tomatoes, skinned and chopped
2 tbsps chopped coriander leaves (optional)

1. Clean and wash the channa dahl or the yellow split peas and soak them for at least 2 hours. Drain well.

2. Melt the ghee or butter over medium heat and fry the onions, cinnamon, cardamom and red chillies until the onions are lightly browned (6-7 minutes).

3. Add the dhal, turmeric, chilli powder and salt. Stir-fry the dhal for 2-3 minutes. Adjust heat to low and fry the dhal for a further 3-4 minutes, stirring frequently.

4. Add the water, bay leaves, coconut and tomatoes. Bring to the boil, cover the pan and simmer for 35-40 minutes.

5. Stir in the coriander leaves (if used) and remove from the heat.

TIME Preparation takes 5-10 minutes plus time needed to soak the dhal, cooking takes 50-55 minutes.

SERVING IDEAS Serve with rice or any Indian bread and Masala Machchi, Kababs or Chicken Chaat.
Suitable for freezing.

Saagwalla Dhal

Spinach and skinless split moong dhal complement each other extremely well. The dish is easy to make and full of essential nutrients. Moong dhal is sold by Indian grocers, but if you cannot get it, use yellow split peas.

SERVES 6-8

170g/6oz skinless split moong dhal or yellow split peas
2 heaped tbsps ghee or unsalted butter
1 large onion, finely sliced
1 fresh green chilli, sliced lengthwise, seeded for a milder flavour
2 cinnamon sticks, 2-inch long each; broken up into 2-3 pieces
½ tsp ground turmeric
½ tsp garam masala
¼ tsp chilli powder
1 tsp salt or to taste
1 tsp ground cumin
2 ripe tomatoes, skinned and chopped
570ml/20fl oz warm water
2 tbsps cooking oil
½ tsp black mustard seeds
2-3 cloves garlic, peeled and finely chopped
1-2 dried red chillies, coarsely chopped
100g/4oz frozen leaf spinach, defrosted and finely chopped or 275g/10oz fresh spinach; hard stalks removed and finely chopped

1. Wash and soak the dhal for 1½-2 hours and drain well.

2. Melt the ghee or butter over medium heat in a non-stick or cast iron pan and fry the onions, green chilli and cinnamon until the onions are lightly browned (6-8 minutes).

3. Add the turmeric and garam masala, stir and mix well.

4. Add the dhal, chilli powder and salt, stir and fry for 8-10 minutes over low heat.

5. Add the cumin and tomato, stir and cook for 3-4 minutes.

6. Add the water, bring to the boil, cover and simmer for 30-35 minutes, stirring occasionally.

7. Meanwhile, heat the oil over medium heat and fry the mustard seeds until they pop.

8. Add the garlic and allow it to turn slightly brown.

9. Add the dried red chillies and then the spinach, stir and mix thoroughly. Cover the pan and simmer for 5 minutes.

10. Add the spinach to the dhal, cover and cook over low heat for 10 minutes, stirring occasionally. Remove the pan from heat.

TIME Preparation takes 10-15 minutes plus time needed to soak the dhal, cooking takes 1 hour 10 minutes.

SERVING IDEAS Serve with rice or Parathas/Rotis. Kababs, Tandoori Chicken and Murghi Jhal Frezi are perfect to complement the meal. Suitable for freezing.

VARIATION Use chunky cauliflower florets instead of the spinach which can be added without the preparation necessary for spinach.

CARROT & COCONUT SALAD

Grated carrots and desiccated coconut make a simple but appetizing salad.

SERVES 4-6

225g/8oz carrots
2 tbsps desiccated coconut
25g/1oz finely shredded onion
1 tbsp lemon juice
2 tbsps chopped coriander leaves
1 fresh green chilli, seeded and coarsely chopped (optional)
½ tsp salt or to taste

1. Peel and grate the carrots.

2. Combine all the ingredients in a bowl except salt.

3. Stir in the salt just before serving.

TIME Preparation takes 10 minutes.

SERVING IDEAS Serve with Kheema Mattar, Meat Vindaloo or Bhoona Gosht.

VARIATION Add 1 tbsp finely chopped fresh mint.

Cabbage & Mint Salad

An unusual touch is given to this salad by the bottled mint and natural yogurt used to coat the ingredients.

SERVES 4-6

275-325g/10-12oz white cabbage
1 small onion, finely chopped
1 fresh green chilli, finely chopped and seeded if a milder flavour is preferred
2-3 tbsps thick set natural yogurt
2 tsps mint sauce
½ tsp salt or to taste

1. Grate the cabbage (use the coarse side of a cheese grater or food processor) and put it into a large mixing bowl.

2. Add the rest of the ingredients and mix thoroughly.

3. Put the salad into a serving dish, cover and chill before serving.

TIME Preparation takes 10 minutes.

SERVING IDEAS Serve with Meat or Chicken Biriani, or rice and curry such as Kofta Curry, Chicken Kohlapuri or Chicken Do Piaza.

Tomato & Cucumber Salad

This salad, with its combination of cucumber, tomato and roasted peanuts makes a mouthwatering side dish.

SERVES 4-6

½ a cucumber
2 tomatoes
1 bunch spring onions, coarsely chopped
1 tbsp lemon juice
1 tbsp olive oil
¼ tsp salt
¼ tsp freshly ground black pepper
1 tbsp chopped coriander leaves
25g/1oz roasted salted peanuts, crushed

1. Peel the cucumber and chop finely.

2. Chop the tomatoes finely.

3. Put cucumber, tomatoes and spring onions into a serving bowl.

4. Combine the lemon juice, olive oil, salt, pepper and coriander leaves and keep aside.

5. Just before serving, stir in the peanuts and the dressing.

TIME Preparation takes 10 minutes.

SERVING IDEAS Serve with any meat, fish, chicken or vegetable curry.

VARIATION Omit the lemon juice and use 3 tbsps natural yogurt.

Carrot & Mooli Salad

This salad has a nutty flavour which is imparted by the mustard seeds fried in hot oil. Mooli is sold in Asian stores and is also available at some green-grocers and supermarkets.

SERVES 4-6

1 tbsp cooking oil
½ tsp black mustard seeds
½ tsp cumin seeds
100g/4oz carrots, peeled and coarsely grated
225g/8oz mooli, peeled and coarsely grated
½ tsp salt
2-3 tbsps finely chopped onion
1 tbsp lemon juice
1 tbsp finely chopped coriander leaves

1. Heat the oil over medium heat and fry the mustard seeds until they pop, add the cumin and remove from heat.

2. Add the grated carrots and mooli and allow to cool.

3. Stir in the salt, onion, lemon juice and coriander leaves before serving.

TIME Preparation takes 15 minutes, cooking takes 5 minutes.

SERVING IDEAS Serve as a side dish with any curry and rice. Avoid serving with rich and creamy curries.

Potato Raita

Raitas normally involve no cooking, but this is one of the few where the potatoes are first cooked in a hot oil and spice mixture, then cooled and mixed with natural yogurt.

SERVES 4-6

2 tbsps cooking oil
¼ tsp fennel seeds
1 clove garlic, peeled and finely chopped
225g/8oz potatoes, peeled and diced
½ tsp ground cumin
½ tsp salt or to taste
125g/5oz natural yogurt
½ tsp sugar
¼ tsp chilli powder or paprika

1. Heat the oil over medium heat and fry the fennel seeds until they are brown.

2. Add the garlic and allow it to turn slightly brown.

3. Add the potatoes and stir and mix. Cover the pan and cook until the potatoes are tender and brown, stirring frequently.

4. Stir in the cumin and salt, mix thoroughly and remove from heat. Allow to cool completely.

5. Beat the yogurt and sugar until smooth. Add the spiced potatoes along with any oil/spice mixture that remains in the pan. Stir and mix well.

6. Put the raita in a serving dish and sprinkle the chilli powder or paprika on top.

TIME Preparation takes 10-15 minutes, cooking takes 10-15 minutes.

SERVING IDEAS Can be served with all types of curry, either chilled or at room temperature.

CUCUMBER RAITA

This raita is rather cooling and the aroma of the roasted cumin seeds is very appetizing.

SERVES 4-6

1 small cucumber
1 tsp cumin seeds
125g/5oz thick set natural yogurt
¼ tsp salt
¼ tsp paprika

1. Peel the cucumber and cut lengthwise into two halves. Slice each half finely.

2. Heat a small pan over low heat and dry roast the cumin seeds until they turn a shade darker. Allow the seeds to cool, then crush them with a rolling pin or pestle and mortar.

3. Beat the yogurt until smooth. Stir in the cumin along with the salt.

4. Reserve a few slices of cucumber for garnish and add the rest to the yogurt – mix thoroughly.

5. Put the raita into a serving dish and arrange the reserved cucumber on top.

6. Sprinkle the paprika evenly on the sliced cucumber.

TIME Preparation takes 15 minutes.

SERVING IDEAS Serve with Meat Vindaloo or Chicken Kohlapuri.

VARIATION Add half cucumber and half finely sliced radish.

Bhindi (Okra) Raita

Crisp fried okra coated with natural yogurt and flavoured with a hot oil seasoning.

SERVES 6-8

Oil for deep frying
225g/8oz bhindi (okra), cut into about one-eighth of an inch rounds
½ tsp salt or to taste
1 fresh green chilli, seeded and coarsely chopped
125g/5oz thick set natural yogurt
½ tsp powdered mustard
1 tbsp cooking oil
½ tsp black mustard seeds
1 tbsp curry leaves

1. Deep fry the bhindi in an electric fryer or a chip pan until they are well browned and crisp. Drain on absorbent paper. Allow to cool completely.

2. Add the salt to the green chilli and crush to a pulp.

3. Beat the yogurt with a fork until smooth, add the powdered mustard and green chilli mixture, stir and mix well.

4. Gently stir in the fried bhindi.

5. Heat the 1 tbsp oil in a small pan and fry the mustard seeds until they crackle, then add the curry leaves and fry for 15-20 seconds.

6. Remove the pan from heat and stir the seasoned oil into the bhindi raita along with all the seasonings.

TIME Preparation takes 15 minutes, cooking takes 5-6 minutes.

SERVING IDEAS Serve with Kheema Palak, Kofta Pilau or Meat Biriani.

Mint & Onion Raita

Raw onions are frequently served with an Indian meal – on their own or occasionally in a yogurt-based dressing.

SERVES 4-6

125g/5oz thick set natural yogurt
1 small onion, finely chopped
1 tbsp chopped fresh mint or 1 tsp bottled garden mint with ½ tsp sugar
1 fresh green chilli, seeded and chopped
¼ tsp paprika
½ tsp salt or to taste

1. Beat the yogurt until smooth.

2. Add the rest of the ingredients, except paprika, and beat again.

3. Put the raita into a serving dish and sprinkle the paprika on top.

TIME Preparation takes 10 minutes.

SERVING IDEAS Serve with Meat Biriani, Mixed Vegetable Pilau or Aubergine Pilau.

VARIATION Add a few finely sliced radish.

CARROT & PEANUT RAITA

A very tasty and easy to prepare side dish which has a high nutritional value.

SERVES 4-6

2 carrots
50g/2oz roasted salted peanuts
1 small clove of garlic, peeled and coarsely chopped
1 fresh green chilli, seeded and coarsely chopped
¼ tsp salt or to taste
125g/5oz thick set natural yogurt
½ tsp sugar
1 tbsp finely chopped coriander leaves (optional)

1. Peel and grate the carrots coarsely.

2. Crush peanuts with a wooden pestle or rolling pin.

3. Mix garlic, chilli and salt and crush to a pulp.

4. Beat the yogurt until smooth and stir in the garlic mixture.

5. Add the carrots, peanuts, sugar and coriander leaves (if using) and mix thoroughly.

TIME Preparation takes 10-15 minutes.

SERVING IDEAS This raita complements almost any meal and can be served as a relish with Kababs or Pakoras.

Cucumber and Onion Raita

Raitas and salads are an integral part of an Indian meal. This raita is particularly easy to make and the roasted cumin seeds add a special flavour.

SERVES 4-6

1 tsp cumin seeds
125g/5oz natural yogurt
3 tbsps finely chopped onions
½ a cucumber, peeled and finely chopped
½ tsp salt or to taste

1. Heat a cast iron or other heavy-based pan and dry-roast the cumin seeds until they release their aroma. Allow to cool and crush them lightly.

2. Beat the yogurt with a fork until smooth, add the rest of the ingredients and half the crushed cumin seeds. Mix thoroughly.

3. Put the raita in a serving dish and sprinkle the remaining cumin seeds on top.

TIME Preparation takes 10-15 minutes.

SERVING IDEAS Serve with any curry, especially suitable to serve with Meat Vindaloo and Meat Madras.

AUBERGINE RAITA

For this recipe, the aubergine is traditionally cooked over charcoal or burnt-down ashes of a wood fire. If you are having a barbecue, then by all means, cook the aubergine on the coals. For the recipe below, grilled aubergine has been used.

SERVES 6-8

1 aubergine (325g/12oz)
½ tsp salt or to taste
½-inch cube of root ginger, peeled and coarsely chopped
1 fresh green chilli, coarsely chopped and seeded for a milder flavour
125g/5oz thick set natural yogurt
2-3 tbsps finely chopped onions
2 tbsps chopped coriander leaves

1. Make one or two small incisions in the aubergine to prevent it from bursting during cooking.

2. Preheat grill to medium. Grill whole aubergine for 10 minutes, turning it over once. Allow to cool completely.

3. Add the salt to the ginger and green chilli and crush them to a pulp.

4. Slit the aubergine lengthwise into two halves and scoop out the flesh. Chop the flesh finely or mash it.

5. Beat the yogurt until smooth. Add ginger/chilli/salt mixture. Stir and mix well. Add the aubergine and mix thoroughly.

6. Stir in the onions and half the coriander leaves just before serving. Garnish with the remaining coriander leaves.

TIME Preparation takes 10 minutes, cooking takes 10 minutes.

SERVING IDEAS Serve with Chicken Biriani, Murgh Dilkush or Chicken Do Piaza.

WATCHPOINT It is important to preheat the grill and cook the aubergine for the specified time. If the aubergine is not well cooked, it will be difficult to scoop out the flesh.

Onion Relish

Raw onions with chillies and lemon juice, often accompany an Indian meal. The flavour of raw onions can be rather strong; if you prefer a milder flavour, wash the chopped onions in cold water and drain them first.

SERVES 4-6

225g/8oz onions, finely chopped
1 fresh green chilli, seeded and minced
1 tbsp fresh mint, minced
1 tbsp fresh coriander leaves, minced
½ tsp salt or to taste
1 tbsp lemon juice

1. Mix all the ingredients together except salt.

2. Stir in the salt just before serving.

TIME Preparation takes 10-15 minutes.

SERVING IDEAS Serve with all types of Kababs, Biriani or Tandoori Chicken, and with rice and meat or chicken curry.

Apple Chutney

A mouthwatering relish with a sweet and sour, slightly hot flavour. Cooking apples are first tossed in a few spices and cooked until they are almost pulpy.

SERVES 8-10

1 tbsp cooking oil
½ tsp black mustard seeds
¼ tsp fenugreek seeds
¼ tsp ground turmeric
Pinch of asaphoetida
2 large cooking apples, peeled and finely chopped
½-¾ tsp chilli powder
1½ tsps salt or to taste
3 tbsps soft light brown sugar

1. Heat the oil over medium heat and fry the mustard seeds until they pop.

2. Add the fenugreek, turmeric and asaphoetida and immediately follow with the apples. Stir and mix thoroughly.

3. Add the chilli powder, salt and sugar, stir and cook until the apple starts secreting juice.

4. Cover and simmer until the apple is tender (5-6 minutes), stirring frequently.

5. Allow the chutney to cool and store in a moisture-free air-tight or screw-top jar. It can then be stored in the refrigerator for 4-6 weeks.

TIME Preparation takes 10 minutes, cooking takes 10 minutes.

SERVING IDEAS Serve with almost all snacks and starters.

Avocado Chutney

Avocado and cottage cheese are combined with a few selected fresh ingredients to make a mouthwatering dish.

SERVES 6-8

1 ripe avocado
Juice of half a lemon
50g/2oz plain cottage cheese
1 clove garlic, peeled and chopped
2 tbsps chopped coriander leaves
1 fresh green chilli, chopped and seeded if a milder flavour is preferred
½ tsp salt or to taste

1. Cut the avocado lengthwise into two and remove the stone. Scoop out the flesh.

2. Put the lemon juice in an electric blender or food processor and add the avocado along with the rest of the ingredients. Blend until smooth, add a little water if necessary, to facilitate blade movement in the blender.

TIME Preparation takes 5-10 minutes.

SERVING IDEAS Serve as a dip with Kababs, Samosas and Pakoras.

Green Coriander Chutney

The wonderful flavour of fresh coriander leaves makes this coconut-based chutney a mouthwatering accompaniment to fried, grilled or roasted dishes.

SERVES 6-8

175ml/6fl oz water
25g/1oz desiccated coconut
1-2 fresh green chillies, chopped and seeded if a milder flavour is preferred
1-2 cloves garlic, peeled and coarsely chopped
½-inch cube of root ginger, peeled and coarsely chopped
25g/1oz fresh coriander leaves, coarsely chopped
½ tsp salt or to taste
1 tbsp lemon juice

1. Bring the water to the boil, remove from heat and soak the coconut in it for 10-15 minutes.

2. Put all the ingredients in an electric blender and blend until smooth. Allow to cool completely.

TIME Preparation takes 10-15 minutes.

SERVING IDEAS Serve with Onion Bhajiyas, Pakoras of any type, Samosas or Hussaini Kababs.

Cumin-Coriander Chutney

The prominent flavour in this chutney is cumin, though equal quantities of cumin and coriander are used. Cumin has a stronger flavour than coriander and the mild and mellow coconut base in the chutney sets off the flavour beautifully.

SERVES 4-6

1 tsp cumin seeds
1 tsp coriander seeds
2-3 dried red chillies
4 tbsps desiccated coconut
55ml/2fl oz water
½ tsp salt or to taste
1½ tbsps lemon juice
2-3 tbsps finely chopped onions

1. Grind the cumin, coriander, red chillies and the coconut in a coffee grinder until the ingredients are smooth.

2. Transfer the ingredients to a bowl and add the water, salt and lemon juice. Mix thoroughly.

3. Stir in the onions.

TIME Preparation takes 10 minutes.

SERVING IDEAS Can be served with almost all fried snacks, Parathas or Rotis, or with rice and any meat, fish or vegetable curry. Suitable for freezing.

VARIATION Use ½ tsp tamarind concentrate dissolved in a little hot water instead of the lemon juice.

MINT & ONION CHUTNEY

This is a delicious relish which will keep well in the refrigerator for 3-4 weeks, provided no moisture is allowed to get in.

SERVES 6-8

2 tbsps cooking oil
1 large onion, coarsely chopped
15g/½oz fresh mint
1 fresh green chilli, seeded if a milder flavour is preferred
1 tbsp lemon juice
½ tsp salt or to taste

1. Heat the oil over medium heat and fry the onions until they are soft but not brown. Allow to cool.

2. Put the onions and the rest of the ingredients in an electric liquidiser and blend until smooth.

3. Put into a moisture-free airtight container or screw-top jar and refridgerate.

TIME Preparation takes 10 minutes, cooking takes 5 minutes.

SERVING IDEAS Serve with all types of snacks.

Date Sauce

A delicious relish with the sweet & sour taste of dates, raisins and tamarind. Tamarind is available from Indian grocers, dried or in ready-to-use form. The latter variety is called tamarind concentrate and is more convenient to use than the dried variety.

SERVES 6-8

50g/2oz stoned dates
15g/½oz seedless raisins
1 tsp ground cumin
1 tsp chilli powder
1 heaped tsp tamarind concentrate or 3 tbsps lemon juice
125ml/4fl oz cold water
¾ tsp salt or to taste
1 tsp soft brown sugar

1. Put all the ingredients in an electric blender and add half the water. Switch on blender and when the ingredients are half ground add the remaining water and blend until fairly smooth.

2. Pour the sauce into a sieve and push it through with a metal spoon until a dry and coarse mixture is left in the sieve – discard this mixture and transfer the sauce to a serving bowl.

TIME Preparation takes 10 minutes.

SERVING IDEAS Serve with Seekh Kababs, Boti Kababs, all types of Pakoras and fried snacks.
Suitable for freezing.

drinks and desserts

Nimbu Pani

Nimbu Pani, or lemon flavoured water is a very refreshing drink for the hot weather or indeed to accompany a spicy meal. The sugar and salt used in the drink are helpful in replacing the energy and natural salt content of the body lost through perspiration.

SERVES 4

570ml/20fl oz water
2 tbsps caster sugar
1 tsp salt
The juice of 1 lemon
Crushed ice
4 slices of lemon

1. Put the sugar and salt in the water and stir until dissolved.

2. Stir in the lemon juice.

3. Put the crushed ice into individual glasses and strain the nimbu pani into the glasses.

4. Top with the sliced lemon.

TIME Preparation takes 5-10 minutes.

Jeera Pani

Jeera Pani (cumin water) has been a popular appetizer from time immemorial. Cumin is noted for its digestive properties.

SERVES 4

2 tbsps cumin seeds
570ml/20fl oz water
2-3 dried red chillies
15g/½oz mint leaves, chopped or
 1 tsp dried mint
1 tsp salt
1 tsp sugar
1 tbsp lemon juice

1. Heat a cast iron or other heavy-based pan and dry-roast the cumin seeds until they are a shade darker, and crush them lightly.

2. Put the water in a saucepan and bring it to the boil.

3. Add the cumin, chillies, mint, salt and sugar.

4. Cover the pan and simmer for 15 minutes.

5. Stir in the lemon juice and remove from heat. Allow the drink to cool, then strain into individual glasses.

TIME Preparation takes a few minutes plus cooling the seeds, cooking takes 15 minutes.

SERVING IDEAS Serve as an appetiser or during meals. Can be served at room temperature or chilled.

Rasam

Rasam is a very popular drink in southern Indian, where it is usually made by boiling a small quantity of lentils in a large volume of spice-flavoured water. It is then enhanced with a hot oil seasoning.

SERVES 4-6

850ml/30fl oz water
50g/2oz masoor dhal (red split lentils), washed and drained
1 tsp coriander seeds
1 tsp cumin seeds
2 dried red chillies
6-8 curry leaves
1 tsp salt or to taste
1 level tsp tamarind concentrate or 1 tbsp lemon juice
1 tsp paprika
1 tbsp cooking oil
½ tsp black mustard seeds

1. Put the water, dhal, coriander, cumin, chillies and curry leaves into a saucepan and bring to the boil. Reduce heat to medium and cook, uncovered, for 6-8 minutes.

2. Cover the pan and simmer for 30 minutes. Remove from heat and allow it to cool slightly.

3. Strain the liquid and sieve the dhal into it. Return the pan to heat and add the tamarind or lemon juice, salt and paprika. Stir until the tamarind is dissolved.

4. Heat the oil and add the mustard seeds. As soon as the seeds crackle, pour the rasam into it or stir the hot oil and the seeds into the rasam. Remove from heat.

TIME Preparation takes 5-10 minutes, cooking takes 35-40 minutes.

SERVING IDEAS Serve as an appetizer or during meals.

Spicy Pineapple Punch

A lovely drink to welcome your guests; serve it warm before lunch, especially at Christmas time, or enjoy it chilled with your barbecue during the long, warm summer evenings.

SERVES 6-8

450ml/15fl oz water
1 litre/36fl oz carton of pineapple juice
5 cinnamon sticks, each 2-inches long; broken up
12 whole cloves
12 green cardamoms, bruised
15g/½oz fresh mint leaves, chopped
175ml/6fl oz brandy

1. Put the water, half the pineapple juice, cinnamon, cloves, cardamom and mint into a saucepan. Bring to the boil, cover the pan and simmer gently for 20 minutes.

2. Remove from the heat and allow to cool. Keep the pan covered.

3. Strain the drink and add the remaining pineapple juice and the brandy. Mix well.

TIME Preparation takes 5 minutes, cooking takes 20-25 minutes.

Spiced Tea

Spiced tea has quite a few variations and is popular in colder regions such as Kashmir, as the ingredients are helpful in creating body heat.

SERVES 2

450ml/15fl oz water
6 whole cloves
6 green cardamoms, bruised
1 cinnamon stick, 2-inches long; broken up
3 tsps tea leaves or 2 tea bags
Milk and sugar to taste

1. Put the water in a saucepan and bring it to the boil.

2. Add the spices, cover the pan and simmer for 10 minutes.

3. Rinse a teapot with hot water and put in the tea leaves or the tea bags.

4. Bring the spiced liquid to the boil again and strain it into the teapot. Brew for 5 minutes and serve with milk and sugar to taste.

TIME Preparation takes 10-15 minutes.

SERVING IDEAS Serve during or after meals.

Mango Sherbet

Mango Sherbet is a delicious and nourishing drink. The quantities used here make a thick sherbet which can be thinned down by adding more milk or water as desired.

MAKES 2 pints

1 × 450g/1lb can of mango pulp
or 2 × 425g/15oz cans of sliced mangoes, drained
570ml/20fl oz milk
4 tbsps caster sugar
1 tsp ground cardamom
1 tbsp rosewater (optional)
300ml/10fl oz cold water

1. Put the mango pulp or slices, half the milk, sugar, cardamom and rosewater into an electric liquidiser or food processor and switch on for a few seconds.

2. Transfer the contents into a large jug or bowl and add the remaining milk and the water.

3. Chill for 2-3 hours.

TIME Preparation takes a few minutes.

SERVING IDEAS Serve during meals or at a barbecue.

VARIATION Omit the milk and use all water. Top the drink with a scoop of vanilla ice cream.

Sweet Saffron Rice

This rice is served as a dessert and is cooked in exactly the same way as a pilau rice; the only difference is that sugar is used instead of salt.

SERVES 8-10

225g/8oz basmati rice
550ml/18fl oz hot water
1 cinnamon stick, 2-inches long, broken into two pieces
4 whole cloves
¼ tsp saffron strands
40g/1½oz ghee or unsalted butter
1 tsp ground cardamom
¼ tsp ground nutmeg
100g/4oz caster sugar
50g/2oz raw cashews, split into halves
40g/1½oz seedless raisins or sultanas

1. Wash the rice and soak it in cold water for 30 minutes; drain thoroughly.

2. Put the water, cinnamon, cloves and saffron in a jug or bowl, cover and heat on high for 3½ minutes or until boiling. Cover and stand aside for 15 minutes.

3. Preheat a microwave browning dish on high for 4-5 minutes. Melt the ghee or butter in the dish on high for 30 seconds. Add the rice and 'fry' on high for 5-6 minutes or until it begins to look fairly dry. Stir frequently during this time.

4. Add the cardamom and nutmeg, stir and mix well. Remove from heat.

5. Put the rice into a 5-pint casserole or basin and add the sugar and the spiced liquid; stir and mix until sugar is dissolved.

6. Stir in the cashews and the raisins or sultanas. Cover with cling film and puncture the film.

7. Cook on high for 10 minutes, then on medium for 2 minutes. Stand for 6-8 minutes.

8. Fork through the rice, remove cinnamon and cloves and serve.

TIME Preparation takes 30 minutes to soak the rice, cooking takes 20 minutes.

COOK'S TIP If you do not have a browning dish use the conventional cooker – melt the ghee or butter over medium heat and fry the rice for 3-4 minutes or until it begins to look fairly dry.
Suitable for freezing.

Kulfi (Indian Ice Cream)

Kulfi is by far the most popular ice cream in India. It is firmer than conventional ice cream and is usually set in small tin or aluminium moulds. You can, however, use either small yogurt pots or a plastic ice cream box.

SERVES 6-8

150ml/5fl oz fresh milk
2 tbsps ground rice
1 tbsp ground almonds
450ml/14½oz tin evaporated milk
1 level tsp ground cardamom
50g/2oz sugar
450ml/15fl oz double cream
1 tbsp rose water or 5-6 drops of any other flavouring such as vanilla, almond etc.
25g/1oz shelled, unsalted pistachio nuts, lightly crushed

1. Heat the milk until it is lukewarm.

2. Put the ground rice and ground almonds into a small bowl and gradually add the warm milk, a little at a time, and make a thin paste of pouring consistency. Stir continuously and break up any lumps, if any lumps remain, sieve the paste.

3. Heat evaporated milk to boiling point and add the ground cardamom.

4. Take the pan off the heat and gradually add the almond/rice mixture, stirring continuously.

5. Add the sugar and cream and place the pan over medium heat, cook the mixture for 12-15 minutes, stirring continuously. Remove the pan from heat and allow the mixture to cool slightly.

6. Add the rosewater flavouring and half of the pistachio nuts, stir and mix well. Allow the mixture to cool completely, stirring frequently to prevent a skin from forming on the surface.

7. When the mixture has cooled completely, put it into a plastic ice cream box or individual moulds.

8. Top with the remaining pistachio nuts and place in the freezer or in the ice-making compartment of a refrigerator for 4-5 hours.

9. Place the kulfi in the refrigerator for 1½-1 ¾ hours before serving. This will soften the kulfi slightly and will make it easier to cut into desired size when it is set in an ice cream box. The time required to soften the kulfi will vary according to the size of the container used.

TIME Preparation takes 10 minutes, cooking takes 15-20 minutes.

Coconut Stuffed Pancakes

Coconut is used for both sweet and savoury dishes in southern India. There is no substitute for freshly grated coconut, but as it is quite time consuming, desiccated coconut is a good compromise.

MAKES 6 pancakes

For the filling

50g/2oz desiccated coconut
50g/2oz soft dark brown sugar
25g/1oz walnut pieces, lightly crushed
1 small tin evaporated milk
1 tsp ground cardamom

1. Mix all ingredients, except ground cardamom, in a small saucepan and place over medium heat. As soon as it begins to bubble, reduce heat to low and let it simmer without a lid for 8-10 minutes stirring occasionally.

2. Stir in the ground cardamom, remove the pan from heat and allow the mixture to cool.

For the pancakes

2 eggs
150g/6oz wholemeal flour
1 tsp ground cinnamon
1 tbsp caster sugar
200ml/7fl oz milk
Ghee or unsalted butter for frying

1. Put all ingredients, except ghee or butter, in a large bowl and beat with a wire beater until smooth. This batter can also be prepared in a liquidiser or food processor.

2. Place a non-stick or cast iron frying pan over low heat, when hot, spread a little (about ¼ tsp) ghee or butter on it.

3. Pour about 2 tbsps of the batter in the pan and spread it quickly by tilting the pan. Pouring off the batter must be done quickly in one go to prevent it from setting before you have a chance to spread it. It is easier to measure each 2 tbsps into a cup or a small bowl before pouring into the pan.

4. In a minute or so, the pancake will set, let it cook for a further minute, then carefully turn it over with a thin spatula or toss it! Cook the other side for about 1 minute (brown spots should appear on both sides).

5. Spread 1 tbsp of the stuffing on one side of the pancake and roll it into a cylinder shape. Make the rest of the pancakes the same way.

TIME Preparation takes 15-20 minutes, cooking takes 50 minutes.

SERVING IDEAS Serve on their own as a tea-time snack or topped with a little whipped cream as a dessert.

WATCHPOINT Use a wide, thin spatula to turn the pancakes; wooden spatulas are too thick and they will squash the pancakes. Steel or plastic slotted spatulas are ideal.

Durbari Malpura

A great delicacy from the courts of the Mughal Emperors, these small pancakes are smothered with dried fruits and nuts and cream, and delicately flavoured with nutmeg and orange rind.

SERVES 6

75g/3oz plain flour
25g/1oz ground rice
50g/2oz caster sugar
1 tsp ground or finely grated nutmeg
Pinch of bicarbonate of soda
Finely grated rind of 1 orange
25g/1oz each of raw cashews and walnuts, lightly crushed
125ml/4fl oz full cream milk
Oil for deep frying
1 tsp butter
25g/1oz sultanas
25g/1oz flaked almonds
300ml/10fl oz single cream
1 tbsp rose water

1. Put the flour, ground rice, sugar, nutmeg, soda bicarbonate, orange rind and the crushed nuts into bowl.

2. Add the milk and stir until a thick batter is formed.

3. Heat the oil over medium heat in a deep frying pan.

4. Put in 1 heaped teaspoon of the batter at a time until the whole pan is filled with a single layer.

5. When the malpuras (spoonfuls of batter) start floating to the surface, turn them over. Fry gently until golden brown on both sides (about 5 minutes). Drain on absorbent paper.

6. Melt the butter over low heat and fry the sultanas for 1 minute. Remove them with a slotted spoon and drain on absorbent paper.

7. In the same fat, fry the almonds until they are lightly browned. Drain on absorbent paper.

8. Put the cream in a saucepan, large enough to hold all the malpuras and bring to a slow simmer.

9. Put in the malpuras and stir gently.

10. Turn the entire contents of the pan onto a serving dish and sprinkle the rosewater evenly on top.

11. Garnish with the fried sultanas and the almonds. Serve hot or cold.

TIME Preparation takes 10 minutes, cooking takes 20 minutes.

VARIATION Use lemon rind instead of orange.

Vermicelli Kheer

In this popular pudding, the vermicelli is first lightly fried in ghee, then simmered gently in milk with sugar and spices to make a rich and creamy dish.

SERVES 6-8

2 tbsps ghee or unsalted butter
25g/1oz plain vermicelli
25g/1oz sultanas
25g/1oz almonds, blanched and slivered
570ml/20fl oz full cream milk
50g/2oz sugar
1 tbsp ground almonds
½ tsp ground cardamom
½ tsp ground cinnamon
1 tbsp rose water or 5-6 drops of other flavourings such as vanilla or almond

1. Melt the ghee or butter over low heat and add the vermicelli, sultanas and slivered almonds. Stir and fry until the vermicelli is golden brown (2-3 minutes).

2. Add the milk, sugar and ground almonds, bring to the boil and simmer gently for 20 minutes, stirring frequently.

3. Stir in the ground cardamom and cinnamon and remove the pan from heat.

4. Allow the kheer to cool slightly and stir in the rose water or other flavouring.

TIME Preparation takes 10 minutes, cooking takes 20-25 minutes.

SERVING IDEAS Serve hot or cold.

Firni (Creamed Ground Rice with Dried Fruit and Nuts)

Although firni is basically a rice pudding, it is a far cry from the western creamed rice or rice pudding. Firni is rich, delicious and temptingly aromatic.

SERVES 6-8

300ml/10fl oz fresh milk
45g/1½oz ground rice
1 tbsp ground almonds
500g/14oz tin of evaporated milk
50g/2oz sugar
1 tbsp rosewater
1 tsp ground cardamom
25g/1oz flaked almonds
25g/1oz pistachio nuts, lightly crushed
25g/1oz dried apricot, finely chopped

1. Put the fresh milk into a heavy-based saucepan over a medium heat.

2. Mix the ground rice and ground almonds together and sprinkle evenly over the milk. Bring the milk to the boil, stirring frequently.

3. Add the evaporated milk and sugar, stir and cook over a low heat for 6-8 minutes.

4. Remove from heat and allow the mixture to cool – stirring occasionally to prevent skin from forming on top.

5. Stir in the rosewater and the ground cardamom.

6. Reserve a few almonds, pistachios and apricots and stir the remainder into the pudding.

7. Transfer the firni into a serving dish and top with the reserved fruit and nuts. Serve hot or cold.

TIME Preparation takes 5-10 minutes, cooking takes about 15 minutes.

VARIATION Add a few raw cashews (coarsely chopped) while cooking the ground rice and ground almonds.

Sweet Vermicelli

A quick and easy sweet dish which is a speciality of the Muslims. This dish is equivalent to Christmas cake or pudding as it is always made during the Muslim religious festival "Idd Ul Fitr".

SERVES 6

100g/4oz plain vermicelli
50g/2oz sugar
25g/1oz raw cashew nuts, split or coarsely chopped
25g/1oz blanched almonds, split whole or coarsely chopped or flaked almonds
25g/1oz sultanas
4 green cardamoms, split open the top of each pod
½ tsp ground cardamom
½ tsp ground nutmeg
300ml/10fl oz water
50g/2oz ghee or unsalted butter

1. Break the vermicelli into small portions.

2. Melt ½oz ghee or butter over low heat and fry the sultanas until they swell up. Remove the pan from heat and transfer the sultanas to another plate with a slotted spoon.

3. Place the pan back on the heat, add all the nuts and stir and fry until the nuts turn slightly brown. Transfer them with a slotted spoon to another dish.

4. Return the pan to heat and add the remaining ghee or butter and adjust heat to medium. Add the whole cardamom and fry for 30 seconds.

5. Add the vermicelli and fry until it turns a rich golden colour (about 5 minutes), stirring constantly.

6. Remove the pan from heat, add the sultanas, half the fried nuts, ground cardamom and ground nutmeg and stir rapidly.

7. Return the pan to heat and add the water and sugar. Bring to the boil, cover the pan and simmer for 5 minutes.

8. Take the lid off, adjust heat to medium and cook the vermicelli for 2-3 minutes or until the liquid dries up, stirring constantly.

9. Remove from heat and serve hot or cold.

10. If serving cold, using a fork, separate the vermicelli strands as they will stick together when cold.

11. Garnish with the remaining fried nuts.

TIME Preparation takes 25-30 minutes, cooking takes 20 minutes.

SERVING IDEAS Serve as a dessert or with tea and coffee.

SPICED MANGO FOOL

In India, mango is considered to be the king of all fruits. The taste of this tropical fruit, which grows extensively in India, is simply delicious.

SERVES 6-8

2 tbsps milk
¼ tsp saffron strands
170g/6oz evaporated milk
50g/2oz sugar
1 level tbsp fine semolina
2 heaped tbsps ground almonds
1 tsp ground cardamom
450g/1lb mango pulp or 2 x 425g/15oz tins of mangoes, drained and puréed
250g/9oz unflavoured fromage frais

1. Put the milk into a small saucepan and bring to the boil. Stir in the saffron strands, remove from the heat, cover the pan and keep aside.

2. Put the evaporated milk and sugar into a saucepan and place it over a low heat.

3. When it begins to bubble, sprinkle the semolina over, stir until well blended.

4. Now add the ground almonds, stir and cook until the mixture thickens (5-6 minutes).

5. Stir in the ground cardamom and remove from heat. Allow this to cool completely, then gradually beat in the mango pulp, making sure there are no lumps.

6. In a large mixing bowl beat the fromage frais with a fork, gradually beat in the evaporated milk and mango mixture.

7. Stir in the saffron milk along with all the strands as these will continue to impart their colour and flavour into the mango pulp. Mix well.

8. Put the mango pulp into a serving dish and chill for 2-3 hours.

TIME Preparation takes 10 minutes, cooking takes 10-15 minutes.

VARIATION Top the dessert with a few strawberries for an attractive look.

Melon Balls in Mango Pulp

After an Indian meal, a light and refreshing dessert makes a nice change.

SERVES 6

1 × 450g/1lb can of mango pulp or 2 × 425g/15oz cans of sliced mangoes
1 medium-sized galia, honeydew or rock melon
Finely grated rind of 1 lemon
2 tbsps caster sugar
2 tbsps cornflour
½ tsp ground nutmeg
150ml/5fl oz double cream

1. Drain the canned mangoes and purée them in an electric blender, or push through a sieve.

2. Using a melon baller make as many balls as possible out of the melon. Scoop out the remaining flesh and put into an electric blender or food processor along with all the juice and blend to a purée.

3. Transfer the purée into a saucepan and add the lemon rind and sugar.

4. Blend the cornflour with a little water and add to the melon purée. Cook over low heat until the mixture thickens. Stir in the nutmeg and remove from heat.

5. Allow the mixture to cool slightly, then mix thoroughly with the mango pulp.

6. Whip the cream until thick, then stir into the mango mixture.

7. Put the melon and mango mixture into a flan dish and arrange the melon balls in 3-4 rows around the entire diameter.

8. Chill for 2-3 hours before serving.

TIME Preparation takes 15-20 minutes plus cooling time, cooking takes 5-10 minutes.
Suitable for freezing.

Mango Delight

If your purse allows it, fresh, ripe mangoes are superb for this dessert. After slicing them, gently scrape off every bit of flesh next to the stones. Though they will not be in neat pieces, they will add a lot to the flavour when mixed with the custard-cream base used for this dish.

SERVES 4-6

2 fresh ripe mangoes or 2 × 425g/15oz tins of sliced mangoes
2 tbsps custard powder
2 tbsps sugar
150ml/5fl oz milk
1 tsp ground cardamom or ground mixed spice
150ml/5fl oz double cream
2 tbsps shelled unsalted pistachio nuts, lightly crushed

1. Drain one tin of the mango slices and purée them in an electric liquidiser or food processor. Now drain the other can and coarsely chop the mango slices. Peel, slice and chop fresh mangoes.

2. Mix custard powder and sugar together, gradually add the milk and blend well. Cook over low heat until the consistency resembles whipped cream.

3. Stir in the ground cardamom or mixed spice and remove from heat.

4. Gradually add the mango pulp to the custard mix, stirring all the time.

5. Whisk the cream until fairly thick, but still pouring consistency. If you buy extra thick double cream, there is no need to whisk it.

6. Stir the cream into the mango mixture and gently mix in the chopped mangoes.

7. Transfer the mango mixture into a serving bowl and top with the crushed pistachio nuts. Serve hot or cold.

TIME Preparation takes 10 minutes, cooking takes 10 minutes.

SHRIKAND

Shrikand is a delicious and creamy dessert which is made of strained yogurt. The yogurt is tied and hung until all the water content has drained off, the result being a thick and creamy yogurt which is rich but delicious.

SERVES 6

3 × 425g/15oz cartons of thick set natural yogurt
¼ tsp saffron strands
1 tbsp hot water
75g/3oz caster sugar
1 heaped tbsp ground almonds
½ tsp ground cardamom
¼ tsp grated or ground nutmeg

1. Pour the yogurt onto a clean, very fine muslin cloth; bring together the four corners of the cloth so that the yogurt is held in the middle. Tie the four corners into a tight knot and hang the muslin over the sink until all the water content has been drained off; 4-6 hours or undisturbed overnight.

2. Add the saffron strands to the hot water, cover and keep aside.

3. Untie the muslin cloth carefully and empty the contents into a mixing bowl. Beat the strained yogurt with a fork, or a wire beater, until smooth.

4. Add the sugar, beat and mix thoroughly. Add the ground almonds, cardamom and the nutmeg and mix well.

5. Stir in the saffron strands and the water in which it was soaked.

6. Chill before serving.

TIME Preparation takes a few minutes plus time needed to drain the yogurt.

VARIATION Top the Shrikand with mandarin orange segments, sliced mangoes or chopped pistachio nuts.

Spiced Fruit Salad

A novel deviation from traditional Indian desserts, but an excellent one to round off an Indian meal. Handle the tinned mango slices very carefully as they tend to be far too soft. Use fresh mangoes instead if you have a friendly bank manager!

SERVES 6-8

425g/15oz tin pineapple chunks
425g/15oz tin papaya (paw paw) chunks
425g/15oz tin mango slices, cut into chunks
425g/15oz tin guava halves, cut into chunks
3 cinnamon sticks, each 2-inches long
3 black cardamoms
6 whole cloves
8 black peppercorns

1. Drain all the fruits and reserve the syrup. Mix all the syrup together, reserve 570ml/20fl oz and drain off remainder.

2. Put the syrup into a saucepan and add the spices, bring to the boil, cover the pan and let it simmer for 20 minutes.

3. Uncover and reduce the syrup to half its original volume by boiling for 5-6 minutes. Remove from heat and allow the syrup to cool.

4. Keep the pan covered until the syrup cools, (in an open pan some of the flavour will be lost).

5. Reserve a few pieces of papaya and guava and all the mangoes. Arrange the remaining fruits in a serving bowl.

6. Arrange the mangoes on top, then put in the reserved papaya and guava.

7. Strain the spiced syrup and pour over the fruits. Cover with cling film and chill.

TIME Preparation takes 10-15 minutes, cooking takes 20 minutes.

VARIATION Use fresh ripe William pear instead of tinned mango. Add 1 tbsp of brandy to the syrup.

SEMOLINA AND ALMOND HALVA

A quick and easy to prepare dessert which is also delicious and filling.

SERVES 6-8

100g/4oz ghee or unsalted butter
100g/4oz fine semolina
100g/4oz ground almonds
100g/4oz sugar
½ tsp ground nutmeg
300ml/10fl oz full cream milk
25g/1oz raw cashews, chopped

1. Grease a large plate and keep aside.

2. Melt the ghee or butter over low heat in a heavy-based pan.

3. Add the semolina and cook until golden brown (6-7 minutes) stirring continuously.

4. Add the almonds, sugar and the nutmeg, stir and mix thoroughly.

5. Add the milk and mix, stirring until the mixture thickens and stops sticking to the bottom and sides of the pan.

6. Put the mixture onto the greased plate and spread it evenly to about ½-inch thickness; use the back of a lightly greased metal spoon to do this. Using a knife, press the sides inwards to form a large square.

7. Sprinkle the chopped cashews evenly on top and press them in gently with the palm of your hand.

8. Allow the mixture to cool and cut into 1-inch squares.

TIME Preparation takes 5 minutes, cooking takes 15 minutes.

SERVING IDEAS Serve as a dessert or as a tea time snack.

VARIATION Omit the ground almonds and use 225g/8oz semolina.

Wheat Fudge

This fudge is made of wholemeal flour which is very fine – atta or chapatti flour is ideal for this recipe. The flour is gently roasted with a generous amount of ghee or butter until the wonderful aroma of the roasted wheat is released.

SERVES 10-12

100g/4oz ghee or unsalted butter
225g/8oz fine textured wholemeal flour
1½ tsps ground cardamom
25g/1oz chopped mixed nuts
100g/4oz light brown sugar

1. Melt the ghee over medium heat and add the flour, stir and mix thoroughly. Cook for 5 minutes, stirring continuously. Adjust heat to low and cook for a further 10-12 minutes stirring continuously.

2. Add the cardamom and chopped nuts, stir and cook for 2-3 minutes.

3. Remove from heat and add the sugar, stir and mix. If there are any lumps, break them up with the back of the spoon.

4. Lightly grease a large plate and spread the flour mixture on it. Using the back of a metal spoon, spread the mixture evenly and form a large square, about ½-inch thick, 6-inches wide and 8-inches long. Allow the mixture to cool, then chill for 20 minutes.

5. Remove from refrigerator and cut into 1½-2-inch squares. Allow to harden before serving. Store in an open container or plate in the refrigerator. They will keep for 3-4 weeks.

TIME Preparation takes 5 minutes, cooking takes 15-18 minutes.

SERVING IDEAS Serve with tea or as a treat with after dinner coffee.

Besan Ladoo

Besan Ladoos are made of roasted besan and like Wheat Fudge, they need constant attention in the first 15 minutes or so. These ladoos have a delicious nutty taste and they really do melt in the mouth!

MAKES 28-30

225g/8oz ghee or unsalted butter
450g/1lb besan, sieved
225g/8oz sugar
1½ tsps ground cardamom
50g/2oz chopped mixed nuts

1. Melt the ghee or butter over medium heat and add the besan. Reduce heat to low and fry the besan for 12-15 minutes stirring continuously.

2. Add the rest of the ingredients, mix thoroughly and remove from heat.

3. Allow the mixture to cool completely and form into small walnut-sized balls.

4. Store in an airtight container, where they will remain fresh for 4-5 weeks.

TIME Preparation takes 5 minutes, cooking takes 12-15 minutes plus cooling and forming the balls.

SERVING IDEAS Try them with morning coffee instead of biscuits or serve with after-dinner coffee or tea.

Stuffed Lychees

Lychees grow abundantly in India and the fruit is normally eaten on its own, when ripe. In this recipe you can use tinned fruit to produce this delicious and refreshing dish.

SERVES 4-6

2 × 425g/15oz cans lychees, sweetened
1 fresh mango or 425g/15oz canned sliced mangoes
2 tbsps cornflour
2 tbsps lemon juice
The finely grated rind of 1 lemon
150ml/5fl oz double cream
1 heaped tbsp ground almonds
A few drops of yellow food colouring (optional)
Roasted flaked almonds to decorate (optional)

1. Drain the lychees and the mangoes and reserve 175ml/6fl oz lychee and 125ml/4floz mango syrup. Mix the syrups together and keep aside. If using fresh mango, reserve all the juice from the lychees and make up to 300ml/10fl oz by adding cold water.

2. Put the cornflour into a saucepan and add a little syrup to make a smooth paste. Gradually add the rest of the syrup and mix thoroughly.

3. Add the lemon rind and juice and cook over low heat until the mixture thickens. Allow to cool.

4. Beat the cream until thick, and stir into the cornflour mixture along with the food colouring. Add the ground almonds and mix well.

5. Remove any broken lychees, chop them finely and mix with the cornflour mixture. Reserve whole lychees.

6. Chop the mango slices coarsely.

7. Stuff each whole lychee with chopped mangoes in such a way that the mango stands about ¼-inch high on each lychee.

8. Mix any remaining mango pieces or pulp with the cornflour mixture.

9. Line a 10-inch flan dish with the cornflour mixture and arrange the lychees on top (the cornflour mixture will line a smaller dish rather thickly and therefore cause the lychees to sink).

10. Chill before serving.

TIME Preparation takes 20-25 minutes.

SERVING IDEAS As it is light and refreshing, it will round off any Indian meal extremely well.

VARIATION Use fresh strawberries instead of mangoes.

glossary

The following glossary of terms is intended to help all Indian cookery enthusiasts to understand the behaviour of each individual spice and the effect it has on the flavour of a dish when used not only on its own, but also in combination with other spices.

Ajowan or Carum Seeds (*Ajwain*) Ajowan is closely related to caraway and cumin and is used in many savoury dishes. Its flavour is similar to that of thyme. It is used in Indian cooking both for its flavour and its medicinal value. Ajowan seeds are often boiled in a little water and the resulting liquid is drunk to settle stomach ailments.

Allspice (*Kabab Cheene*) Jamaica practically has a monopoly over the supply of allspice to the rest of the world but, although allspice is native to the West Indies, it is now grown in many other tropical countries.

Allspice is not a combination of different spices, but is produced from the dried berries of the Jamaican pimento which has a flavour and aroma similar to that of cardamom, cinnamon and nutmeg. It is not a traditional ingredient in Indian cooking, but has come to be used in many pilau, biriani and Mughlai meat and poultry dishes.

Aniseed or Fennel Seed (*Sonf or Saunf*) Aniseed or fennel can safely be substituted one for the other, as they have a similar flavour. Aniseed is similar to cumin seeds but are rather a dull greyish colour. They have a sweetish liquorice-like flavour and are used widely in Bengal and Kashmir.

The fennel plant is native to the Mediterranean, though it has been cultivated in India since Ancient times. Both aniseed and fennel seeds are either gently fried or ground with other spices. They are also often chewed at the end of a meal as an aid to digestion and as a breath sweetener.

Asafoetida (*Hing*) This is obtained from the resinous gum of a tropical plant which is closely related to the fennel family. It can be bought from Indian grocers in solid pieces or in powder form.

Asafoetida is used very sparingly because of its very strong flavour. It has quite a powerful smell, but when fried in minute quantities in hot oil with other spices, it imparts a certain distinctive flavour which is an integral part of the strict vegetarian diet of the Brahmins. It is never used in recipes for meat and poultry dishes.

Bay Leaf (*Tej Patta*) The bay leaf is not traditional to Indian cooking. It is a common mistranslation, for Western bay leaves are quite different from *tej patta,* which are the tender leaves obtained from the Cassia tree and which have a flavour similar to cinnamon. In the West, bay leaves, obtained from the sweet bay laurel, are more easily available and have become a popular substitute.

Indian bay leaves can be crumbled easily to blend with other spices. Western bay leaves are brighter in appearance and are always whole. They also have a stronger flavour than Indian bay leaves.

Black Pepper (*Kali Mirchi*) Black pepper comes from the pepper vines grown in the tropical forests of monsoon Asia. The berries are picked when they are green, and then dried in the sun to give us the familiar black pepper. Pepper loses its flavour rapidly and so it is always advisable to buy whole peppercorns and grind them in a pepper mill as and when required. Preground pepper does nothing to enhance the flavour of a dish.

Caraway Seeds (*Shahjeera*) Caraway seed is closely related to cumin, but has a milder flavour. Unlike cumin, caraway does not dominate the flavour of the dish in which it is used. The flavour of caraway blends easily with meat. Sometimes the seeds are used to flavour the oil before cooking vegetables, pulses, pilaus and birianis.

Cardamom (*Elaichi*) The cardamom plant is a perennial of the ginger family and grows abundantly in southern India. The ripe cardamom seed pods are dried in the sun before being sold commercially.

There are two varieties of cardamom pods: large dark brown, almost black, ones, known as *Badi Elaichi* and small green ones referred to as *Choti Elaichi.* The dark brown variety is used in certain curries, pilaus and birianis and the inner seeds are often used for making garam masala. The small green variety is used in most curries, pilaus and some sweet dishes. When a recipe calls for whole cardamom, the pods should always be opened up slightly to extract the full flavour of the cardamom, for it is the seeds that have the maximum flavour. The same method can also be used in judging the quality of cardamoms. Good quality cardamom seeds will always appear a rich brownish-black, slightly sticky and have a strong aromatic smell.

Cardamom is sold whole or ground by Indian grocers. Ground cardamom is often used in Indian sweets. It is best to grind small quantities at home using a coffee mill. Ready-ground cardamom is not only expensive, but because cardamom loses its natural oil quickly, it also loses its flavour.

Chapattie or Atta Flour This is a fine-textured, wholemeal flour which is used in making most unleavened Indian bread. The whole kernel is a good source of dietary fibre as it contains a high proportion of bran and wheatgerm.

If real chapatti flour is not available, then a fine-textured wholemeal flour or a mixture of equal quantities of wholemeal and plain flour can be used to make Indian breads.

Chickpea Flour or Gram Flour (*Besan*) This is a very fine-textured flour, creamy yellow in colour and made by dry-grinding chickpeas. It is a very versatile medium which can be used as a base for many sweet dishes, to prepare a batter with which to coat onions and other vegetables before frying to make bhajiyas (as distinct from bhaji), and as a garnish in the final stages of cooking vegetables. Besan should be stored in a cool dry place.

Chillies, Dried Red (*Lal Mirchi*) These vary a great deal in shape and size. Usually, the tiny ones are very hot, so use them sparingly. They are also paler in appearance. The rich red ones, which are long and flat, are less hot and have more flavour.

When chillies are ripe they are usually a rich red colour. These are then dried in the sun to give us the dried red chillies, which are very different in flavour from fresh green or fresh ripe chillies.

Chillies, Fresh Green (*Hari Mirchi*) Fresh green chillies have a delicious capsicum-like flavour. They also vary a great deal in strength and unfortunately it is difficult to judge the strength and this has to be discovered by trial and error. They are a good source of vitamin C, but have to be eaten in small quantities. Chillies are often added to a dish towards the end to obtain a deliciously different flavour without the dish being hot. More often they are ground with other ingredients to make chutneys or are used for pickling.

Fresh green chillies vary a great deal in shape and size. It is the long slim variety that are commonly used in Indian cooking. They can be frozen after washing thoroughly and can be used straight from the freezer.

All chillies, red or green, should be seeded if a milder flavour is preferred, as the seeds are the hottest part of the chillies.

Cinnamon (*Da Ubini*) The cinnamon sticks used in Indian cooking are different from those used in the West. Indian cinnamon sticks have the texture and feel of tree bark, and are actually obtained from the bark of the Cassia tree, which is grown in most tropical countries. True cinnamon sticks, which are in the form of a scroll, are available in most supermarkets and have a much more delicate flavour than Cassia bark. True cinnamon is native to Sri Lanka. Both Cassia tree cinnamon and true cinnamon, however, are from the same botanical family.

Cinnamon is an essential ingredient in garam masala. It is also often used whole in certain curries, pilaus and birianis, and is brewed with cloves and aniseed as a medicinal drink to fight the symptoms of colds, coughs and flu. It should be stored in an air-tight container.

Cloves (*Lavang*) Cloves are the buds of the dried flower of the clove tree, which is native to southern Asia. They have a strong and distinctive flavour and are an essential ingredient in garam masala. They are also used whole in certain curries, pilaus and birianis. Whether used whole or ground, cloves should be used in carefully measured quantities as the flavour is rather overpowering.

Cloves should always be bought whole, as ground cloves do not contain the essential oil that flavours a dish.

Cloves are highly antiseptic and are often chewed to relieve toothache.

Coriander (*Nhania* or *Kotmil*) Coriander is the single most important spice in Indian cooking. Its mild and slightly sweet flavour blends well with almost all Indian dishes and it controls their basic flavour.

Traditionally, coriander is gently roasted before grinding as this brings out its full flavour as well as making it easier to grind finely. Ground pre-packed coriander, if roasted gently and cooled before storing in airtight containers, will significantly enhance the flavour of dishes.

Coriander Leaves (*Hara Dhania*) Fresh coriander leaves are an essential flavouring and garnishing ingredient in Indian dishes. They are also used for many delicious chutneys.

The leaves can be frozen if they are to be used for flavouring a dish or grinding with other spices for chutneys. Fresh leaves should be used for garnishes as frozen ones do not look attractive. The freshness of coriander can be preserved for at least two weeks if, as soon as the bunch is bought, the roots and any yellow/black leaves are cut off and the remaining good leaves are dried on absorbent paper until all moisture is removed. These should then be wrapped in aluminium foil, sealing all edges, and stored in the refrigerator. During storage it is advisable to remove any yellow/black stalks or leaves that appear as these will spoil the rest of the bunch.

The tender stalks of coriander have the same flavour as that of the leaves. They can therefore be finely chopped and used along with the leaves.

Coriander is easy to grow in any type of soil and can therefore be grown it in a window box throughout the winter and out in the garden in the summer.

Cumin (*Jeera*) Cumin is a pungent and aromatic spice, which is also very powerful. There are two varieties: black cumin (*kala jeera*) and white cumin (*safed jeera*). Although both are widely used, one cannot be substituted for the other as they each have their own quite distinctive flavour.

Sometimes black cumin is confused with caraway seeds, which are quite different.

Cumin is used whole to flavour the oil before cooking vegetables, pulses and some rice dishes. Ground cumin, because of its powerful flavour, should be used in carefully measured quantities. A better flavour is obtained by gently roasting the seeds before grinding. Ground prepacked cumin, if roasted and cooled before storing, will produce more satisfactory results, than if used straight from the packet.

Coconut, Desiccated (*Kopra*) Desiccated coconut offers a convenient alternative to the rather time-consuming process of preparing fresh coconut for use in a recipe.

Whenever desiccated coconut has to be ground with other spices, it should first be ground dry in a coffee mill to obtain the finer grain structure essential for making a good sauce. When used for chutneys, it can be ground along with other ingredients as chutneys do not need to be finely ground.

Coconut, Fresh (*Nariyal*) The coconut palm grows along tropical coasts all over the world. The vast coastline of India produces an abundant growth of coconut, and Indian cooking is well known for its use of coconut in savoury as well as sweet dishes.

In India, fresh coconut is generally cracked open and the juice inside the coconut is drunk as a cooling beverage. Various manual gadgets are available to grate the coconut flesh, which is then ground with other spices. Sometimes the juice, or coconut milk, is extracted and used when making a rich sauce. Creamed coconut sold in blocks is a very convenient substitute for fresh coconut milk.

If you wish to use fresh coconut, a very convenient way to prepare it is as follows:
Preheat the oven to 200°C/400°F/Gas Mark 6. Crack the coconut shell by striking it smartly with a hammer or other heavy object until the juice starts trickling out. Take care not to shatter it. Carefully drain the juice and place the cracked whole coconut in the centre of the oven for about twenty-five minutes or until the crack on the shell is visible. Remove the coconut from the oven and gently tap it all the way around with a hammer or meat mallet. The hard outer shell will come away very easily, leaving only the pure white flesh, which has a dark brown outer skin. Cut the coconut into conveniently-sized pieces and peel the skin. Grate the flesh in the food processor. This can be frozen in small quantities ready to use. Coconut prepared in this way will, of course, need to be blended or liquidised in the same way as desiccated coconut.

Curry Leaves (*Curry Patta*) These are sold dried or fresh. The leaves are small and shiny and are used in many different ways. They can be crumbled before being added to a dish or used whole. Alternatively, they can be fried whole in hot oil and then added to the dish.

Curry leaves are used extensively in southern Indian cooking and are one of the main ingredients in commercially prepared curry powder, especially Madras curry powder.

The dried leaves can be stored in a screw-top jar and the fresh ones can be frozen and used straight from the freezer.

Fenugreek (*Methi*) Fenugreek seeds have a slightly bitter flavour and must be used in the specified quantities. They are either fried in hot oil or gently roasted and ground with other spices – each method produces its own distinctive flavour. Whichever method is used, the seeds should not be overdone, or a very bitter flavour will result. Fenugreek is widely used in vegetable, lentil and some fish dishes.

The seeds are brownish-yellow in colour and rectangular in shape. The fresh green leaves, which are very much like watercress, are used as a vegetable. They cannot be substituted for the seeds. The leaves are also dried for use as a herb with vegetables and for stuffing breads. In northern India, fenugreek biscuits are a great delicacy.

Garam Masala Garam Masala is a combination of hot spices. The word *garam* signifies heat and *masala* means a mixture of various spices.

Garam masala is known to create body heat which helps the body to retain warmth in a cold climate. It is frequently used in northern Indian cooking where the temperature in winter is significantly lower than in the rest of the country.

Garam masala is used in many different ways. It is sometimes used together with other spices, or it can be sprinkled on as a condiment at the end of the cooking time. Cardamom, cinnamon and cloves are the main ingredients which govern the taste of the final mixture when ground. These spices are also used whole in pilaus and birianis and in certain curries and dry-spiced vegetable dishes.

The recipe for garam masala can vary a great deal; other spices such as whole black peppercorns, coriander seeds, and cumin seeds may be added to to the three basic ingredients.

The garam masala used in this book consists of cinnamon, cardamom, cloves and nutmeg. The quantity of each spice used is: 2 tbsps cinnamon sticks, broken into small pieces, 11/2 tbsps green cardamoms with the skin, 1 tbsp whole cloves and 1/2 a whole nutmeg, broken into pieces for grinding.

Heat a cast-iron or other heavy-based pan. When the pan is hot, add the above ingredients and reduce heat to low. Stir and roast the ingredients until they release their aroma. Remove from the heat and allow to cool completely; stir during the first half of the cooling time to prevent them from browning as the pan will remain hot for a while. When completely cool, grind the spices to a fine powder in a coffee mill and store in an air-tight jar. Garam masala prepared in this way is much more aromatic and has a fuller flavour than ready-packed garam masala.The latter does not have the required aroma and flavour because the main ingredients – cinnamon, cardamom and cloves – lose their essential oils very rapidly.

Garlic (*Lasoon*) Fresh garlic is a vital ingredient in Indian cooking. Powdered garlic or garlic salt cannot be substituted as the flavour is so very different.

Fresh garlic will keep well if it is stored in an earthenware pot and the pot kept in a cool, dry and reasonably dark place. Garlic is usually either ground to a paste or used finely chopped. It can be prepared and frozen in ice cube trays. Garlic paste can be made in a blender or in a herb mill.

Garlic also has extremely good medicinal properties. The antiseptic substances in garlic help to tone up the digestive system. Garlic also reduces the cholesterol level in the blood and thereby reduces the risk of high blood pressure.

Clarified Butter (*Ghee*) Ghee is used extensively in Indian cooking, especially in pilaus, birianis and Mughlai dishes. It is the primary ingredient that enhances the richness of Mughlai dishes. Ghee has a distinctive flavour and can be heated to a much higher temperature than ordinary butter without burning because the clarifying process uses unsalted butter. Concentrated butter offers a very suitable and convenient alternative to ghee.

It is not difficult to make ghee at home, the most important point to watch out for is the temperature. You will need about 450g/1lb unsalted butter, cut up into small pieces. If you wish, you can use a smaller quantity, and once you have mastered the art, the quantity can be increased to suit your needs. Put the butter in a heavy-based saucepan over a low heat and allow it to melt without sizzling. Adjust the heat to a slightly higher setting to allow the butter to simmer gently for ten to fifteen minutes, during which time all the milk solids will separate and the moisture will be released from the butter. A layer of foam will appear on the surface during this time. When the foam subsides, this is an indication that there is no more moisture left. Let the butter simmer until the milk solids settle at the bottom of the pan and turn brown. Watch carefully so that the milk solids do not burn; keep the heat down on low. Once the milk solids have turned brown, remove the pan from heat and allow the clarified butter to cool until it is comfortable to handle. Strain the ghee through a fine muslin cloth and store in a moisture-free jar. There is no need to refrigerate ghee. The freshness of this ghee is assured for about three months.

Ground Mixed Spice This needs no introduction as it is widely used for baking, especially apple-based puddings. The mixture contains the same basic ingredients as garam masala and a teaspoon of mixed spice, fried in hot oil, will enhance the flavour of any curry. It is therefore a good substitute for garam masala.

Ginger (*Adrak*) Root ginger is an almost indispensable ingredient in Indian cooking. Powdered ginger can be used for convenience, but will not produce the same flavour as it does not contain the essential properties of fresh root ginger. Fresh ginger adds a hot taste to the dish and also acts as a thickener. It is either scraped and ground to a paste or grated. The method used to prepare and freeze fresh garlic can also be used for root ginger.

Root ginger will keep well for about four to five weeks if the same process of storage is followed as for fresh garlic.

Mustard Seed (*Rai or Sarson*) Mustard seed has been used as a spice for many thousands of years. There are three different types of seeds: black mustard, brown mustard, which is also known as Indian mustard, and white or Alba mustard.

Brown or black mustard seed is commonly used in Indian cooking. It is not easy to differentiate between the two though the brown variety is slightly lighter in colour.

Powdered or crushed mustard is used in pickles and the whole seeds are used to flavour vegetables and pulses, and are fried in hot oil to give a nutty flavour. The green leaves are used as a vegetable.

Mustard oil, which is extracted from the seeds, is a popular medium of cooking in Assam and Bengal, the two north-eastern states in India. It is also used for making pickles.

Onion (*Pyaz*) Onion is one of the oldest vegetable flavourings to be commonly used all over the world. With a few exceptions, no Indian dish is complete without the use of onions. When a recipe calls for the onions to be fried gently until golden brown, the onion should never be allowed to brown, but should be a pale golden colour. Browned onions have a different flavour and are used only for garnishing dishes, and not for making sauce.

While preparing onions in the blender or liquidiser, no water should be added at first. Once the onions start secreting their juices, blending becomes easier. The addition of water makes the onions rather soggy. If necessary, however, about one tablespoon of water could be added to make the blending easier.

Onions which have been cut should not be exposed to air for any length of time as this causes the onions to develop a rather stale flavour. Onions should be chopped or sliced as finely as possible for Indian cooking. The finer the onions are prepared, the better the flavour and the texture of the dish will be.

Spring onions and shallots are also used in Indian cooking, except in northern India.

Onion Seeds (*Kalonji*) Onion seeds are used whole for flavouring pickles and vegetable dishes. They are also used in savoury snacks and Tandoori-baked bread, such as Naan or Tandoori Roti. In Assam and Bengal, onion seeds are used along with other whole spices to flavour dhals and fish curries.

Onion seeds are not actually derived from the onion plant, but because of their close resemblance to actual onion seeds, they are referred to thus. They actually come from the *Nigella* plant, which is grown in India and the Middle East.

Paprika Indian paprika comes mainly from Kashmir where this mild and sweet variety of chilli, known as *deghi mirchi*, is grown extensively. Its brilliant red colour does not indicate the same pungency as the other chillies used in Indian cooking. Paprika is primarily used to add that wonderfully rich colour to a dish.

Poppy Seeds (*Khus Khus*) Various kinds of poppy flowers are grown all around the world, but the poppy seeds used in Indian cooking come from the opium poppy, which flourishes in tropical climates. The seeds are pale cream, almost white, in appearance and they add a nutty flavour to the dish, as well as improving its texture by thickening the gravy. They should not be substituted for the black poppy seeds used in baking as these impart a bitter flavour to the dish.

Rose Essence and Rose-water These are used in many Indian dishes, especially those of Mughal origin. Rose essence is used in sweet dishes and rose-water has its use in both sweet and savoury dishes.

The essence is extracted from a special variety of roses cultivated solely for the purpose of making essence. Rose-water is made by diluting rose essence.

Rose-water is also sprinkled on guests to welcome them as they arrive for a wedding.

Saffron (*Kessar*) Saffron consists of the dried stigma of the saffron crocus flower. Though saffron is grown in most Mediterranean countries, the type used in Indian cooking comes from the foothills of the Himalayas.

Saffron is used in Mughlai, Kashmiri and northern Indian cooking to add both colour and flavour to dishes. The long and laborious process of collecting the stigma makes saffron one of the world's most expensive flavourings. Between 75,000 and 250,000 stigmas are required to produce just one pound of saffron.

Saffron should always be bought in strands. Powdered saffron is often adulterated and will therefore not impart an authentic flavour. Just a pinch of saffron is enough to flavour any dish.

The strands should be soaked in a little hot water or milk for ten to fifteen minutes. Both the infusion and the strands should be used in the dish for maximum flavour. Saffron is used for both sweet and savoury dishes.

Do not be tempted to substitute turmeric for saffron, as it has its own distinctive flavour.

Sesame Seeds (*Til*) Sesame is one of most important oil seeds in the world. It is native to India, which, together with China, is the largest grower and exporter of sesame oil to the West.

The sesame seed used in Indian cooking is a pale creamy colour and has a nutty flavour. The black variety used in baking in the West is never used in Indian cooking.

Tamarind (*Imli*) Tamarind plants grow all over India. The tamarind pods resemble pea pods, but are six to eight inches long, half-an-inch thick, and are a dark brown colour when ripe.

Tamarind pulp is sticky and sour and is added to a whole range of Indian dishes to add a distinctive tangy taste. The pod is broken up and the seeds are removed before being packed and sold. The pulp is soaked in hot water and the juice extracted for use.

Ready-to-use tamarind concentrate, a highly concentrated tamarind pulp, is sold in all Indian grocery stores and is much more convenient to use.

Turmeric (*Haldi*) Turmeric is native to India and it is the turmeric root which is cleaned, boiled, dried and ground to give us the powder. Turmeric adds colour as well as flavour to a dish. It is closely related to the ginger plant and it aids the digestive system, as does ginger. Turmeric is also used as an antiseptic.

Turmeric has a certain religious and social significance and is used as a sacred ingredient by the Hindus. In north-east India a bride and a bridegroom are 'purified' by being bathed in turmeric paste; it is believed that this prepares them for their new life together. In certain Hindu marriages, a thread, dipped in turmeric water, is tied around the bride's neck by the bridegroom.

Yogurt In India, natural set yogurt, most of which is home-made, is always used for cooking and general consumption.

Yogurt finds its way into the Indian diet in numerous different guises. A vegetarian would always finish off a meal by eating yogurt on its own or by having a yogurt-based drink. Yogurt is used to make salads (raitas) of different kinds and also to tenderise meat and poultry. The enzyme contained in the yogurt breaks up the tissues so that the spices can then penetrate deep into the meat and poultry. Yogurt also thickens and enhances the flavour of the gravy in many Indian dishes.

As it is made from buffalo milk, which has a higher fat content than cows milk, Indian yogurt has a rich, creamy taste. The most suitable yogurt for use in Indian cooking is one which is thick set and is made with whole milk. Other types of natural yogurt have a high water content and will make gravy watery and do little to enhance the flavour of dishes.